LISTEN TO THE VOICES

LISTEN TO THE VOICES

Conversations with Contemporary Writers

JO BRANS

Southern Methodist University Press

DALLAS

FIRST EDITION, 1988

Requests for permission to reproduce material from this work
should be sent to:
Southern Methodist University Press
Box 415
Dallas, Texas 75275

Library of Congress Cataloging-in-Publication Data

Brans, Jo.
Listen to the voices.

Includes index.
1. English fiction—20th century—History and
criticism.   2. American fiction—20th century—
History and criticism.   3. Authors, English—20th
century—Interviews.   4. Authors, American—20th
century—Interviews.   5. Fiction—Authorship.   I. Title.
PR882.B73   1988   823'.91'09   87-42939
ISBN 0-87074-265-5
IBSN 0-87074-266-3 (pbk.)

Design and production by Whitehead & Whitehead

For Bailey Devine

CONTENTS

Acknowledgments ix

Introduction xiii *What the Voices Say*

Saul Bellow 1 *A Feeling for Where the Nerves Lie*

John Cheever 33 *The Fragrance of Morality*

Eudora Welty 57 *Struggling against the Plaid*

Donald Barthelme 77 *Embracing the World*

D. M. Thomas 103 *The Grass Captain*

Margaret Atwood 125 *Using What You're Given*

Erskine Caldwell 149 *Book Burning*

Iris Murdoch 171 *Virtuous Dogs and a Unicorn*

William Gass 193 *Games of the Extremes*

Margaret Drabble 215 *Beasts of the People*

About the Author 243

Index 245

ACKNOWLEDGMENTS

FOR THE ART IN THEIR BOOKS, as well as for the generosity with which they talked to me about their art, I want to recognize first the ten writers whose words form the substance of this volume. To them, my unending thanks and admiration.

Suzanne Comer of the Southern Methodist University Press had the vision to see the underlying coherence in a series of apparently disparate interviews. Her energy, intelligence, and tact make her a model editor.

The student organizers of the Southern Methodist University Literary Festival were always sympathetic to this project. I particularly appreciate the help of Jack Myers, the faculty sponsor of the event who year after year arranged interviews for me with the writers who came to the campus during the annual week-long Festival.

My gratitude to *Southwest Review,* which published slightly abbreviated versions of seven of these interviews, goes back a dozen years. For the quarterly's John H. McGinnis Award, given in 1977 in recognition of the Bellow interview, I am grateful to the late Margaret Hartley, then editor, and to her associate and successor, Charlotte Whaley. More recently, Willard Spiegelman and Betsey McDougall, the current editor and managing editor of the *Review,* have lent their good sense to this enterprise.

Robert Compton, book editor of the *Dallas Morning News,* made the meeting with D. M. Thomas possible; I used portions of the interview in a story I wrote for the *News*. Marshall Terry, Bonnie Wheeler, and George Zeiss helped me to get to England and thus to Iris Murdoch. As book reviewer for *D Magazine,* I "discovered" Margaret Drabble's work; Jane Holahan and Pamela Lange of the Dallas Public Library put me in touch with Drabble herself. Pascal Covici introduced me to Saul Bellow.

Finally, for reading, thinking, listening, and questioning with me during the years I worked on this book, I will always be grateful to my former colleagues and students at Southern Methodist University, to my family, and to such smart and steadfast friends as Shelby Hearon, Bill Porterfield, Muriel Seldin, and most especially—she knows why —Molly Friedrich.

LISTEN TO THE VOICES

INTRODUCTION

What the Voices Say

ANYONE WHO LOVES FICTION, as I do, as you probably do if you are reading this, must have some desire to know why and how the writer writes. When I began interviewing writers, I suppose I hoped to elicit an explanation as startling and as magical as the one William Faulkner made to Malcolm Cowley during the course of a car trip the two took in 1948: "I listen to the voices, and when I put down what the voices say, it's right. Sometimes I don't like what they say, but I don't change it." I haven't been disappointed. Though no one has spoken of listening to voices, I have heard over and over that writing is something more than a natural process. I have listened to startling and, yes, magical things.

"I write as I do," Saul Bellow told me a sunny November day in Dallas twelve years ago, "because I am what I am. I can't really help myself." Bellow's words have become my rationale for this collection of interviews: the belief that in some mysterious but significant fashion, beyond style and craft, the writer and the work are one. If the writer writes what he or she is, the unspoken but central question in every interview must be, "Well, then, what are you?"

With Leon Edel, the biographer of Henry James, I am persuaded that "if the writer's work counts, it is like the breath of the human body, and that body counts as well. A writer writes out of his whole physical as well as mental being." But for me, the impulse to know the writer came before the theory. This book began the fall of 1976 when I learned that Bellow was to speak at the annual Literary Festival at Southern Methodist University, where I was then teaching. A serious fan of his work, I felt that somehow I must meet Bellow while he was on campus. So, quickly, before I could lose my nerve, I wrote to him in Chicago and requested an interview.

To be honest, I was not quite sure at that early stage why I wanted to interview Bellow. In my query, I claimed to be eager to publish the interview. But I thought of publication only when a friend cautioned me that Bellow would not necessarily want to see me just because I wanted to see him. I had to give the writer a reason, a sensible reason if not the real reason. Publication was a sensible reason.

The real reason I found hard to fathom if not downright frivolous. Was I any different from a rock star groupie or a movie star fan, I worried? Weren't Bellow's books enough? Would I next want an autographed eight-by-ten glossy or a lock of hair, like the finger bone of a saint? How could an interview, my ploy, enhance the pleasure I got from *Herzog* or *Henderson the Rain King*? Brought up as I was on the New Critical sufficiency of the text, I knew that, logically, loving Bellow's books didn't mean I "must meet Bellow."

But logic was not the issue. Like many readers, I have a touch of Holden Caulfield in my makeup. In *Catcher in the Rye,* you will remember, Holden says, "What really knocks me out is a book that, when you're all done reading it, you wish the author that wrote it was a terrific friend of yours and you could call him up on the phone whenever you felt like it." All I knew in the beginning was that I had been knocked out by Bellow's books, and here was my chance to call up Saul Bellow. I certainly wasn't going to miss the chance, or, later, the chance to call up John Cheever, Eudora Welty, and the others included here.

I was lucky to have the chance. During the last decade that I taught at Southern Methodist, almost every year I interviewed one or two of the writers who came to the campus to speak at the annual Literary Festival. Other writers I pursued independently. The interviews, which are published here in chronological order, were taped, the tapes were transcribed and edited to remove the blips and glops of speech, and upon request the transcriptions were given back to the writers for final changes. Seven of the interviews here were published, as each was completed, in a somewhat abbreviated form in the university's literary quarterly, *Southwest Review.*

In spite of the academic environment surrounding this enterprise, however, these interviews aren't really intended to be "academic." That is, they do not offer enlightenment on deconstruction or other hot issues in recent literary criticism. "I'm quite illiterate," Holden says, "but I read a lot." In other words, he is a representative reader. I wanted to ask Holden's questions, which were mine too—the questions not of a critic but of a reader. Maybe then, I hoped—and when I reached this point in my thinking I was beginning to see dimly what this interviewing was all about—maybe then these very particular conversations would be transformed into universal dialogues, of interest to other readers as well.

Though I wanted the questions to be representative, I did not try to make a "representative" selection of writers. Because I admire the work of many writers I have not had a chance to interview, on the eve of publication I am almost as dismayed by who is not here as grateful for who is. Nevertheless, the ten who are included are both critically and commercially among our most successful contemporary authors. They have been awarded, in addition to Bellow's Nobel Prize, the highest literary honors in England, Canada, and the United States. Even a cursory look yields a Booker McConnell Prize and two James Tait Black Awards in England, the Canadian Governor General's Award, and in this country three Guggenheims, five National Book Awards, three Pulitzers, and two Howells Medals, as well as other awards too numerous to mention.

In addition to such readily apparent critical recognition, all ten of these writers, even the most "esoteric" or "difficult" or "regional," have had the huge mass market sales that indicate popular recognition also. Their large followings prove beyond a doubt that each has, as Bellow says of himself, "some feeling for where the nerves lie" in the human psyche. They are writers you want to call up.

What did we talk about? Anything that flourishes within the realm of the artistic imagination, such subjects of fiction as family life, erotic love, friendship, alcoholism, divorce, suicide, feminism, clothes, gardening, mining, cooking, cotton picking, the importance of work, illness, Darwinian survival, Communism, capitalism, fascism, Freudianism, American foreign policy, religion, meditation, the good life, the nature of reality, death, the after-life, metamorphosis, the uses of mythology, the varieties of human personality, the fraternity of other writers—all these topics were gleaned from the fertile fields of the writers' work.

Literary form, except for a few brief references here and there, is covered by John Cheever's sweeping, "It seems to me that when one has an impulse to communicate something in fiction the form and the length of it are inherent." Easy for him to say, of course. But what I'm getting at is that, for all the magic of their powers, these writers are not magical aliens but human beings who write stories. They possess, as another writer has remarked, a good bit of the human condition. Here, in this book, they talk about their work in broadly humanistic terms.

In such humanistic terms, the interviews demonstrate interesting contrasts between the work of various writers. To begin with, there are contrasts of character. Bellow, the son of Russian immigrants, creates urban American figures, but his Herzogs, Sammlers, and Fleishers often have their roots in Jewish folklore. Cheever's frustrated Wapshots and Farraguts, on the other hand, represent the decline of the white Anglo-Saxon Protestant, usually in suburbs or small towns on the Eastern seaboard.

Even the treatment of characters ostensibly from the same region differs widely. Both Eudora Welty and Erskine Caldwell have been labeled "Southern writers." But how unlike Welty's comic and mythic vision of a poor but proud and traditional people is Caldwell's naturalistic view of a defeated race reduced to a hardscrabble existence.

The methods too are diverse, even for writers supposedly in the same camp. Both D. M. Thomas and Donald Barthelme have been called "experimental," for example.

But Thomas's novels, which focus on the inner life of characters caught up in history, are deliberately associative and Freudian, surreal. Barthelme, on the other hand, focuses on the "dreck" of society itself, "the trash phenomenon" with which his often simplistic characters must cope. Though his "collages" may be closer to visual art than to conventional fiction, Barthelme insists he is a realist.

Ideological differences of course spring up everywhere. Both Margaret Atwood and Margaret Drabble have been called "feminist" writers, but neither accepts the label comfortably; neither wants to write or indeed has written anything so narrow as didactically feminist fiction. Both are concerned with individual freedom and identity, for men *and* women, defined against the constraints of society, but their emphases and methods differ considerably.

As another example, both Iris Murdoch and William Gass are philosophers whose books proceed in some fashion from their philosophical views. But their views are diametrically opposed even as to the purpose of writing fiction. Murdoch would like, through the vehicle of fiction, to revitalize the categories of good and evil, which she claims have been corrupted and dissipated by the moral relativism of modern philosophy. Gass sees fiction as a place for the writer to play "games of the extremes," to create amoral and asocial characters who are as powerful and convincing as he or she can make them, and to let the reader worry about how to resist them.

Yet there is common ground. I don't want artificially to force into a few basic themes the wide range of topics or the highly complex issues that came up in these conversations. Just the same, reading the interviews again, I find that, diverse as the writers and their works certainly are, our discussions insistently circle back to two common concerns to which the reader might wish to be alerted in this introduction. Let me call the first of these common concerns the creative process, the second the morality of art.

"I listen to the voices, and when I put down what the voices say, it's right," said Faulkner, describing his own creativity. Each writer here approaches the alchemy of literary creativity with some personal variant on Faulkner's voices. Bellow says that the writer has clairvoyant powers. Margaret Drabble talks about "a passport into other people's minds." Defining himself as a Muse poet, Thomas declares that he writes from the "feminine part" of himself, and that his imagination finds its expression through a woman, like Lisa in *The White Hotel*.

Margaret Atwood reveals that her work begins with images, and she refuses the closure of a final explanation of the symbolism. Caldwell says he writes to let elemental life express itself, and that the characters themselves, without guidance from the author, perform the action in a story. For William Gass, writing is an intuitive process enabling him to see another reality. Cheever says his stories come from "a force of memory" which all human beings share.

For Eudora Welty, the source of her inspiration remains a mystery. Barthelme finds his in a "mulch pile" of life's fragments, Iris Murdoch in "a vision that holds the world together."

Clairvoyance, the Muse, elemental life, a force of memory, a vision—these things are not dreamt of in ordinary philosophies. But the ten writers here have dreamed them and felt them and enacted them on the page. They have published them far and wide for our pity and fear and wonder. Like Faulkner, in one way or another they have listened to the voices of their own creativity.

Can art which depends on mysteries like those described above be made to serve a moral purpose? The issue of morality in art, which goes back to Plato, constantly reemerges in the history of aesthetics. It enjoyed a heyday in Victorian England, and is very much in the air today. Superficially, at least, artists seem to be sharply divided on the subject between those who think that art has nothing to do with morality, and those who think that all art inevitably, and rightly, takes a moral position.

Faulkner, of the first persuasion, was critical of his voices, on what grounds we don't know, but he did not tamper with what they said to him. "Sometimes I don't like what they say," he told Cowley, "but I don't change it."

Plato would have banished Faulkner, of course. In Plato's Republic, storytellers like Faulkner could not be counted on to do party-line obeisance to the Good, the True, and the Beautiful, so for the preservation of the ideal state Plato would have excluded the entire subversive, possibly irrational, body of poets. In Freudian parlance, we would say today that Plato's banished storytellers were in touch with the unconscious. Morality, Plato thought, is a supremely conscious activity.

But in Plato, as in Freud, to confront human life is inevitably to conceive of a duality. With what Leon Edel calls the "whole physical as well as mental being," the writer puts his or her words to work in the world. As human beings may experience a conflict between mind and body, writers may face a disparity between the claims of inspiration and the demands of an ordinary human conscience. And so these interviews return from time to time, both through my questions and the writers' remarks in passing, to a second common concern, the moral value of art.

From the Cheever interview on, I began to ask for an opinion of John Gardner's *On Moral Fiction,* a controversial, strongly worded book that after its publication in 1978 helped shape many discussions, some not so polite, about writers in America. Writers found the book infuriating—Barthelme calls it here "a Saint Valentine's Day Massacre"—because in it Gardner assesses his peers individually on how moral he, as arbiter of literary ethics, finds their work to be. Gardner's basic stance, however, is nothing new: simply that a writer has an obligation to write "moral fiction."

That argument called forth a variety of responses. I have already mentioned Gass's theory that writing is an elaborate "game," through which fiction deliberately casts the reader off from moral certainty. Gass admires Bellow because Bellow makes his villains as strong and convincing as his heroes. Barthelme sides with Gass by saying that art should not try for some calculated moral effect, but Barthelme thinks that making art is itself a moral activity.

At the other end of the spectrum, Drabble flatly says that art is *"not a game,"* but is intimately connected with morality. Murdoch comes out, as I have mentioned, for "the reality of virtue." Almost all of human discourse, in her view, consists of making moral judgments: "religion is breathing." How can art be different?

Most of the writers fall somewhere between the two extremes. Caldwell says morals are just customs, a view earlier made respectable by Montaigne. If the writer shocks, he adds, it's because life itself is shocking.

Atwood says moral neutrality doesn't exist, so the writer must take care what sort of experience he or she inflicts on the reader, and must be sure that the game is worth the candle. Thomas sees the world of the novel, like the actual world, as a Manichaean battle constantly being waged between the forces of light and dark. He would like to add to the forces of light, which he sees as having a slight, a very slight, edge over evil.

Bellow resents the notion that he must root around "like a truffle hound" in the unconscious for the sake of art. For him, art, a spiritual transmission to the sacred part of another person, resides on a higher moral level. Close to Bellow in spirit are Eudora Welty, who points out that we learn to love others by hearing their stories, and John Cheever, who claims that "storytelling is one of our most rudimentary means of being alive, and of comprehending our lives."

Cheever, in fact, suggests a synthesis which puts the central position between extremes into a form with which I am certain all these writers could agree. Cheever doesn't think any morality which is "forced and inflexible," mixed up "with legislatures, with social pressures," belongs in art. Instead he speaks, most beautifully, of "the fragrance of morality," of an almost sensual apprehension of that in human conduct which is "fitting and decent." It is the fragrance of morality which pervades the best fiction, and which places fiction solidly on the side of life.

"To be alive, to be the whole man alive," D. H. Lawrence once wrote. Or to be the whole woman alive, for that matter. But Lawrence is right, I think, as I follow the turns and nuances in these questions of art and the good life: to be alive, wholly alive, that is the point. And I remember the moments of real human life that emerged in the interviews. When Bellow talked about the suicide of his friend John Berryman, his voice grew husky and his

eyes suspiciously bright. Iris Murdoch, with a philosopher's perennial curiosity, began at one point to interro-
gate her interviewer. William Gass vividly relived the rage
he felt when the first draft of *Omensetter's Luck* was stolen.
If he had caught the thief, Gass said, "I would have killed
him." John Cheever was especially, touchingly, human. I
knew when Cheever told me of the problematic relationship with his brother Fred that he was hinting at the secret
depths of his own life. However, only since Cheever's
death have I come to understand what those depths were,
or what Cheever perhaps meant when he confided quietly
that he felt lonely and frightened almost every day of
his life.

Not for the first time, it occurs to me that I am indeed a
representative reader, that I share with many people the
idea that great writers know something that I need to know
to help me live more fully. Then I realize that I have found
what I sought in these interviews, what I really had in
mind when I called these writers up, what I wanted to
know when I began to listen to their voices.

SAUL BELLOW

A Feeling for Where the Nerves Lie

S AUL BELLOW is the dean of American letters in the
second half of this century. In ten novels and two
collections of short stories, he has reigned over
American fiction for more than forty years, and is the only
novelist ever to win three National Book Awards. He has
also won a Pulitzer, and was awarded the Nobel Prize for
Literature in 1976 "for the human understanding and subtle
analysis of contemporary culture that are combined in his
work." Asked by the press how he felt about winning the
Nobel, Bellow remarked that the child in him was delighted but that the adult was skeptical.

That kind of split is familiar to Bellow readers. The
typical Bellow hero is a fellow intent on bringing into harmony the childish enthusiasms of his heart with the skepticism of his adult head. The skepticism emerged in the
Nobel acceptance speech in which Bellow, a good Pla-
tonist, sounded major themes of his fiction: the cultural
decline in the present age; the vagaries of existence; the human aspiration to reach a higher level where the spirit is
satisfied.

I

The novel lacks the greatness of the epic or Greek drama, Bellow told the celebrants, "but it is the best we can do just now. It is a sort of latter-day lean-to, a hovel in which the spirit takes shelter." Like every human being, the novel moves between two worlds, the everyday world of action and the rarer world of spirit which we visit only through "glimpses." By showing us the two worlds united in art, Bellow concluded, the novel testifies to the diversity of human existence and "promises us meaning, harmony, and even justice."

Bellow's background makes him too a citizen of two worlds, the Old World from which his parents came, trailing, he has said, taffeta petticoats, long gloves, and ostrich plumes, and the New World Bellow both loves and chastises. He was born in 1915 in Canada, of Jewish parents who had emigrated from Russia two years earlier. The youngest of four children, he spent his early years in an old and impoverished section of Montreal. In 1924, the family moved to Chicago's South Side, and Bellow grew up speaking French, Russian, Yiddish, and English. He took a degree with honors in anthropology and sociology from Northwestern University in 1937, did graduate work in anthropology at Wisconsin, and served a two-year stint in the merchant marine during World War II.

Bellow spent a year in Paris on a Guggenheim, and has taught at New York University, Princeton, and the University of Minnesota. For years he has taught occasional courses at the University of Chicago and served as a member of the prestigious Committee on Social Thought there. A certain amount of emotional chaos, however, has come into the life of this most intellectual of writers, most notably in the form of four marriages, with sons from each of the first three, and four divorces.

The author of plays, nonfiction, and two collections of short stories, Bellow has made the novel his chief mode of expression in a writing career that began in the thirties at a bridge table in a Chicago back bedroom "while all rational, serious, dutiful people were at their jobs." His apprentice novels *Dangling Man* (1944) and *The Victim* (1947), written in the manner of Flaubert, he has disparaged as "small and correct."

His third book was anything but. Bursting with event and character, rioting in language, *The Adventures of Augie March* (1953) was the great comic novel of the fifties. With it, Bellow won a National Book Award, and, more important, found his own voice.

Seize the Day (1956) has been called the best of Bellow's books by critics who prize compression and the rich but precise use of language. However, *Henderson the Rain King* (1959) is better Bellow, a superb spoof of hero stories (and perhaps Ernest Hemingway), yet a sympathetic review of the spiritual cravings of the American character. His second National Book Award–winning novel *Herzog* (1964) advanced this theme. Herzog, searching for "a good five-cent synthesis" of soul and body, of present and past, writes letters to the living, the lost, the great, and the dead, a device unparalleled in American fiction.

Doubles abound in Bellow's fiction. *Mr. Sammler's Planet* (1970), which also won the National Book Award, chronicles the interior landscape and the external adventures of Artur Sammler, a one-eyed European Jew, over seventy, who has survived the death camps of Europe only to find life in Chicago almost as horrific. *Humboldt's Gift* (1975), the book whose publication immediately preceded our interview, recounts the friendship of two American writers, Von Humboldt Fleisher and Charlie Citrine. *The Dean's*

December (1982) moves between two cities, Chicago and Bucharest, and the action of a double crisis in the soul of Albert Corde, the Dean of Students in a Chicago university. "The whirling souls of Chicago" are viewed perceptively by a narrator, like Mr. Sammler, who is familiar with another terrifying milieu.

Bellow's most recent novel *More Die of Heartbreak* (1987) revolves about the erotic adventures of the botanist Benn Crader. But under the rapid humor and the tragicomic plot, Bellow is up to his old tricks: the examination of the soul of a man whose brilliant mind cannot save him from error. "I am a phoenix," Benn says, "who runs after arsonists."

This conversation took place on a November Sunday in 1976 at the home of Pascal Covici, the son of Bellow's first editor and a colleague of mine in the English department at Southern Methodist University. After a pleasant lunch for six or eight Bellow admirers provided by Pascal's wife Joan, the others withdrew, leaving us to the interview amid frequent applications of white wine for me and bourbon for Bellow. Bellow is a trim, handsome man with a finely chiseled face and heavy-lidded brown eyes. His manner was gravely courteous, and he responded to the questions with an air of wanting to say everything exactly right.

BRANS: You said recently that you began to write books because you love literature. And I thought that was the best answer to the question of "why" that anybody had given. But it seemed to be a strange answer. You didn't say anything about expressing yourself or revealing your feelings. None of that Rousseau stuff.

BELLOW: If I thought the project was about myself I would value it less. It isn't really about myself. What I have discovered over the years is that although it began with me, it is an activity that affects other people, and that I have the knack of expressing some of their unexpressed thoughts and feelings. For instance, for many years I had fantasies in which I wrote letters to people. Then I thought, Oh, what an odd thing. Wouldn't it be amusing if I wrote a book about a man who, going out of his mind, is writing letters to everybody? And then I discovered that hundreds of thousands of people were doing just that—always had been doing that.

BRANS: Writing mental letters?

BELLOW: Yes. And so this was some evidence to me that I enjoyed some "clairvoyant powers." I had had that before, from my very first book. When I published *Dangling Man,* many people wrote me and said that they found their own situation in this. And then I began to realize that I had some feeling for where the nerves lie. That the enterprise was not really about me, that I was on loan to myself, as it were, and that I was doing something that expressed common needs, common preoccupations.

If it were just about myself I don't think that it would have meant so very much to me, because I haven't all that much use for myself—myself as such, my own ego, pride of accomplishment, or what you like. I think I have not an abnormal amount of such pride, but a relatively low amount. I would have been satisfied with a far more modest success. I never wanted to uncork the genie, or raise the lid of Pandora's box. I began to see some years ago that it was a Pandora's box.

BRANS: You mean your success? Or the connection that you made with people?

BELLOW: No, the connection was important, but the success was something else again, because the success meant that I was supplying a need, a public need—of a cultural kind. And that I was expected to act the culture figure, to be a public utility, an unpaid functionary, something between a congressman and a clergyman. And I saw that people felt they had a right to bring to me everything that troubled them in this province.

BRANS: That's what Sammler says about himself—that he is a priest or a psychologist.

BELLOW: Yes, you begin to feel that way pretty soon.

BRANS: When you say "clairvoyant," do you mean that intuitively or mystically you speak for other people? That you are a kind of scapegoat figure as a writer and you bear the burden of other people, and you write about that?

You have sometimes quoted Whitman, that the poet in America must create archetypes of Americans. Are you creating archetypes that come from all the people?

BELLOW: Well, I used the word *clairvoyant*. I might have chosen simpler, less mysterious language and said that because I'm concerned with what affects so many people, I have trained myself in an attitude of mind which provides just that sort of material. It may not be clairvoyance, but I have sometimes definitely sensed that it's a little more than a natural process. Something beyond positivistic, rationalistic common sense, or the clear light of day.

BRANS: That seems a curious thing for you to say, when your books are so full of ideas.

BELLOW: Well, not all ideas are clear and rational. And not all ideas belong to the modern idea system of scientific provability, or whatever you want to call it.

BRANS: It seems really remarkable to me for a writer

somehow to feel that he speaks for all kinds of people with whom he's never come in contact.

BELLOW: I think it's true, though. And I don't like to question the sources of my own ideas and feelings too closely. That is to say, I avoid the assumption that I know the origin of my own thoughts and feelings. I've become aware of a conflict between the modern university education I received and those things that I really felt in my soul most deeply. I've trusted those more and more. —You see, I'm not even supposed to have a soul.

BRANS: Who says you can't have a soul?

BELLOW: The soul is out of bounds if you have the sort of education I had. I got my bachelor's degree as an anthropologist. And I read Marx and Bertrand Russell and Morris R. Cohen; I read the logical positivists. I read Freud and Adler and the Gestalt psychologists and the rest. And I know how a modern man is supposed to think. The hero of *Humboldt's Gift* says, "If you put a test before me I can get a high mark, but it's only head culture."

The fact is there are other deeper motives in a human being, which I don't like to call unconscious, because that's a term preempted by psychoanalysis, but I say to myself, "I have always behaved in such a way that I cannot escape the conclusion that I believe things I'm not consciously aware of believing. That I have hopes I can't justify. And that I have affections I can't explain by the modern system in which I was trained."

Then you come to the point of choice. Do you believe the psychoanalytic explanation of your deeper motives? Or do you simply say, "These are my deeper motives, I don't care what psychoanalysis has to say about them"? I've made the second choice. I don't care any longer whether my ideas square with the modern canon, which I have taken to calling the canon of head culture.

I know that people live by something far deeper than head culture; they couldn't live if they didn't. They couldn't survive if they didn't. What a woman does for her children, what a man does for his family, what people most tenaciously cling to, these things are not adequately explained by Oedipus complexes, libidos, class struggles, or existential individualism—whatever you like.

Now, I know that psychoanalysis has found a natural preserve for poets and artists called the unconscious. A writer is supposed to go there and dig around like a truffle hound. He comes back with a truffle, a delicacy for the cultural world. The poet is a wonderful Caliban, the analyst is the Prospero who knows how to put his discoveries to a higher purpose. Well, I don't believe that. I don't believe that we go and dig in the unconscious and come back with new truffles from the libidinous unknown. That's not the way it really is.

BRANS: How do you think it really is? If you act on what you get from this part of yourself . . .

BELLOW: There are persistent ideas, the truth of which we recognize when we meet them in literature. You read Tolstoy—it's not uncommon that a character of Tolstoy will hear an inner voice. We all know what that is. We immediately recognize it. We know how the soul of a child speaks to the child. We've experienced it ourselves, only there's no room for it in the new mental world that we've constructed, which is less and less a world and more and more a prison, it seems to me.

But we know all these things when people talk to us about them. Our immortal hopes we know. We understand what they are. We don't dismiss them out of hand.

And it's not just because of ancient superstition, it's because there is some unacknowledged information that we have. It's about time we simply dealt with it directly and without being so evasive.

BRANS: Now you're being Rousseau. You use this "we" so bravely. Aren't you making the assumption that what you think is really what everybody thinks? Isn't that a sort of Rousseau claim: I know my heart, so I know men?

BELLOW: "Je sens mon coeur, et je connais les hommes." Well, there's a good deal to it.

BRANS: How do you know that I'm not completely unlike you, and that you can talk about "we" all you want, but what you really mean is "I"?

BELLOW: I sense that when I say these things you don't actively disagree with me. At least, you're agnostic enough not to dispute them immediately. You'll think matters over.

BRANS: You're quite a teacher. Tell me about your teaching. What has been the importance of your teaching to your writing? You taught Tolstoy last year, didn't you?

BELLOW: Yes, and Conrad.

BRANS: Do you feel as frustrated about teaching as I do sometimes? What do you think about it? You teach graduate students all the time, who presumably feel lucky to be there, and who are dedicated to ideas—to what you have to say to them.

BELLOW: I suppose so. In Chicago it's very hard to find people to talk literature to. You find them at the university, and that's the long and the short of the thing. There is no literary culture in the United States. There are no colleagues to discuss novels with. Most of the critical articles that you read in magazines or newspapers are scandalous. And there is no community, so you talk to young people who know something. It's a great comfort.

And, after all, why should one lock these things within one's bosom? I can't even talk to my wife about them. She's a mathematician. She's wonderful—she knows all kinds of things, but she doesn't know this, just as I don't know pure mathematics.

BRANS: But you both are using symbols, symbol systems.

BELLOW: Yes, but I'm dealing in broad human facts to which all human beings have access. Only an elite has access to what she does. I think there are only twenty people in the world who actually understand her theorems—this eliminates most mathematicians.

BRANS: So she really has to keep it locked within her bosom, whether she wants to or not.

BELLOW: Yes, it's hard for her—hard for her to live with a man who doesn't understand these things. We have other kinds of understanding, but her situation with me is not very different from my situation with most people in Chicago—mechanics, secretaries, lawyers, dentists, engineers, criminals, stockbrokers, or hoodlums. I can meet with them, we can find common ground, there's a lot we *can* talk about. But we don't talk about what matters most. Neither they nor I can do that.

BRANS: Can you talk to your students about that?

BELLOW: Not directly. I have to talk to them about *The Red and the Black,* which is what I am doing this term, but one can put a lot of things into that, and they understand.

BRANS: So in your teaching, then, you find this common ground where you can meet, and where you can really exchange experiences safely.

BELLOW: I think that the university contains all that

there is left in this country, or indeed in most countries, of a literary culture.

BRANS: Maybe what we do in classrooms in a university is really our religion.

BELLOW: No, I wouldn't go so far as that. It's not my religion. But it really is the only avenue I have for expressing certain feelings and thoughts—or for talking shop, which can be important if you're deprived of it. I never much liked talking shop, but occasionally one does like to discuss one's trade.

BRANS: And this gives you a chance to do that.

BELLOW: I do it indirectly. I never talk about myself, and I never talk to students about what I'm writing, or what I'm thinking about my own work. But that I can obliquely touch upon some of these questions gives me nearly the kind of gratification I'm looking for. That's what it's meant to me all these years. Perhaps students learn something from it too.

BRANS: Yet you've been very critical of academics. Isn't there a contradiction here?

BELLOW: I'm critical of academics who take masterpieces and turn them into discourse in the modern intellectual style. I'm against that, of course. I am not for the redescription of *Moby Dick* by Marxists and existentialists and Christian symbolists, respectively. What does that do for *Moby Dick* or for me? It doesn't do anything. It only results in the making of more books—King Solomon has already warned us against that in Ecclesiastes.

BRANS: You make me very uncomfortable because I don't know exactly where you draw the line. And when I was coming to talk to you today I felt that somehow I might be doing some kind of disservice to your books by asking you questions about them. I thought, I'm supposed to take these books that mean a great deal to me—I'm supposed to understand what they mean. If I ask direct questions about them, maybe it's sacrilege.

BELLOW: I'm well prepared to defend myself against these incursions, if that's what they are. But there's no reason why people shouldn't talk about books. There is a prerequisite, though, which is that they should be deeply stirred by the books. They should love them or hate them. But not try to convert them into—

BRANS: Theory?

BELLOW: Yes. Or chatter. There's no need to babble about these things. They *can* be talked about. But so much of literary criticism is babbling.

BRANS: I'm not sure I understand exactly what you mean by babbling. Do you mean using special terminology? Or talking about little things and ignoring big ones?

BELLOW: Critics often translate important books—write them again, as it were, in the fashionable intellectual jargon. And then the books are no longer themselves. They have been borrowed by Culture, with a capital C.

There are two things here that we must clearly distinguish. One is the work of art with its direct effect on people. The other is a work of art as a cultural commodity, as a piece of society's property in Culture. In the second form, art becomes a fertilizer for the cultivation of languages, vocabularies, intellectual styles, ornaments, degrees, honors, prizes, and all the rest of that.

And this is what always happens. Our model for it is the Christian religion, which started with faith and ended with churches.

BRANS: Are you afraid you will become a Culture Object?

BELLOW: I think we must all be on guard against it. I don't want to become a support of the new clergy. Why should I? It's none of my business!

BRANS: You think sometimes that you might be drawn into writing for these people?

BELLOW: You're on the right track. The public has changed. It now includes more people who have gone to college. Until recently, contemporary literature was not part of the curriculum. If you were a lawyer with a good education, or an engineer, or a physician, or a clergyman, it was assumed that you could read a novel. You didn't need ten manuals in order to read it. There is a process of mystification associated with this, you see.

BRANS: Do you think writers are tempted to contribute deliberately to this process of mystification?

BELLOW: I feel no such temptation. But many modern writers do. They reflect the rise of the intellectual level of the public. There is a public of professional intellectuals for whom poets and novelists perform a function. Take somebody like Joyce, especially in *Finnegans Wake*. He is writing for a small public of intellectuals—of highly skilled readers, people who know the history of modern literature and are amused by puzzles. The same thing is true of Thomas Mann. Of Eliot. Of all the small public writers.

BRANS: Is this what Stendhal called his "happy few"?

BELLOW: The "happy few" in Stendhal were people of spirit and energy and genius and passion and imagination and all the rest of that. They weren't necessarily intellectuals.

BRANS: Not the literary intelligentsia?

BELLOW: In the modern sense, you see. But Joyce was trying to please a certain kind of public, to which he himself belonged. These were scholars, or amateur scholars—people who liked mental games, people who would not be put off by a multitude of references to Homer or to Vico or Thomas Aquinas, or to Irish history; and this reflects a change in the public and the writer's relation to that public.

I don't blame writers for this; I'm simply pointing to the fact that modern art has a far larger intellectual burden than it ever had. And at certain points it really becomes an exercise in the history of the art itself, so that it's for people who know that history.

I'm not against an elite literature, mind you. That's not really what I'm talking about. What I'm talking about is the amount of modern intellectual freight in literature and painting. One can find this agreeable, but you can't say that it is literature in the older sense.

BRANS: Which was intended for the man in the street?

BELLOW: Yes, at least the novel was.

BRANS: Do you see yourself, then, as writing for that man in the street?

BELLOW: I don't know him well enough to write for him in that direct way. But I have a good deal of feeling for him. I know that at bottom I'm just the same kind of human being. There are cultural differences, but I know they are only that. They may not be differences of the heart. I don't like the snobbery implicit in the idea of the "mass man" developed by Ortega, his German predecessors, and his recent successors.

BRANS: This mindless creature who goes around cultivating his body—you don't think he exists?

BELLOW: In some respects. I don't think that it fully characterizes anyone.

BRANS: I really could argue with you. What about people who go habitually to singles bars, that sort of thing? Instant Dionysus.

BELLOW: Yes, well, they are standardized in their quest for joy or diversion. But how do we know what their souls suffer in abreaction from this? We don't know. Do we really think that in their secret human agonies over what they do, they are still standardized? We don't know that.

BRANS: But surely if their sufferings are real there should be some way of finding something—something more particular.

BELLOW: It would be nice if they had a language for it. A wonderful liberation. Unfortunately "education" and the mass media fill them up with formulas.

BRANS: You don't want to write for a literary intelligentsia. And your books sell beautifully. Do you think of yourself as somehow serving all of those people?

BELLOW: No, I write as I do because I am what I am. I can't really help myself.

BRANS: You're not trying to teach people how to live?

BELLOW: No.

BRANS: But your books seem so much as if you have the answers. Before I met you I thought, "Here's a man who has the answers, and if I can just ask him the right questions, then he'll give me the right answers." And I wondered if maybe you had that sense of yourself at all. And when you began talking about clairvoyance, I thought that's what you meant, partly. So you don't see yourself as a teacher of the masses?

BELLOW: Not necessarily. Although when I think about it, I do believe that I have something of importance to transmit. Just how to name it, I don't know. But I think of myself as speaking to an inviolate part of other people, around which there is a sort of nearly sacred perimeter, a significant space, if you like, a place where the human being really has removed to, with all his most important spiritual possessions.

Yes, that I do think about. I'm not very clear about it, but I don't have to be because I'm not a philosopher. All I have to do is feel it, and that I do feel.

BRANS: That you're talking to someone other than the social being?

BELLOW: Yes, I'm talking to human beings who have certain permanent attributes—that there is something in them—as in myself. I've never doubted it. I don't think of myself as different in that way. On the contrary, I think of myself as ordinary in many ways.

But when I say "ordinary," I don't mean what people commonly mean by ordinary. I mean something extraordinary which is in every human being. At the moment there is no place for this extraordinary universal possession. It's rushed out of sight by material preoccupations (which I have too), by fear, by fashion, which is the child of fear.

But I really do think that I am talking to a part of people that I know is there and that they know is there. Though my books may not make sense to many readers. Perhaps the sound of my voice communicates this sense of things.

BRANS: I've been curious about that. I've wondered why people bought *Herzog* so enthusiastically, because it's hard to believe that most people feel quite as fragmented or as confused as Herzog, and yet the book has sold millions of copies. So evidently there is something—

BELLOW: I think they recognized certain things in it. The theme of divorce, the feeling of being shut out, their humanity denied by the arbitrary acts of those who are very close to them, evicted, deprived of a connection that they thought they had. And in Moses Herzog a kind of self-critical comic sense, an amused objectivity toward himself, almost amounting to courage.

BRANS: The straw hat, and the striped jacket, and the whole bit?

BELLOW: Yes, putting up a resistance to these crushing antagonists. Even if it's only a comic resistance.

BRANS: That's the best kind. But I don't think it is only comic. Do you? It ends with Herzog sitting out in the sun, the flowers, the candles, the whole thing. The whole thing about grace. Do you think your life is touched with grace?

BELLOW: Not exceptionally. But I think of Herzog in a different way. I think of him as a man who, in the agony of suffering, finds himself to be his own most penetrating critic. And he reexamines his life, as it were, by reenacting all the roles he took seriously. And when he has gone through all the reenactments, he's back at the original point.

BRANS: That's wonderful! I never thought of that. Okay, reenactment of what?

BELLOW: The professor, the son, the brother, the lover, the father, the husband, the avenger, the intellectual—all of it. It's an attempt really to divest himself of all of the personae—

BRANS: The social selves?

BELLOW: That's right. And when he has dismissed these personae, there comes a pause.

BRANS: But that's grace—"Thou movest me." Or is Herzog just like a cat, accepting the life of the universe, or something?

BELLOW: It's better than his trying to invent everything for himself, or accepting human inventions, the collective errors, by which he's lived. He's decided to go through a process of jettisoning or lightening. That's how I saw the book when I was writing it. And I wrote it with passion, because I believed in it with a passion. I thought, "Enough of this."

BRANS: Then is Madeleine necessary to him because she causes all these things? Is she like Proust's *madeleine,* the thing that makes you think, remember all the past—reenact the past?

BELLOW: Oh, he loved her deeply. She wounded him horribly, and he is trying to live with the wound. And he's also very angry, of course, and critical.

BRANS: And he's wrong about her, isn't he? I mean, she's not what he said she was, is she?

BELLOW: No, she's both better and worse than he said she was. But of course he's at war and he can't be fair. But he loves her, and he loves the child, and he feels that she's replaced him with Valentine, a liar, a phony, and there's something of the phony in her, to which the phony Valentine appeals.

BRANS: But he's such a loser! You know, no woman can take such a loser. At a point, you just have to get away from somebody like that.

BELLOW: Well, it isn't that he's a loser. It's that he's so chaotic; no woman can stand so much disorder. It's not the losing at all, it's the chaos, and the complexity of life which would tire a woman out, just trying to follow it. This complexity is intolerable, I agree.

BRANS: Right. You mean simple losing would be okay, but complicated losing not so good. But tell me about Humboldt—he's even more complex. I tried first of all to fit Humboldt into John Berryman. But of course biographically he's very close to Delmore Schwartz.

BELLOW: Yes.

BRANS: And I began to see that he probably wasn't either of those men exactly.

BELLOW: No, he's not.

BRANS: There seem to be stories about both of them in the character. The thing I remember is something about pushing the big girl downstairs that you wrote about Berryman. And that sounded like Humboldt chasing the girl through her apartment. But you're saying something about the artist and what the writer has to expect in that book.

BELLOW: American society likes its artists and writers, certainly, it's proud of them, it rewards them, but it doesn't know what the hell they're all about—and there's a sort of vulgar cheerfulness in its relation to them. Some of the writers share this same vulgar cheerfulness. They make something of it at times. Think of Allen Ginsberg's line, "America I'm putting my queer shoulder to the wheel."

BRANS: You mean writers feel responsible.

BELLOW: It isn't just that they feel responsible. They feel attached. Attachment. Piety. Even when they think it awful. When Humboldt feels his talent leaving him, he begins to clown. He's putting his poet's shoulder to the wheel. We too are America's children. It's this part that Citrine finds Humboldt guilty of playing.

BRANS: You mean the artist-in-residence?

BELLOW: That's right, when there's a slackening of the talent, then there come all these other games that the poet invents.

BRANS: Like the whole con thing about going to Princeton.

BELLOW: Exactly. Or the automobile, or the farm, or the relations with women.

BRANS: Which are often the things that sell books of poetry. Don't you think that's true?

BELLOW: That's right. But there's something really promotional, exhibitionistic, and impure about it. And Charlie knows that, you see.

BRANS: But Charlie is successful.

BELLOW: Charlie is not really successful. Charlie is a man who, by having success, has excused himself from success. Charlie is like Julien Sorel in *The Red and the Black*. When he gets to the top of society, there's nothing to do but shoot Madame de Renal and get his head cut off.

BRANS: He doesn't care anymore.

BELLOW: Of course not.

BRANS: I like that.

BELLOW: That's exactly the Charlie position in the book. That's why he'd rather hang around with card players and bums and tramps.

BRANS: Does he think they're more genuine?

BELLOW: It isn't that he thinks they're more genuine. No, everybody's equally genuine or false. It's just that he thinks they express the ludicrousness of the position.

BRANS: The games are all out in the open.

BELLOW: That's right.

BRANS: Charlie resembles you a lot in the outward aspects. I think of a matador executing dazzling veronicas, with the cape very close to the real human body. Tell me how not to see Citrine as Bellow.

BELLOW: I would have to suffer from dissociation of personality to be all these people in the books. I can't possibly be all of them. I lend a character, out of pure friendship, whatever he needs, that's all.

BRANS: The amazing thing about Charlie is all the love

he has, for these bums, and for the people in his past, for almost everyone.

BELLOW: True. Nobody has noticed the amount of affection in that book. The critics are unaware of that sort of quality in a book.

BRANS: He loves his past, in a way that seems so accurate. You focus on these things in the past that seem important to me but that many current writers don't care about. Do you think that the ability to remember, or to create memory, is important for a novelist?

BELLOW: In my own case these memories serve to resurrect feelings which, at the time, I didn't want to have. I had them. They were very powerful. But they were too much for me to deal with, and I covered them over with cynicism or wit or whatever. And now I realize how much emotion was invested in them, and I bring them back.

BRANS: You mean in loving your family?

BELLOW: Yes.

BRANS: Did you feel at the same time that they were really not you, and that you were trapped in this family?

BELLOW: No. I always had a great picty about my life. I always thought my life—I didn't think about it as my life when I was a kid—I thought it the most extraordinary, brilliant thing in the whole history of the universe that we should all be together. And there was so much unusable love that in the end it turned against itself and became a kind of chilliness, and for many years it stayed that way. The Marxist attitude toward the family, the modern attitude toward mothers, or fathers, or—

BRANS: Mothers can't do any good. There's no way!

BELLOW: And all the rest of it. And then I realized that I was simply fooling myself. That it had really been a feast of love for me which I couldn't persuade the others to share. They weren't aware of it in me. Mostly not. Sometimes they were.

BRANS: Do you really think it would have made them uncomfortable? You say that sometimes in the novels. Citrine, for example, feels that Julius is uncomfortable with the love that Charlie has to give him—that it really is superfluous or shouldn't be expressed. It might be there, but it shouldn't be shown in any sort of overt way.

BELLOW: Yes, because Julius has made his way in life as a tough business operator.

BRANS: Why do you so often have your heroes the brothers of all those tough-minded businessmen who've made lots of money?

BELLOW: Because they're all over the place. After all, I am a historian. Every novelist is a historian, a chronicler of his time. Of course I write about business types.

BRANS: People making lots of money? Being successful?

BELLOW: Well, it's the history of the United States, in a way. Here we sit in Dallas. Isn't it the history of Texas?

BRANS: Can we talk about *Sammler*?

BELLOW: Sure.

BRANS: That was the first one of your books that I read. I think it came out in the *Atlantic*. As I began reading it, I was absolutely dumbfounded.

BELLOW: Why?

BRANS: I thought it was a real accusation. I thought I was supposed to take all this stuff about the mass man to heart.

BELLOW: No, not really. I'll tell you how I saw it. There's enough European in me to be able to look at America as a foreigner.

BRANS: Is that true? You really still feel close enough to Europe?

BELLOW: Yes, I do, through my family. My parents were immigrants. They spoke Russian. In 1920 their table talk was still about the Czar, the war, the Revolution.

BRANS: Well, I thought *Sammler* was just a gripy old man's opinion of the world, when I first read it. Then I read it again, and I began to see that you had a distance from Sammler, and that he was not your spokesman. At least I imagined that he was far grouchier than you would have been. And I finally decided that the book was a limited affirmation of America. And that what people like Angela had was a kind of energy, a kind of creativity, that Sammler could only grudgingly recognize.

BELLOW: *Sammler* would have been a better book if I had dealt openly with some of my feelings, instead of filtering them through him.

BRANS: You mean everything had to come out with a kind of bias because of him?

BELLOW: Not a bias in the ordinary sense. But he is a Lazarus—a man back from the dead.

BRANS: You were talking earlier about these experiences, these feelings that we all have, and you think there are certain of those experiences that Sammler no longer has. Is he disenfranchised somehow?

BELLOW: Well, I think he's cold, because he's known the grave.

BRANS: I think *Sammler* is a wonderful book. I don't have any reservations about it. Once I discovered that Sammler wasn't the voice of God, or something, then I was comfortable enough with it. It was only when I thought that he had all the answers that I was . . .

BELLOW: Oh, he doesn't have all the answers. If he had had all the answers he would have been the religious man he wished to be. In reading Meister Eckhart he was feeling his way. He was only beginning to acknowledge the first stirrings of religion.

BRANS: He was terribly bound to being a human creature, in spite of all his mysticism and so forth.

BELLOW: Yes, but then you see it was really a sort of exotic report on life in the United States; it was not condemnatory.

BRANS: It was misread, then.

BELLOW: Of course it was misread. We started out earlier by talking about criticism. One of the troubles with criticism is that it's simply linear, if you know what I mean—sketchy. The novelist never feels he's got anything until he has it in all the density of actual experience. Then he looks at a piece of criticism, and all he sees is the single outline of thought. It's not the same thing. And you can't deal with a phenomenon that way. So he never really trusts criticism, because it lacks the essential density.

BRANS: Well, the critic has to make a point. He has to take a line, and then he has to develop the line. You feel all these things rushing in upon you from the book, and yet you can't, for your own sanity's sake, try to say all there is about the book, and what you finally want to keep saying is, "Go read it. Go read this novel, and you'll see what I mean."

BELLOW: Or, "Don't go read it."

BRANS: Do you think of yourself as a survivor, like Sammler or Citrine?

BELLOW: No, I think of myself as horribly deprived of people whom I loved and who are dead.

BRANS: You know, I really loved John Berryman. I never even knew him, but I believed in him, in Henry. I hate to face what he became at the end. But you must have known that bad side of Berryman. I'm sure he called you late at night, and all that—the terrors.

BELLOW: I know, but he was full of feeling.

BRANS: Would I have liked him if I'd known him really?

BELLOW: Well, he would have gotten drunk and made passes at you and wanted you to nurse him and do things for him.

BRANS: I have very little patience with that. I like healthy people around me who don't get in my way.

BELLOW: "Sleek-headed men and such as sleep o' nights." But John was a real man. He and I were very close in spirit as writers, I think. He knew it, and we would sometimes talk about it. He wrote a little piece once after *The Adventures of Augie March* came out, in which he said that this book had cleared the way for him to do certain things. Maybe it was so. But he loved literature. That is rare even among writers. John gave himself to it, heart and soul.

BRANS: Why was he such a disaster, though? Why did his life have to be such chaos? Your life is not like that. You've controlled your life.

BELLOW: Yes, I know. Oh, I didn't have to face the kinds of things he faced—the suicide of a father—coming out on the porch and seeing his dead father in the morning.

BRANS: Don't you think at a certain point you just grow out of that? Or you move away from that? You take control of yourself.

BELLOW: Well, he lacked control.

BRANS: But in his poetry he had fine control.

BELLOW: Yes, in his poetry he had the control. In his life there was none at all. Then because he decayed physically he knew he must die soon. He was really sick. He had no liver anymore, he lacked muscular coordination. He was getting dirty. And it was getting to be pretty pukey. And he knew it. His pride suffered from it. And he probably said, Well, enough. He was a derelict, in hospitals. And he just stopped it.

BRANS: It seemed to me a deprivation for the rest of us that he should do that. I felt really angry because he'd do it.

BELLOW: He thought he was on the wagon, and he thought he was straight with his wife, and he thought he was out of the woods, and all of that Boy Scout optimism of somebody who feels, "At last, I'm on the right path." And then he went off completely, got drunk again—horribly drunk. Disappeared for days, and found himself in bed with some strange girl.

BRANS: But you see, I don't buy this "found himself" thing. I mean, he got there. He did it.

BELLOW: Yes, but in disgust with himself. Of course he did it. He had no further use for himself. And I believe he thought he didn't want to write, that he had done it all.

BRANS: The death of the poet. Like Humboldt. But Rinaldo Cantabile survives. Now there's a name! I can't say it without rejoicing that you thought of it. Why a musical name for a thug?

BELLOW: I know the common people in Chicago, the bums or whatever you like, all have these unfathomed cultural and intellectual ambitions, and they don't know what to do about them really. They bring the greatest enthusiasm and devotion to these things, but at the same time they're clumsy, stupid, arrogant, ambitious.

BRANS: You mean like Rinaldo, who thinks he's going for the big time, and then somehow it all . . . I never have enjoyed anything as much as when Citrine bests Rinaldo. It was so marvelous. I was so afraid that somehow he was going to be in service to Rinaldo forever.

BELLOW: Oh, no.

BRANS: And Rinaldo really gets put down. But he's a splendid character.

Is he a sort of antihero, a Rameau's Nephew? You suggest in *Dangling Man* that you have been influenced by Diderot and I see evidence everywhere. Your interest in opposites, the philosopher and the criminal—in *Sammler*, in *Humboldt*. I feel often that your novels are dialogues in the fashion of Diderot.

BELLOW: I read *Rameau's Nephew* when I was very young and I got terribly excited by it. I thought it was just a marvelous book. I especially admired the speed and energy of the formulations and Diderot's talent for hitting all the high spots without any waste of time, and the amount of feeling. It just made a great impression.

It was also a way of combining the writing of a story with a great deal of thought, not philosophical thought but the thought of an imaginative man about someone's career and about what it meant to be a parasite and a failure in an elite society and to be low man among the aristocrats. All of that really appealed to me.

BRANS: The Nephew—*Lui*—is not the victor, do you think? Students usually argue that he carries the day.

BELLOW: Because he's the energetic man; he's the man of passion. Diderot probably holds himself too aloof and reserved in that book. I've sometimes had the wild idea of writing a *Rameau's Nephew* in which the central character is a modern woman.

BRANS: Tell me—you're a daring writer, why *haven't* you ever used a modern woman as your protagonist? I don't agree with some of your critics who say that you don't understand women, and that you have only a Schopenhauerean attitude toward women.

BELLOW: I don't. No, unfortunately I just struck the women's movement at a bad time.

BRANS: But why haven't you ever written from the point of view of a woman? Why do you always have to have a Madeleine as interpreted by Herzog, and Renata as interpreted by Citrine?

BELLOW: I sometimes think of doing it; I just never got around to it. I was working out problems that couldn't be worked out that way. The only thing I ever wrote about a woman directly was a story called "Leaving the Yellow House." About Hattie. I loved her. But of course you could say she's an older woman. She's an old lady.

BRANS: But your women do seem to be around mostly just to stick on Band-aids at opportune times, or they leave when things get rough. There's this attitude toward women. I think it's because the women always are filtered, or falsified, through the minds of the heroes.

BELLOW: Maybe. But I thought there were some rather nice women in *Humboldt's Gift*. I thought Demmie Vonghel was an awfully nice woman.

BRANS: Oh, she's fine. I loved Demmie.

BELLOW: She's a real sort of American—you know— young lady.

BRANS: But she dies. And then there's Renata. I imagine all the men who talk to you about your books like Renata. I really don't like Renata very much.

BELLOW: Well, Renata is a delight. She's not supposed to be a marvelous "woman," only a grand female.

BRANS: What was all this stuff about her marrying death—what's his name? Flonzaley? Why didn't Citrine get the girl? I think Citrine should—it's American for Citrine to get the girl.

BELLOW: I think it's American for a swinging girl like that to make the best match she can.

BRANS: With a mortician?

BELLOW: Oh, well, that's just poking fun at poor Charlie, not at Renata. I was not poking fun at Renata.

BRANS: I like to think that Demmie is what you really think women are. And Renata is just a sort of—

BELLOW: Renata is the nympholeptic dream of elderly gents like Charlie Citrine, who still want to be accepted as virile and desirable, as a wonderful man for a beautiful woman to have.

BRANS: Why couldn't you have told the story of Charlie Citrine, say, from Demmie's point of view? I'm just asking that as a possibility. Could Demmie have told that story?

BELLOW: Yes, she could. I could have done it, too.

BRANS: Yes, she's a fully realized character. You could have talked from her. There are passages in there where she speaks . . . You know, she has the wonderful ability just suddenly to haul off and knock Charlie in the chops.

BELLOW: Yes.

BRANS: But you've never tried this, really?

BELLOW: No, I think I could. I know I could, as a matter of fact. All this stuff about my prejudices is just nonsense. I probably have certain prejudices. I mean, never believe what a man says about his own prejudices. Because he doesn't know. That's why they're prejudices. But . . . I do have the kindliest, closest feelings to certain women. I always have had, and it just hasn't come out that way, that's all.

BRANS: I think it has come out that way. I really think that people who read your books with any attention know that. It's just that you do always have this kind of Schopenhauerean female figure, standing there in all of her curves.

BELLOW: Take somebody like Ramona in *Herzog*. Now Ramona is nice, an awfully nice girl. She just happens to be realistically portrayed, and this is what people can't take. She is the good-hearted (and she *is* good-hearted), giving, charitable, but ideological female. She is an ideologist. She makes speeches. She thinks she knows what's best for Moses.

BRANS: But it seems that at the end of the book he's pretty much disposed toward her point of view. He's waiting for her, after all.

BELLOW: He's going to forgive her all this ideological stuff. It is a matter of forgiving, because he has no use for it. He's gotten rid of his own. And why should he consent to listen to hers?

BRANS: But her ideology is all about love, and renewing the spirit through the flesh.

BELLOW: He doesn't believe that!

BRANS: He doesn't? At all? Well, then, he really doesn't find the solution. He's just sort of at a way station, is that the idea?

BELLOW: He's come to a point of rest, which is saying a lot for anybody these days.

BRANS: But it won't last.

BELLOW: No, he's going to have to assume roles again, and deal with people again. He's just come to a well-earned interregnum. Don't grudge poor Moses *that*.

BRANS: Do you equate those two things? Assuming roles and seeing people?

BELLOW: Well, you have to deal with them. You have to make allowances for them. You have to make allowances for their vanities and their weaknesses and so on, even though at bottom they're really okay. But there are so many vain struggles, and there's so much wrangling, and so much nonsense. Most of what passes between human beings, except in their finest moments, is nonsensical. And it gets more nonsensical all the time. The more books we read about conduct, self-regulation . . .

BRANS: What books?

BELLOW: I'm thinking about those deep books, those heavy works which tell you what to do at every moment of your life. Americans seem to be unable to live without prescriptions.

photo by Nancy Crampton

JOHN CHEEVER

The Fragrance of Morality

JOHN CHEEVER concludes his first novel *The Wapshot Chronicle* (1957) with the posthumous "Advice to my sons" of Leander Wapshot. Leander's instructions cover various aspects of life: pleasure—"Never make love with pants on"; taste—"Never wear red necktie"; health and ritual—"Avoid kneeling in unheated stone churches"; and character—"Fear tastes like a rusty knife and do not let her into your house."

Finally, Leander sums up this moral legacy with four imperatives which are the touchstones of Cheever's fiction as well: "Stand up straight. Admire the world. Relish the love of a gentle woman. Trust in the Lord." True, Cheever's work often depicts a fallen world where men are bowed under banal lives, a gentle woman is hard to find, and God too is temporarily out of touch. But, in a distinguished career that began at seventeen with the publication of his first short story and that ended at seventy with a novel published in the last year of his life, Cheever the writer never changed his mind about those aims.

33

"The Chekhov of the suburbs," as he has been termed, Cheever is like Chekhov not only in his mastery of the short story form but in his compassion for characters who long for tradition in the midst of disruptive times. Caught between the comforting verities of the small New England towns in which they grew up and what they see as the threatening amorality of the cities which provide their livelihood, his people inhabit emotional and ethical as well as geographical suburbs. Just as Chekhov's characters yearn for the old days before the cherry orchard was in danger, Cheever's characters too, in the words of Joan Didion, yearn "always after some abstraction symbolized by the word 'home,' after 'tenderness,' after 'gentleness,' after re-membered houses where the fires were laid and the silver was polished and everything could be 'decent' and 'radi-ant' and 'clear.'" Nostalgia, "homesickness," is a constant theme in the work of both Cheever and Chekhov.

One of two sons of Frederick and Mary Cheever, Chee-ver was born in 1912 in Quincy, Massachusetts, where he grew up. His formal education ended when he was ex-pelled from prep school for smoking in his senior year. He decamped to a cold-water walk-up in New York where he worked at teaching himself to write short stories. During the thirties, Cheever lived mostly in Manhattan, publish-ing stories in the *New Republic,* the *Atlantic, Collier's, Story,* and, most often, in the *New Yorker.* In 1941, he married Mary Winternitz; they had three children, Susan, Ben-jamin, and Federico, and eventually settled in Ossining, New York, in a house which was built in 1799.

At the end of four years of military service during World War II, Cheever brought out his first collection of stories, *The Way Some People Live* (1943). Over the next thirty years, he published five more: *The Enormous Radio* (1953), *The Housebreaker of Shady Hill* (1958), *Some People, Places, and Things That Will Not Appear in My Next Novel* (1961), *The Brigadier and the Golf Widow* (1964), and *The World of Apples* (1973). *The Stories of John Cheever* (1978) includes all of his stories except "the most embarrassingly immature."

No one has described those stories better than Cheever himself. They picture, he says in the preface to the 1978 collection, "a long-lost world when the city of New York was still filled with a river light," Benny Goodman sounded from stationery-store radios, and "almost everybody wore a hat." But "that generation of chain smokers who woke the world in the morning with their coughing, who used to get stoned at cocktail parties and perform obsolete dance steps like 'the Cleveland Chicken,'" were "truly nostalgic for love and happiness" and worshiped gods "as ancient as yours and mine, whoever you are."

Cheever published five novels. *The Wapshot Chronicle,* which won the National Book Award for 1958, is set largely in St. Botolphs, a New England port town, and contrasts the inglorious present with the glorious past of one of its first families. Leander Wapshot, whose heroic ancestors sailed the globe, captains a decrepit excursion launch which, in its last days, his wife converts into a "Floating Gift Shoppe." A sequel, *The Wapshot Scandal* (1964), traces the further decline of the family after Leander's death, though individually the Wapshots have their triumphs and the novel is ambiguously hopeful. This book earned Cheever the prestigious Howells Medal for Fiction in 1965, presented by the American Academy of Arts and Letters for the best work of fiction in a five-year period. *Bullet Park* (1969), as heavy-handedly symbolic as the names of its two main characters, Hammer and Nailles, suggest, is a savage exposé of the secret horrors that lurk beneath the apparent placidity of suburban life.

Falconer (1977) takes place in a prison, a metaphor for the degradation to which the protagonist Ezekiel Farragut has sunk. The descendant of a patrician Yankee family, Farragut has fallen from the traditional attitudes that Cheever admires through addiction to drugs and alcohol, the failure of his marriage, and the murder of his brother. The most sexually explicit of Cheever's books, *Falconer* traces the homosexual love affair with a fellow prisoner which redeems Farragut and returns him to human closeness.

If a human being is rescued in *Falconer,* a pond being used as a dump is rescued in *Oh What a Paradise It Seems* (1982), completed not long before Cheever died. Just "a story to be read in bed in an old house on a rainy night," as this short modern fable begins and ends, *Paradise* nevertheless sounds poetically once again the sweet, sad note Cheever played so well: life is beautiful—and fragile.

A short, gnomish man with neatly combed blond hair and bright, birdlike eyes, John Cheever was dressed in a good and well-worn tweed jacket during this interview in a Dallas hotel in 1979. Although he was a recovering alcoholic, perhaps already harboring the cancer that would kill him in 1982, his manner was jubilant and his wit irrepressible. He lavished his stories so freely that I felt they would never run out.

BRANS: I felt like a character in a John Cheever story, suggesting we go up to your room for this interview. That was indelicate of me.

CHEEVER: You remind me of an interview a woman did with me years ago. I was terribly tired. I'd done something like five interviews, and I said, "I'm absolutely bushed, so why don't you lie on that bed, and I'll lie on this bed, and then we'll just do it lying down." And she said that was great.

Then, could she take some photographs of me? And I said yes. And she said, "Would you mind taking off your shirt?" And I said, "Well, yes, as a matter of fact I would, since I look like hell with my shirt off." And then presently she seemed to get into my bed, and then she wanted to flirt around me without any clothes on at all. And finally I said, "Get the hell out of here."

And then she didn't want to get out, and she had a mink coat. So I opened the door and threw the mink coat out, and she followed it.

BRANS: That was clever.

CHEEVER: I called up. She represented a substantial magazine. And I said, "Listen, you know, I just kicked the interviewer out of the room." And they said, "Oh, oh, horrors."

BRANS: You *didn't* tell them the story.

CHEEVER: Yes, I did. I said, "I'm going to tell you and I won't mention it to anybody else." And I didn't until some fifteen years after the fact. She wrote an extremely flattering account.

BRANS: You poor man, all these aggressive interviewers.

CHEEVER: No, I'm not a poor man, not at all. Why? I mean it's much harder for them. (That sounds a little pious, doesn't it?)

BRANS: It must be a wonderful high for you, though, to know . . .

CHEEVER: I mean, this morning everybody said, Well, I'm terribly sorry, but you have to go off and do the morning show in Fort Worth. And then I said, If you hadn't asked me to do the morning show in Fort Worth, I would wonder: Had I not shaved? Had I not bathed? Is my breath bad? Because I've done the morning show in Toronto, in Moscow, in London, in Boston, in New York—absolutely a constant waking up in the morning. And some of them have been terribly funny. There used to be something called the Dave Garroway Show. You probably don't remember.

BRANS: Oh, I do remember.

CHEEVER: It used to be in a storefront in Radio City, and if you wanted to get on television you appeared and held up signs. It was a riot outside. I went on with Red [Robert Penn] Warren. We had both won the National Book Award—this was twenty-three years ago. There was also a chimpanzee on the show, called Joe, and he was fully dressed, much better dressed than either Red or I, and much more composed.

Red and I had terrible hangovers, and Garroway said, "Mr. Warren, you write poetry, and you write prose. Would you explain why you choose one medium and then the other?" And Red said, "Ah scratches where Ah itches."

The audience were all standing outside the windows holding up signs that said, "Send money, pregnant." The talk shows in those days were really wild.

BRANS: What were you asked this morning in Fort Worth?

CHEEVER: The questions were pretty good, except for the first one which was, How do you write a novel? I said, as in any profession, you would inform yourself on what has been accomplished by others in the field and then sit down and do it.

Another interview I had recently was fairly funny. I was asked, as I frequently am, "What are your three favorite titles? What three books do you owe your life to?" There are so many thousands to which I'm indebted that it would be untruthful to name three. So I said, oh, something like a combination of the *Aeneid* and *Tom Swift*.

And then the man said that he was reading Homer, and I said, "I'm very pleased to hear it. Whose translation?" And he said he was reading it in English.

BRANS: Good heavens. How *do* you write a novel? Where do all your stories come from? You can't have observed them all. They must just come to you—the man in *Bullet Park* who is sucked under the train, and all that's left is one loafer, for example.

CHEEVER: My feeling, of course, is that in working with literature we are dealing with the force of memory, not the reservoir but the force of memory. This force is not understood, but the one thing about it is that one can speak of the man who disappeared under the train and nothing is found but his loafers, and you respond to it. That is the marvelous thing, that it's a mutual thing. If you didn't respond to it, it would have no reality.

But it isn't only memory, it's also the music of language, whether there are too many *th*'s or *r*'s in a sentence, and so forth. Yet, when one gets it right, then the reader recognizes it. But one never knows precisely what it is that we can put our finger on beyond the fact that it is in the nature of an illumination.

BRANS: You don't mean personal memory, then.

CHEEVER: No. I'm talking about a force that is not understood, beyond the fact that we can use it.

BRANS: So that you can remember whatever is human, in some way.

CHEEVER: Of course, it's "subconscious," a word which

Saul Bellow uses scornfully. That's a Freudian contribution. And it's Jungian. The universal subconscious is perhaps, if you're going to accept that sort of a definition, the best that we have. But I think our concept is so much richer than anything Jung ever dreamed of.

As to the stories, perhaps the first thing in the world that I can remember is being told a story. And then in my childhood I was either told or read stories. And upon being bewildered by any turn of events in life I've tried to put it into the language of the story, to see if I could comprehend it. Faced with love and faced with death.

I suppose the last thing I will do in the world, with my last breath, I will be telling myself a story about whatever the circumstances are as I lie dying. Storytelling is one of our most rudimentary means of being alive, and of comprehending our lives. The capacity to tell a story seems to me to have begun civilization.

BRANS: When you tell a story, what does that involve?

CHEEVER: It involves using the past, the present, that which I anticipate, and, I believe, such racial memory as I may possess. Absolutely everything I've got.

BRANS: So you're really putting yourself into connection with all those forces out there. Have you always been—as I read through the collected stories again it seemed to me that they were always Christian.

CHEEVER: Yes, I've been a Christian.

BRANS: Have you ever rebelled?

CHEEVER: Well, yeah, when I was thirteen, or something like that. I thought, What a pack of rubbish! But then it seems to me that I allied my reconversion with falling in love. The force of love is quite plainly put upon people. And I think rather early in my love life I rejoined the church.

BRANS: What do you mean by your love life?

CHEEVER: Oh, my love for the human race, or for any member of it.

BRANS: Is Christianity to you—I noticed that you're very caught up in mythology, that there are other kinds of mythology that you use. Is Christianity to you another myth? Is it a great myth of death and resurrection?

CHEEVER: I hadn't thought of it that way. And as a Christian, of course I couldn't say yes. I must believe that God gave his only son. And since I'm not an early Athenian, the Greek myths—no, I can't say that.

BRANS: So you don't think of it as another expression of—

CHEEVER: No. I don't mix it up with Diana, no.

BRANS: I withdraw that. I don't want you to be a heretic. I love that whole Christian vision in your work. Just the moments of light that are always there in every kind of darkness, always something unexpected and beautiful. I don't see your stories as cynical. Some people say they are, though.

CHEEVER: Well, time seems to have changed the emphasis on the stories. I like to think people thought they were cynical because they used to run in narrow columns between pages of the most expensive advertising in the world. But perhaps the world itself has changed, or the stories have changed. No, they're thought to be quite compassionate now. And I expect presently I'll be charged with sentimentality. Since everything in a story is organic, and the organic changes, you know, it fluctuates. But no, I've never thought of myself as being particularly cynical. I can be nasty.

BRANS: In some of the stories you have been consciously nasty?

CHEEVER: Oh, yes.

BRANS: A particular target in mind?

CHEEVER: I can't remember ever writing a libelous story. I have them in my notes, but I almost never publish them because people recognize themselves, and are unduly crushed.

BRANS: It must be terribly wounding to recognize yourself.

CHEEVER: It's frightfully wounding, yes. So, I try never to do anything that someone can identify with—although people do, of course, identify.

BRANS: I suppose people do see themselves and don't recognize the universality—

CHEEVER: They never take on the heroic attributes.

BRANS: Tell me something. When the age became more liberal, toward sexual explicitness and that sort of thing, was this a liberating thing for you? The *New Yorker* stories would have had to be fairly circumspect, but people are shocked by the sex in *Falconer,* you know.

CHEEVER: Are they? Well, there is the masturbating scene.

BRANS: Yes. A teacher in our department told me, "I put *Falconer* on my reading list, and then I read the book again, and I thought, I can't talk about this to students. So I told the students how I felt, and they said not to worry, they could talk about it with *me.*"

But the masturbation scene was the one I meant. The trough.

CHEEVER: The trough? Yes, of course. I went back to Sing Sing last year, and the prisoners I had taught said, "What the hell did you write that for? We don't do that." And I said, "I know you don't do that."

BRANS: Oh, you mean you made that all up?

CHEEVER: No, it goes on in railroad stations and airports in the United States.

BRANS: See what I know! I thought that was absolutely—

CHEEVER: Well, I cannot say that it goes on *here,* in the outside world. That would be indecorous. But I can say that it is performed by prisoners. Then it becomes acceptable. The only people who were offended were the prisoners, who were quite indignant and said, "We do nothing of the sort!"

BRANS: Then it really didn't happen at Sing Sing?

CHEEVER: No, no. Why should it? I mean they enjoy a great deal of freedom as far as that sort of thing goes. But of course it does go on—

BRANS: *Falconer* is dedicated to your son?

CHEEVER: Yes. He was entering Stanford as a freshman, and I said, "Do you want this kind of book dedicated to you?" And he said, "Well, I'd better read it, hadn't I?" And he went upstairs and read it. When he came down the next morning, he said, "No, no, I want it dedicated to me."

And I said, "You're up to it? You mean you're going to enter college as the son of the fellow that wrote this?" And he said, "Yeah, I am." And he had no trouble.

BRANS: What were you saying with the masturbation trough?

CHEEVER: I don't remember. But there is some revelation in there, that perhaps the strongest statement in the book involves a margin of decency. Decency is the word I used in the book. It's a sense that there are certain things that one simply does not do, and I'm not speaking of heaven or hell. There are two scenes that were terribly important in the book. One is the masturbation scene, and the other is where they are undressed for a venereal examination. Both scenes were meant to be, as far as I've been able to comprehend them, the mysteriousness of one's mortality.

I do remember writing that scene. But I can't even remember the image beyond that it's territorial—there was a border, an edge. I suppose I'll be reading the book to find out.

BRANS: So you haven't felt liberated as a writer by the freedom of the age?

CHEEVER: No. Some of that freedom is misleading. I've never been disposed to describe sexual intercourse. Why describe, as if you were changing a tire, the most exalted human experience?

And as far as decorum goes in the *New Yorker,* anything I've ever wanted to do, I do. Then if people want to take it out, they take it out. And I can put it back in when the stories are collected.

BRANS: What do you think about John Gardner and that whole way of thinking of fiction as moral—his standing at the door to the gas chamber presumably telling the authors that they had to go in or not go in, depending on whether or not they were moral writers?

CHEEVER: I think John's book, *On Moral Fiction,* was an approach to opinions that we all possess. That fiction, of course, is on the side of life, with conspicuous exceptions—the men who are dedicated to satanic practices.

BRANS: What do you mean?

CHEEVER: Oh, I'm thinking of Huysmans, of course.

BRANS: The dead-end sort of thing.

CHEEVER: The self-declared decadence. And I don't mean the self-declared suicide. It seems to me that fiction is a striving toward life. It is the only history we have of man's struggle to be illustrious. It does deal with nobility—with heroism. Basically, it seems to me that all great fiction deals with potential greatness.

BRANS: What makes fiction moral, in your mind?

CHEEVER: I wouldn't link morality to fiction.

BRANS: You don't think that the act of writing is itself a moral act?

CHEEVER: No, "creative," of course, is the word we use as much as the word "moral." Both words have unfortunate connotations. And yet I don't know of any other words in English.

BRANS: I suppose I'm thinking of moral as something that's life-sustaining, life-perpetuating.

CHEEVER: Well, the connotation it has for me, coming perhaps from New England, is something forced and inflexible. It is mixed up in my mind with legislatures, with social pressures.

BRANS: If you tell undergraduates that a book is moral, they usually think it has something to do with sex, and it's against. I suppose that's the sort of thing you're talking about.

CHEEVER: I am self-centered, of course, and I believe I came out rather badly in Gardner's book.

BRANS: No, you came out very well.

CHEEVER: How did Saul Bellow come out?

BRANS: Gardner said he was an essayist—his books were extended essays.

CHEEVER: What you might call the fragrance of morality is extremely strong in Saul's books. A sense of that which is fitting and decent. I can't think of a contemporary writer who possesses it more uncompromisingly than Saul.

BRANS: Maybe he wants to be a leader.

CHEEVER: Well, here again "leadership," like "morality" and "creativity," involves connotations that are uncontrolled. I had to make a speech at the donation of Malcolm Cowley's manuscripts to the Newberry Library in Chicago. All I could think of was literature. And I genuinely think of it this way, as something to which one makes a contribution. That is really all one can do. The vastness of literature and its importance to any civilization is inestimable, and one's contribution can be very fleeting or lasting or large or small. It doesn't really matter, so long as one recognizes the vastness and the power of the stream. (How does a man make a contribution to the stream other than to spit in it or urinate in it? I did notice that when I spoke at the dinner about the passionate wish to make a contribution to the stream, it was understood that I would explain which I intended.)

And that is the way I see it, which of course doesn't involve leadership at all. In his Nobel Prize speech, Saul spoke of literature as being perhaps—and my feeling is that this is true—the first sign of civilization.

BRANS: How long have you known him?

CHEEVER: Saul? Oh, I've not known him well ever. That is, we see very little of one another. I'm always delighted to see him. The assumption is that we met in some other life and we'll meet again, so why bother to spend any time together in this world. Then he lives in Chicago and I live in Ossining.

I remember when we first met, but I can't remember the date. It must have been about thirty-five years ago. We met at Eleanor Clark's before she married Red Warren.

BRANS: So long ago. But you see him—what, once or twice a year?

CHEEVER: Right. We meet roughly twice a year. He was driving me home once in Chicago, and he said, "That's the beach where, when I was a young man, people used to play ukuleles, cover themselves with oil, and stand on their hands."

And I said, "You know, that's why writers don't meet. Because when you give me a series of three, then I have to rival and match you with three."

I remember some years ago, when I picked up *Dangling Man*—I don't think I had read anything else by him—I knew at the end of perhaps the third sentence that some tremendous talent had come into the English language. And I remember putting it down at the end of the first page and running upstairs saying, "Something terrific is going on here!" . . . There are some lovely things in there—the description of the woman washing windows. What was of interest, of course, was the voice. He has one of the great voices.

BRANS: You read Bellow. Do you read Cheever?

CHEEVER: I don't happen to read my own work over, because I find it all embarrassing or boring. I find it all quite dull.

BRANS: Are you serious about that? You really don't pick up the Wapshot books and read them again? But you must have read all of the stories again when the anthology came out, or when you were working on it? No?

CHEEVER: Absolutely not. I would read three lines, and if they were all right . . . Somebody asked me about "The Geometry of Love," a story that's full of bitterness. I have never, I think, held the story in my hand since the manuscript was mailed out. I'd simply thrown it aside then.

BRANS: I remember that in those conversations that Faulkner had at Virginia, he was always getting confused about what had happened in some of his novels. He would have to be corrected. It was so funny. The students would jump up, and they'd say, "Oh, no, you've got that wrong," or "That's not her name." I thought at the time I read it that he was shamming but maybe he didn't reread his work either. He really had forgotten, maybe.

CHEEVER: One wouldn't want to be affected. I don't really know why, but this is very much work that has been accomplished. When the new edition of the Wapshots came out, I had a long train trip to make, and I thought, well, I'll take it, and I can read the *Chronicle*. I really don't mind the *Chronicle*. But I couldn't even get through the Fourth of July morning. It's like some sort of generative process that has already taken place and as far as you're concerned is exhausted.

I will enjoy reading "The Death of Justina" tomorrow night. And I rather enjoy reading "The Swimmer." I've read "Justina" everywhere, wherever I've been, even Japan and Moscow. The references are quite limited to suburbs of the Northeast, but for some reason or other it's right wherever—I don't know why. It's because bureaucracy is always recognizable, I guess.

BRANS: You really love Justina as a character, too, don't you? I can just feel—the way she dies is such an enviable way to die. She has had a good life. She's sitting on the couch with a glass of, I think, brandy. And she dies sitting straight up. Her eyes are still open. It's a really wonderful death.

CHEEVER: It was. Justina is like my mother-in-law. I adored my mother-in-law, and her last request was for a good drink of vodka. I think she died before it got to her.

"Justina" was originally to have been part of a book called *The Wapshot Footnotes*. I was going to go into what had happened to all the Wapshot characters. But after I did "Justina," I decided that the book didn't justify itself.

BRANS: You've said the same thing about "The Swimmer," that you intended it as a novel, but that you didn't think you could really spend three hundred pages having the constellations change in the north sky. What are the differences in your mind between writing a novel and writing a short story? How do you decide?

CHEEVER: It's really the emotion that one wants to communicate that establishes the form. "The Swimmer" was the only one in which I felt an ambiguity. It was the first time that it had taken me a long time to write a short story. It was obviously a turning point in my—gestation, let's say. It was virtually a book when I finished. And then when I started to cut it back I realized the whole thing turns on the moment when time remains totally mysterious to him—and to me. It seems to me that when one has an impulse to communicate something in fiction the form and the length of it are inherent.

BRANS: The first thing I read of yours that I really sat down and thought about was *Falconer.* I remember thinking, Gee, I thought John Cheever wrote short stories for the *New Yorker.* I wasn't prepared, and it just bowled me over.

CHEEVER: I still think *Falconer* is a tremendous book. I absolutely wrote it in a state of hysteria from the opening line to the end, "Rejoice, rejoice." And it took me about eight months. I must have been horrible to live with.

BRANS: I was just about to ask you a really ugly question. Are you braced? I was going to ask you about this brother thing, about Farragut's killing his brother. But fratricide is all through your fiction. I'm not trying to pry into—

CHEEVER: Well, evidently I loved my brother very much.

BRANS: But in a very curious way. I keep picking up all these clues, and I don't understand the story of you and your brother, or how this has affected the fiction.

CHEEVER: Well, I don't understand it either. I took it very seriously at the advice of Freudians years ago. That I loved my brother, and very likely would not love anyone else. And that I had to learn to live with that.

BRANS: Do Freudians really say things like that?

CHEEVER: Yes. And they would say, "Let's mine the early material, right?" And this would go on and on and on. So then I sort of drew away from my brother. But he really is very much a part of my life.

BRANS: How much older was he than you?

CHEEVER: Seven years older. And drank himself to death about five years ago, I guess it was. Yes, I loved my brother. I very much enjoyed being with him.

BRANS: Was he on the decline for a number of years before he died?

CHEEVER: Yes. We broke off when it was quite apparent that this love was going to come between us and any sort of decent relationship with women. I simply packed my bag. That's when I left Boston.

BRANS: You were seventeen?

CHEEVER: Yes. Then he followed me.

BRANS: You mean it was such an absorptive relationship that you didn't think there was room for women in your life as long as . . . ?

CHEEVER: Yes, except as a convenience. It all struck me as being destructive—self-destructive.

BRANS: Were you wiser about this than he was?

CHEEVER: I don't think so. It would have been very possible for two men, two brothers, to live in Boston. We used to be asked out together. It's a society that accommodated two brothers' lives.

BRANS: So that it didn't even seem peculiar to other people?

CHEEVER: "In the eccentricities, Mr. Hollingsworth," quoth the society, "two brothers are quite acceptable." As a matter of fact, it's just as right as any other eccentricities of Boston society. We were looking at a house, we were going to live in an old house in Boston. I was going to write novels and he was in the cotton textile business, and it was a perfectly acceptable situation.

BRANS: How did that become such a continuing motif in your fiction? For example, the fratricide in *Falconer*.

CHEEVER: I doubt that I will ever escape from it. But it doesn't in any way strike me as an interference.

BRANS: Do you think that in having Farragut kill off his brother you were killing off a part of yourself?

CHEEVER: Very likely. I don't know. I have been hitting this character on the head with rocks and sticks for years. I said to my brother when I last saw him— We said good-bye. He'd started to drink again. He was standing on the threshold of my house, and I said, "By the way, Fred, I killed you in my last book." I had just finished *Falconer*. And he said, "Good, good."

BRANS: He liked it?

CHEEVER: He laughed, and he said, "That's fine." He was pleased.

BRANS: You had a compulsion to write it, perhaps. Tell me about the discipline of writing. Is it a chore for you, or does it come naturally? Denise Levertov recently said that poetry chooses you, you do not choose to write poetry. Do you feel that way about fiction, that it chooses you?

CHEEVER: I'm not as bold as Denise in these matters. I was astonished to hear her say that sentence that she de-livered. After having had a gestalt, or an inscape, she felt, the poet had the form revealed to him. Now to go into the field of revelation is to step into a wilderness that I'm not prepared to go into, nor into the premise that fiction chose me.

BRANS: It makes you sound like one of the elect.

CHEEVER: Well, you get into an entirely different stratum, where you can't count on what you touch, or breathe, or—you don't know where you are. I think it's admirable that she has this, but I certainly don't share it with her.

BRANS: But you did decide very young that you wanted to write fiction.

CHEEVER: But that wasn't so uncommon a task. Very often people find woodwork irresistible, or musical instruments. I certainly wouldn't say that the novel or the short story had chosen me.

BRANS: It was a very brave thing for you to go to New York at seventeen, and live in a grim little room, and begin to write.

CHEEVER: Well, the kindness that one has received is one of the most astonishing things one finds in life, actually. The most enormous help that comes from almost everyone.

BRANS: Who was helpful to you in particular?

CHEEVER: One of the reasons I went to New York was that E. E. Cummings, who came from Boston, encouraged me to. I was taught by my family that if you were going to succeed anywhere you would do it in Boston. And if you died of boredom, it was entirely a lack of character on your part. You were what is known as a good sport: that is, the Cheevers *never* die of boredom in Boston. And the rest of the world was full of Jews who ate white eggs and made a lot of money and stock down there and committed suicide. I mean, New York was just a dreadful place. You didn't go there. The idea was that to leave Boston marked you as a character who was lacking, not in any way an estimable character.

And it was Cummings who said, "Joey, Joey," which is what I used to be called, "get out." And in this wonderful wind-up-the-chimney voice, "Get out!" And of course Cummings was a Yankee. He was a perfectly comfortable Yankee; his mother was a Little. And I said, "Well, why, Cummings?" And he said, "Boston is a city without springboards, for people who can't die. Get out! Get out!" And I was met everywhere with understanding and magnanimity. And still am, and it seems to me, so are you, so are we all.

BRANS: How did you meet Cummings?

CHEEVER: I met him through a couple named Hazel and Morey Werner. Morey Werner was a great friend of Cummings. I met Hazel Werner because Lincoln Kirstein bought a story of mine when I was about eighteen. Lincoln and Morey took me and Hazel Hawthorne to lunch, and we were both quite sloppily dressed. We'd gotten together the best we had in clothing. I had on white buckskin shoes and my good gray flannels and a blue button-down shirt. I don't know what Hazel had on, she'd gotten up some sort of— We went sailing down the street after Lincoln and Morey, these two gorgeous creatures—you know, fur collars on, and derby hats. And Hazel was a friend of Cummings. I met her at that extraordinary lunch. I think we both got blind drunk.

BRANS: In self-defense.

CHEEVER: And sort of giggled at one another. Lincoln was going on about Balanchine. He was just then organizing the School of American Ballet. He's done wonderfully for ballet. He was terribly nice to me, and I couldn't have been ruder or more unpleasant.

BRANS: I've seen the picture Walker Evans made of your grubby little room.

CHEEVER: It was, of course, extremely rugged. And I was cold and hungry much of the time. At the ceremony for the honorary degree at Harvard a Russian woman sat next to me. She said, "Of course you graduated from Harvard?" And I said, "No, madame, no." And she said, "Where did you spend your college years?" And I said, "In furnished rooms on the Lower West Side." She said, "What was it like?" We'd just met her. I said, "I was cold and hungry and lonely." And she said, "But that is all over." And I said, "I'm not at all sure, madame." And then she kissed me on the mouth.

BRANS: Were you afraid in New York because you weren't going to school and you weren't doing the—?

CHEEVER: Never more frightened or lonely than I am today.

BRANS: Surely you're not afraid now?

CHEEVER: Yes, I'm frightened and lonely now. Not at this moment. But before I go to sleep tonight I will be both frightened and lonely.

BRANS: Is that true?

CHEEVER: Yes, that's true.

BRANS: That's really a daily thing for you?

CHEEVER: Well, it's not daily—but it is part of my life. The mystery of loneliness I think is a part of my life. There are weeks, of course, when I am quite happy and quite thoughtless. But I find life no less perplexing, no less bewildering, than it was when I was an adolescent—much more so, actually. Because when you're young you have the drive, the desires.

BRANS: And then you know you're not going to die.

CHEEVER: Yes.

BRANS: That helps a lot. What are the roles of suffering and pain in creating?

CHEEVER: The common assumption is that the artist is a man who is tormented to the point of doing some works of great art, and then presently destroys himself, because there is no other way out of his torment. This idea is very gratifying to the layman, because then one wouldn't after all want to be an artist, would one? The glee with which the self-destruction of someone like Jackson Pollock or Hart Crane is pursued and followed becomes obscene. It's not so gratifying to the artist's colleagues. Saul Bellow has contributed enormously by being the first American writer to win the Nobel Prize who is not an alcoholic suicide.

BRANS: So you don't think that such suffering is really necessary for art?

CHEEVER: Well, suffering, yes. That's very much a part of life. But I don't think self-destruction, which shouldn't be confused with suffering, is.

EUDORA WELTY

Struggling against the Plaid

EUDORA WELTY has recreated her early life and the experiences that shaped her writing in three lectures delivered at Harvard and published as *One Writer's Beginnings* (1984), which surprisingly became a national bestseller. The Welty family was not Southern in origin. Her Republican father came from Ohio and her mother from West Virginia. As Eudora, born in 1909, and her two younger brothers were native Mississippians, cheerful differences of opinion often arose. "It was a good family to grow up in," Welty has said. "I learned early there wasn't just one side that was right."

She attended college in Mississippi, but graduated in 1929 from the University of Wisconsin, and then for a time studied advertising at Columbia University's Graduate School of Business. Back home, after a brief stint in journalism Welty took a job as a publicity agent during the Depression for the Works Progress Administration. The travel the job demanded brought her into contact with the diversity of people in her home state. She took hundreds of snapshots, some of which she published much later in

One Time, One Place: Mississippi in the Depression (1971). As Welty clicked the shutter, however, she became aware that "what I needed to find out about people and their lives had to be sought for through another way, through writing stories."

Just as Welty's collection of essays and reviews *The Eye of the Story* (1978) reveals her empathy and generosity for other writers, from the beginning her stories excited praise and support from others. Over the years, she has won six O. Henry awards, and no less an eminence than Katherine Anne Porter wrote the introduction for her first collection, *A Curtain of Green* (1941). Three other collections followed: *The Wide Net* (1943), *The Golden Apples* (1949), and *The Bride of the Innisfallen* (1955). *The Collected Stories* (1980) was her first bestseller; the year it came out, Welty received both the Presidential Medal of Freedom and the National Medal for Literature. Her stories are characterized by photographic precision of details, the mastery of colloquial and lyrical language, compassionate humor, and a suggestion of the poetic depths and infinite complexity of human experience.

The most constant theme in her five novels, as well as in the stories, is the unpredictability of human character and the multiplicity of life. Jamie Lockhart, the enigmatic protagonist of *The Robber Bridegroom* (1942), is the attacker, the defender, and the husband of fair Rosamund; he is highwayman, businessman, and lover. Or, as Welty concludes, he is "a hero" with "the power to look both ways and to see a thing from all sides."

If a single person is many-sided, so is a family, and indeed a family is embellished by taking in the alien. Unmarried herself, Welty frequently shows fictional marriages that bring together contradictory values and kinds of people. *Delta Wedding* (1946) revolves around the coming wedding of Dabney, the beauty of the aristocratic Fairchild plantation family, to the overseer Troy Flavin, and the "unsuitable" previous marriage of the family favorite George to Robbie, one of Welty's numerous little have-nots. The varying responses of the tightly knit clan to these two outsiders reveal "how deep were the complexities of the everyday, of the family."

In *The Ponder Heart* (1954), the mystery of the marriage of Uncle Daniel Ponder, who constantly gives his money and possessions away, to his child bride Bonnie Dee Peacock, who is enamored of "things," is "pondered" by the narrator, Daniel's niece Edna Earle. Edna Earle sides with Daniel, yet expresses muted affection for the greedy little Bonnie at the end: "She's the kind of person you do miss. I don't know why—deliver me from giving you the reason."

The central marriage of *Losing Battles* (1970) is that between young Jack Renfro, prince of the proud, poor Renfro clan, and his young wife, Gloria, the orphan protégée of Miss Julia Mortimer, an unmarried schoolteacher long the bane of Renfro lives. Over a day and a half, the Renfros celebrate Jack's return from prison and Granny's ninetieth birthday with a family reunion. While Miss Julia is buried, the Renfros are going strong, and family ranks close to take in Gloria.

The Optimist's Daughter (1972), which won the Pulitzer Prize for 1973, explores, less benignly, some of the same tensions. Here, the marriage of old Judge McKelva to Fay, a much younger have-not, is complicated by the point of view, that of the Judge's grown daughter Laurel, which allows the comparison of Fay to Laurel's dead mother. Fay says she made the Judge happy; Laurel is sure Fay hastened his demise. The issue, raised when Laurel comes back for her father's funeral, is never resolved, though the reader feels that the author's sympathies lie with Laurel. In a rare autobiographical admission, Welty has said that the dead Becky is patterned after her own mother.

When I first read Eudora Welty, she was my neighbor. Two blocks from the Mississippi state capitol, the Tudor brick house her father built in the twenties sits right across the street from Belhaven College, where I went to school. We girls would read her stories and crane out our high dorm windows for a glimpse of the writer, said to be shy.

Sometimes, downtown—Jackson was like a small town then, in the fifties—I would run into Miss Welty. I never said hello. Instead, mute with respect and as shy as she, silently and I hope invisibly I would follow her tall, angular figure home: drift down the quiet streets in her wake, catch the North State Street bus if she did, sit behind her peering out as she did at the big old houses, the little "colored" shacks, the ugly new brick moderns. Where was her secret? Back in my dorm room, I would read her stories again, watch her windows, and wonder.

When, twenty-five years later, with a smile behind her bright blue eyes, she told me, "I don't lead a very dramatic life myself, outwardly," I could have said I knew that. But I didn't. Instead, shy as ever, both of us, we stayed where we belonged, with the stories.

BRANS: The thing that especially impressed me in the conversation yesterday was that you said you wrote because you loved language and you love using language. I know you are a photographer, and you've painted too.

WELTY: I was never a true or serious painter, just a childhood painter.

BRANS: How does writing compare in your mind with those other art forms?

WELTY: Oh, it's in the front. The others are just playthings. I didn't have any talent for photographs. I was strictly amateurish. I think the book I did [*One Time, One Place*] has a value in being a record, just because it was taken in the 1930s. And I was in the position of being perfectly accepted wherever I went, and everything was unselfconscious on the part of both the people and myself. There was no posing, and neither was there any pulling back or anything like that. Our relationship was perfectly free and open, so that I was able to get photographs of things as they really were. I think today the book has a sort of historical value, which has nothing to do with any kind of professional expertise in taking pictures, which I knew I didn't have.

But I am a professional writer. That is my work and my life, and I take it extremely seriously. It isn't just the love of language, or love of the written word, though that is certainly foremost, but the wish to use this language and written word in order to make something, which is what writing is. It's a tool. It's the tool, not the end result. So I guess that would be how you could describe what I'm trying to do.

BRANS: To create a reality with words. Why is dialogue, spoken language, so important to you—say, in *Losing Battles*?

WELTY: I tried to see if I could do a whole novel completely without going inside the minds of my characters, which is the way I do in most of my writing. I didn't tell how anyone thought—I tried to show it by speech and action. I was deliberately trying to see if I could convey the same thing by speech and outward appearance as I used to do by going inside people's minds.

BRANS: It seems to me that in your writing you're hardly ever autobiographical. I've heard you say that you're working out of your feelings, but not your own experiences. Are there any stories that are autobiographical?

WELTY: I don't deliberately avoid being autobiographical. It's just that when I'm writing a story I have to invent the things that best show my feelings about my own experience or about life, and I think most of us wouldn't be able to take our own experience and make a dramatic situation out of that without some aid. And I do much better with invented characters who can better carry out my feelings.

I don't think you can describe emotion you have not felt. You know, you have to know what it's like—what it is to feel a certain thing—or your description or your use of these emotions will be artificial and shallow. So I certainly understand what my characters are feeling, but I try to show it in a way that is interesting dramatically.

And I don't lead a very dramatic life myself, outwardly. So it's not that I'm concealing myself, it's just that I'm using whatever—a lot of the details come out of my own life, things that I've observed. There was a scene in my novel, *The Optimist's Daughter,* about a three-year-old child in West Virginia, a whole section in there that I suppose you could call autobiographical, but actually it was my own memories of being at my grandmother's, on the farm, and all the things that the child felt—the rivers and the mountains and all those things. Nothing like that could be made up, you see. If you've never been in the mountains you wouldn't know how to say what it was like to be in the mountains. But it was not me as the character. It was my feelings, my memories, my experiences, but it was that character that was feeling them, not me. The character was not me. So, that's an example.

BRANS: You sort of projected your feelings into this creation.

WELTY: Yes, and used them to describe this character. I didn't use all that I had, I used just what would help me to explain the character.

BRANS: How do those characters come to your mind? Do they just spring full-blown into your mind? Or do you work them out—?

WELTY: It's just part of the whole process of making a story. I mean, they are all one with the plot and the atmosphere of the story and the weather and the location. They don't exist apart from the story—they're not even in the world outside the story. You can't take a character out of this story and put it into another.

BRANS: It doesn't work?

WELTY: They wouldn't live. So the characters are all integral parts of the story in which they occur. Of course you can use many sources to make a character—occupation, memory, knowledge, dreams, newspaper articles, many things. You may get little bits here and little bits there, because the character is a sort of magnet and attracts different kinds of observations. Not just any, you know; it's just what applies to the character. So how can you tell where they come from, any more than you can tell where anything comes from—where a tune comes from to a composer?

BRANS: Do you have any set pattern of working? That is, do the characters occur to you first, or a trick of plot, or some idea that you want to express? Is there any particular order that seems to be the same?

WELTY: It's different with every story. It just depends. Sometimes the story begins with the idea of a character and then you invent a plot which will bring this out. Take that one story that's used lots of times in schools called "A Worn Path." That character called up the story. Such a person as that would take a trip like this to do something. That's a good simple case.

BRANS: What I love about "A Worn Path" is not so much the endurance of the walker as the windmill or whatever you call it at the end. For me that was the beauty of the story, that all of a sudden old Phoenix does move above the . . . just the endurance . . .

WELTY: I love that, too.

BRANS: And walking all the way back down the path holding the little windmill up. I have a clear picture of that. It made the trip into town worth the coming.

WELTY: Absolutely.

BRANS: In one of your essays you say that Faulkner has a sense of blood guilt about the Indians [in the South] and then about the blacks. In your own work you don't have that.

WELTY: Well, it's not my theme. You know his work encompassed so much and so many books and so many generations and so much history, that that was an integral part of it. I don't write historically or anything. Most of the things that I write about can be translated into personal relationships. I've never gone into such things as guilt over the Indians or—it just hasn't been my subject. My stories, I think, reflect the racial relationships—guilt is just one aspect of that. Certainly I think any writer is aware of the complicated relationship between the races. It comes out in so many even domestic situations.

BRANS: Very few of your stories deal directly with blacks, though. And those that do, I've wondered if the blackness is a necessary part of the character. For example, old Phoenix. Why is she black?

WELTY: It's not a deliberate thing, like, "I am now going to write about the black race." I write about all people. I think my characters are about half and half black and white.

BRANS: Really?

WELTY: I would guess. Considering the novels and everything. I think it's the same challenge to a writer. It doesn't matter about color of skin or their age or anything else. Then again, I never have thought about "A Worn Path" as being anything but what it was; but one thing may be that when I wrote that story, what started me writing it was the sight of a figure like Phoenix Jackson. I never got close to her, just saw her crossing a distant field early one afternoon in the fall. Just her figure. I couldn't see her up close, but you could tell it was an old woman going somewhere, and I thought, she is bent on an errand. And I know it isn't for herself. It was just the look of her figure.

BRANS: It's not true, then, what I read—that you were the lady old Phoenix asked to tie her shoe?

WELTY: Oh, no. I was out with a painter who was painting his landscape and so we were sitting under a tree. I was reading, and I watched her cross the landscape in the half-distance, and when I got home I wrote that story that she had made me think of. She was a black woman.

But then I suppose it would be more likely to be a black woman who would be in such desperate need and live so remotely away from help and who would have so far to go. I don't think that story would be the same story with a white person. The white person could have the same character, of course, and do the same thing, but it wouldn't have the same urgency about it.

BRANS: Well, old Phoenix does fox white people. You know, she takes the nickel from the hunter, then asks the lady to tie her shoe.

WELTY: It wasn't because they were white, though. Those are two different things altogether. It was the desperate need for the money and for the child that she needed that nickel—she knew it was a sin, too. But asking the lady to tie her shoe—she knew who would be nice to her. She picked a nice person, because she was a nice person, and she picked one. Those are two entirely different motives, taking the nickel from this really nasty white man and asking a favor of a nice lady. She knew in both cases.

BRANS: She had a wonderful graciousness.

WELTY: She knew how to treat both.

BRANS: One of my students went to your reading Sunday night, and she came in with a paper on it. She had misunderstood the title of the story called "Livvie," and she referred to it as "Living," which showed she understood the story anyway.

WELTY: That's very cute. I'm glad to hear that.

BRANS: A misprision, I guess, but a nice one. What I'm saying is, I know sometimes I fix interpretations on the things I've read.

WELTY: Well, I do too. We all do that. And I don't feel a thing bad about it, because a story writer hopes to suggest all kinds of possibilities. Even though it may not have been in the writer's mind, if something in the story suggests it, I think it's legitimate. You know, it doesn't have to be exact.

The only way I think to err is to be completely out of tone or out of the scope of the story or its intention. No, it doesn't bother me one bit if someone interprets something in a different way, if I think the story can just as well suggest that as not, because you try to make it full of suggestions, not just one.

BRANS: As a teacher I'm very sensitive to this whole question, because students frequently say, at the end of the discussion of the story where you really are trying to get at all the things that make the story possible, "Now do you think that Eudora Welty really intended all of that?" And of course there's no defense for a teacher, and all I can say is, "How do I know?"

WELTY: That's all we can say when we read anybody's work.

BRANS: How can I know what she intended? But if we find it here in the story, the story belongs to us when we're reading it.

WELTY: Exactly. The only thing that I know bogs a lot of students down, because I get letters all the time, is in the case of that dread subject, symbols. You know, if they get to thinking, This equals this, and this equals that, the whole story is destroyed. Symbols are important, I think, but only if they're organic—you know, occur in the course of the story, are not dragged in to equal something.

BRANS: No, no. It takes all the life out to do that.

WELTY: Of course. And symbols aren't equivalents.

BRANS: —not algebraic equations!

WELTY: I know it. But, you know, some students get the idea, and it's very troubling to them. And what I hate about it is it might discourage them from ever enjoying reading stories, if they think they're supposed to make an algebraic interpretation, as you said.

BRANS: In connection with "Livvie," let me ask you something that's really off the wall, probably: Was there any thought in your mind at all of reflecting Faulkner's *As I Lay Dying*? Just the name of the character Cash, and then the fact that Livvie—

WELTY: No, that was a coincidence. No, indeed—I mean, I wouldn't—you're not aware of any other person's work when you write your own. At the time I wrote that story I didn't know about Faulkner's Cash. When did he write *As I Lay Dying*?

BRANS: I think about 1930.

WELTY: You know, Faulkner was out of print when I was growing up.

BRANS: For a long time, right.

WELTY: It was about 1940.

BRANS: When Malcolm Cowley did *The Portable Faulkner*.

WELTY: Everything I have of Faulkner's I've bought through searching in secondhand bookstores in order to read them. He wasn't in the libraries. He wasn't to be had—at least in Mississippi. I don't think he was to be had anywhere. He was out of print, for a long time.

BRANS: That's right. I had forgotten that. That's important.

WELTY: Well, I guess I hadn't read him until I had been writing for some time. But, at any rate, the presence of Faulkner's writing in Mississippi—I was glad he was there, and I loved his work, but he wasn't hovering over my work. Because when you're writing, you're just thinking about your story, not how would Faulkner do it, how would Chekhov do it, how would Katherine Anne Porter do it?

BRANS: I wasn't really asking you that. I know that's not true.

WELTY: A lot of people do wonder, just because he lived there, and of course it is a formidable thing.

BRANS: His shadow.

WELTY: I wish that he could have helped me.

BRANS: What I was thinking was just that sometimes I feel that you've taken some of the same themes. I suppose that was inevitable.

WELTY: Because we get them out of the same well.

BRANS: But that, in your mind, is more or less unconscious. And you give them a comic twist. In *Losing Battles,* for example, all the Beecham kin decide at one point that Gloria might be a Beecham, and that her father might be one of the Beecham brothers, and they seem to be delighted with the whole idea.

WELTY: Yes, they're thrilled. That makes her okay.

BRANS: Right. Even though by Mississippi law at the time that would make the marriage incest. But that's kind of a Faulknerian—I'm thinking of *The Sound and the Fury,* where Quentin says he'd rather have slept with his sister Caddy himself than have an outsider—incest would be better. I always think of Faulkner in connection with that idea, because I got my first gasp of shock from him.

WELTY: Well, I didn't mean anything serious and tragic at all. I just meant it to show what the Beechams were like. That is, to be a Beecham made everything all right. That was what I was showing.

BRANS: You have commented that Faulkner's comedy may have more of the South—more of the real life of the South—in it than his tragedy.

WELTY: I think it has everything.

BRANS: And it seems to me that your writing is basically

comic. There is almost always that sense of harmony and reconciliation at the end.

WELTY: Yes, I think it's a part of tragic things. It intrudes, as it does in life, in even the most tragic situations. Not comedy—I would say humor does. Yes, I like writing comedy. It's very difficult and it's much harder, because one false step—and I've made many of them . . . That's why I have to work very hard on the comic theme, because it's so much more difficult to do. One false step and the whole thing comes down in a wreck around you.

BRANS: When I think of comedy, I don't so much think always of humor, as I think of the something at the end that suggests that the world will continue—that life will continue. A kind of optimism for the species. You always suggest this, usually with a synthesis of opposing elements. I love that line in *Losing Battles*—in Miss Julia's letter—"The side that loses gets to the truth first."

WELTY: Oh, yes, that's when she was in her desperate state.

BRANS: Had she thought of herself at that point as having lost?

WELTY: Oh, I'm sure. She did.

BRANS: She did lose?

WELTY: Look at all the people around her. All her class, all the people she'd taught, they didn't know a thing, except the thing that mattered most to them, which I think is most valuable—that is, their love for one another and dependence upon one another, and their family, and their pride, and all of that. But nothing Miss Julia had tried to teach them had even taken root. Nothing.

BRANS: In your mind is she like Miss Eckhart in *The Golden Apples*?

WELTY: She filled a function in the story perhaps that would be kind of similar, in that she was a person unlike the world in which she lived, trying to teach and help somebody. But Miss Eckhart was a very mysterious character. Julia Mortimer was much more straightforward and dedicated and thinking of the people as somebody she wanted to help. Miss Eckhart was a very strange person.

BRANS: Could I ask you what your sense is of the differences between male and female characters in your stories? I keep thinking about that line from "Livvie," "I rather a man be anything, than a woman be mean." And also, in *Delta Wedding,* say, the women are obviously making the demands on the men.

WELTY: Well, men and women are different. I don't mean they're not equally important. But they're different. That's the wonderful thing about life. No, in those different stories I'm not writing about them as men versus women.

In the Delta it's very much of a matriarchy, especially in those years in the twenties that I was writing about, and really ever since the Civil War when the men were all gone and the women began to take over everything. You know, they really did. I've met families up there where the women just ruled the roost, and I've made that happen in the book because I thought, that's the way it was in those days in the South. I've never lived in the Delta, and I was too young to have known what was going on in anything in the twenties, but I know that that's a fact.

Indeed it's true of many sections of that country after the Civil War changed the pattern of life there. So I've just had that taken for granted—it was part of the story. That was something the men were up against.

I think that in many of my stories I do have a force, like Miss Julia Mortimer or Miss Eckhart. But those two are so poles apart in their characters that I can't see much connection.

BRANS: There's a real passion in Miss Eckhart.

WELTY: There certainly is. It's a passion for getting some people out of their element. She herself was trapped, you know, with her terrible old mother. And then no telling what kind of strange Germanic background, which I didn't know anything about and could only indicate. I mean we don't know—they had tantrums in that house, and flaming quarrels.

BRANS: There's that one quarrel that surfaces when the girls are there. She hits her mother, doesn't she, or—?

WELTY: Or something. I think her mother hits her. But anyway, I wanted to indicate that they were passionate people. And Miss Julia was passionate too. Most of my good characters are. Virgie Rainey had it too, and Miss Eckhart saw it, that Virgie had that power to feel and project her feelings, and she wanted her to realize all of this.

BRANS: Do you think Virgie does?

WELTY: I think at the end of the story she is saying goodbye to the life there in Morgana. I think she's got it in her to do something else.

BRANS: Remember that line about Virgie's sewing? Virgie is cutting out a plaid dress, trying to match up the rows, and Miss Katie says, "There's nothing Virgie Rainey likes like struggling against a good hard plaid."

I'm thinking of the struggle in *Losing Battles* too—Jack and Gloria, who in a way have come from separate worlds. Although Gloria resists it, she's very much the child of Miss Julia Mortimer. She was brought up to be the teacher.

And Jack is very much the hope and promise of the Renfro clan, and yet I felt reading the book that even though they've been apart most of the time they've been married, they've already impressed their worlds on each other. Is that what you intended?

WELTY: Yes, indeed, I certainly did. That's exactly correct. And why Gloria—I think every instinct in her wants them to go and live to themselves, as they put it there.

BRANS: Yes, in that little house.

WELTY: It's going to be mighty hard to do. But she knows where she stands all right, and she's not intimidated at all. And Jack, of course, is just oblivious to the fact that there could be anything wrong with his staying there and having the best of both.

BRANS: He wants her to love Granny. Granny is just so unlovable.

WELTY: Granny doesn't want to. "She didn't say anything, she nodded. She would love you."

BRANS: I thought Granny was just as mean as she could be.

WELTY: Well, she's living in her own world, too.

BRANS: And she wants to be a hundred instead of ninety.

WELTY: She thinks she is a hundred.

BRANS: But the most amazing thing is that Jack is willing to love Miss Julia Mortimer.

WELTY: Yes. He's willing to.

BRANS: Nobody else in his family is.

WELTY: No. He is. I really love Jack.

BRANS: When I asked you in the panel yesterday which of your characters you thought spoke for you, I kind of expected you to say Jack.

WELTY: Oh, I was thinking about stories yesterday, I wasn't thinking about the novel. Well, Jack is really the reason I went on and made a novel out of this. Because when I first began it, it was a short story which was to end when Jack came home. The story was about why he happened to go to the pen. All that crazy story about the fight. And he was to come home and wonder why they thought anything was wrong. You know, "What's happened?" Well, as soon as he walks in the door I think, "No, I want to go on with him." I had to start all over and write a novel.

Yes, he's willing to love Miss Julia. In fact, he says in there, "I love her. I feel like I love her. I've heard her story." I think that's very direct and penetrating: because he's heard her story, he knows what's happened to her.

BRANS: And she has a reality for him even though he "never laid eyes on her."

WELTY: And the people who have gone to school to her didn't really see her. Jack is really a good person, even though he is all the other things.

BRANS: I don't see anything bad in Jack.

WELTY: No, except that he allows himself to be used by everybody.

BRANS: But that comes out of his goodness.

WELTY: It comes out of his goodness and it's so typical also, I think, of just such situations. Haven't you known people like this? We all have. Yes, I really like Jack. He's a much better person than Gloria.

BRANS: Well, she's a little have-not. Don't you see her in that way? A have-not, so that she's clutching.

WELTY: An orphan.

BRANS: And that's what Miss Julia represents too. But when Jack says, "I've heard her story," he's really—

WELTY: They're all living on stories. They tell each other the stories of everybody. And he heard her story. They were blinded to her by having gone to school to her. They just took her as their bane. They're struggling against her. But he *heard* her story.

BRANS: Now Virgie Rainey—she struggles against herself. Isn't Virgie essentially a wanderer, who really wants to wander, but for years she makes herself stay there in Morgana for her mother's sake?

WELTY: I guess so. I use that term rather loosely because it also means planets, and I have got a number of characters that I try to suggest can move outside this tiny little town in the Delta, though it's not a cut-and-dried kind of thing. It's not A, B, C, D. But I wanted to suggest it.

BRANS: They could make it in a larger world.

WELTY: Yes. That there was a larger world. Whether they could make it or be broken like Eugene MacLain is something else. They know something else is out there. It's just an awareness of the spaciousness and mystery of—really, of living, and that was just a kind of symbol of it, a disguise. I do feel that there are very mysterious things in life, and I would like just to suggest their presence—an awareness of them.

BRANS: Is the sense of mystery and magic related to your use of mythology?

WELTY: I think it is. Exactly, that's what it is. Because I use anything I can to suggest it.

BRANS: And myths then seem to suggest something timeless?

WELTY: Yes, or something—

BRANS: Perpetually reborn or recreated?

WELTY: I think so. Something perhaps bigger than ordinary life allows people to be sometimes.

I find it hard to express things in any terms other than the story. I really do. Some people can, but I can't. I never think that way. I only think in terms of the story. Of this story.

Embracing the World

NOT SINCE HEMINGWAY has a writer had as much influence on the American short story as Donald Barthelme, who has frequently been called America's most brilliant contemporary writer, as well as the father of minimalist fiction in this country. After Barthelme, the short story will never be the same; his work anticipated the affectless fiction of Raymond Carver, Ann Beattie, and his brother Frederick Barthelme, as well as a group of younger writers like Amy Hempel. Though one hears the influence of Kafka, Borges, Lewis Carroll, Gertrude Stein, even Ring Lardner, in his wildly witty stories, Barthelme is unique. "Nobody could have predicted Barthelme," the late John Gardner once remarked. "He wasn't a possibility."

More than any other writer in English, Barthelme has freed fiction from the strictures of linear plot, comprehensible character, and even coherent design. He allies fiction instead with stand-up comedy, newspaper reports and headlines, advertising slogans, parody, and other cultural

photo by Nancy Crampton

detritus. "The principle of collage is the central principle of all art in the twentieth century in all media," Barthelme believes. In well over a hundred short stories and three novels, he has created verbal collages. By tossing repetition, unrelated and often fantastic episodes, a variety of voices and kinds of language, onto the page, as a visual artist might apply paint or bits of straw or paper to a canvas, Barthelme confounds traditional expectations of what a piece of fiction ought to be.

Like his father, an avant-garde architect, he seeks to bring new forms into existence. The son, however, is motivated by a deep-seated pessimism. His stories fail in "meaning" in order to imply the failure of meaning in contemporary life. They are composed of fragments in order to reflect the fragmented quality of modern existence; they explode on the page in order to mirror the explosion of ephemera under which we are sinking. Melvin Maddocks has written perceptively, "A lapsed Catholic, Barthelme is a poet of order gone. His stories are metaphysical rebellions against the petty chaos, the near-madness they report. In almost every respect but technique, he is—or at least he longs to be—a traditionalist."

The oldest of five children, Barthelme was born in Philadelphia, where his father was studying architecture, but grew up in Houston, Texas. He graduated from the University of Houston, where he founded a literary magazine, and worked as a reporter on a Houston paper. After army duty, he returned to Houston, worked in public relations at the university, and later directed a contemporary arts museum. In the early sixties he came to New York to launch his literary career and in 1963 and 1964 published ten stories in the *New Yorker,* where most of his stories have appeared before publication in book form.

Readers and critics alike were baffled but impressed by the first books of short stories, *Come Back, Dr. Caligari* (1964) and *Unspeakable Practices, Unnatural Acts* (1968). However, his first novel *Snow White* (1967), which places the fairy-tale heroine in the pop culture of the sixties—she and the seven live in a commune and have meaningful encounters in the shower—became a campus and popular favorite. With *City Life* (1970), which contains his most daring and brilliant stories, especially "Brain Damage," his critical reputation soared as well.

Other, less pyrotechnical collections followed. *Sadness* (1972), like *City Life,* uses irony as a defense against the dreck of the modern world. *Guilty Pleasures* (1974) consists largely of hilarious parodies. *Amateurs* (1976) is a modern fable and *Great Days* (1979) a new dialogue form. *Sixty Stories* (1981) brought together in one volume his best work over twenty years, and was followed by a rash of critical books and articles. All the stories in *Overnight to Many Distant Cities* (1983) are masterly but not groundbreaking, and *Forty Stories* (1986) is a collection of pieces published elsewhere, with the addition of nine new stories.

After *Snow White,* Barthelme has written two more novels. *The Dead Father* (1975) presents the question of the authority of the past in the person of a giant father, who though "dead" continues to exact duty from the next generation. *Paradise* (1986) may or may not be the projected novel *Ghosts* alluded to in the interview which follows.

Just as Barthelme has turned the form of the short story inside out, all three of the novels are alike in their use of a familiar mythic narrative pattern turned inside out in order to show the pattern's essential absurdity. Thus Snow White, the beautiful maiden, is trapped in drudgery and in the sequential sex of the sixties with her seven, and the "dead" father issues instructions as to his proper burial. One of my great regrets here is that, when Barthelme himself brought up his interest in Joseph Campbell's myth studies, the interviewer was asleep at the wheel.

When this interview was done in 1981, Barthelme, a big genial man with a red beard going white, was teaching part of the year at the University of Houston. After he visited a contemporary literature class I was teaching, the two of us closed the door to my poky, booklined office for this conversation.

BRANS: You have said that your father's example, as an innovator, as a modern architect, was important in your career somehow.

BARTHELME: Oh, yes, it was very important.

BRANS: Could you elaborate on that?

BARTHELME: It was an attitude toward his work. First, he was very much involved in the early modernism. He went to architecture school—his degree is from the University of Pennsylvania, which is why I was born in Philadelphia. He met my mother there—she was also a Penn graduate. He was trained in architecture school entirely in the Beaux Arts tradition. No whiff of modernism was allowed to penetrate the Penn architecture school at that time. And he got out of school and suddenly the whole world changed for him. But he is, for example, a marvelous draftsman, because that's one of the things the Beaux Arts system stressed, those meticulous wash drawings and so on. It was very fine training, but it had nothing to do with what was really going on in architecture. So he went through a complete reversal—his world turned upside down, in a way.

Remember, at that time—we're talking about the late twenties and early thirties—the architecture of the country didn't look like it does today. The modern building was quite, quite rare. To get hold of Le Corbusier's books was a task. You had to write to France for them, or find some wonderful shop that had already written to France for them. So his task was to do an entirely new thing, which was contrary to his training in important ways.

And he did it with great enthusiasm, with great zest, and he did it very, very well. It was the whole atmosphere of the home, because, when he built our house, it was a terrible anomaly amidst all the houses around it. It looked weird, although it was a very beautiful house, somewhat similar to Mies's Tugendhat house. And then, inside the house, the furniture was all Alvar Aalto stuff. It was not like real furniture, in a way. I mean we all know what real furniture is, and this stuff was weird-looking. Now this has been assimilated all over the country. You've got Aalto-derived furniture in airport waiting rooms, for example. But it was unusual then, and it had to have been, both visually and spiritually, important.

BRANS: Were you ever tempted by architecture yourself? You've got a very strong visual sense.

BARTHELME: No, I always wanted to be a writer, even when I was small. A couple of my brothers tried it. Rick started off in architecture at Tulane, and my brother Pete started off in architecture at Cornell, but both of them went into other things.

BRANS: Was there a time in which you felt you had to throw off your father's influence? I can't help but think about you and *The Dead Father* in connection with your own family situation, because a strong father is not an easy person to live with.

BARTHELME: Well, we had, when I was an adolescent, a series of, let us say, temperamental clashes, and I think that was the process of getting away, for me.

BRANS: Karl Kilian has been quoted as saying that he was impressed with your family, because it was like a family of giants. I think he meant physically—he had the impression that all of you were big people.

Then he also went on to say that all kinds of things were going on. That you actually talked to each other—genuine discussions—it was a very volatile atmosphere.

BARTHELME: Kidding Father was an activity that took about seven of us to do, and there were only six of us. Putting Father down was the main family sport.

BRANS: Is there any particular reason for the number of fathers in your work who are being done away with in one form or another? I'm thinking of *The Dead Father*. Using a father and beating him—is there anything autobiographical—?

BARTHELME: Well, not directly. The relation is the universal problem. You remember, I think in Gertrude Stein there's a story about the guy who seizes his father by the hair and drags him out of the house into the orchard, and at a certain point the father who is being dragged says, "Stop, stop. In my time I did not drag my father beyond this tree."

BRANS: I had the idea that *The Dead Father* was a lot like Faulkner's *As I Lay Dying*, except with you it's the father that has to be buried, and in Faulkner it's the mother.

BARTHELME: Someone also pointed out to me that in Kafka's letter to his father, the image of a giant father presents itself. And I haven't gone back to reread it to see how Kafka handled it. But in Kafka the father obliterates the son.

BRANS: In *The Dead Father* it's quite clearly the son's victory. Of course you do kind of wonder what the father's going to do even after he's buried. He may be buried, but he's not dead. He's still sending up lustful feelings.

Speaking of the lustful father makes me want to ask you something about the relationship between the sexes in your work. I was just thinking of Hogo's remark in *Snow White,* that it's not enough that we have all these problems with women; now we have to acknowledge that *they* have thoughts and feelings.

BARTHELME: The book has been read as sort of anticipating the great feminist activity of the sixties and seventies. And male resentment is a theme that's there.

BRANS: I don't think of that necessarily as male resentment, but just that men like Hogo, say, seem to have fairly simple notions about women and the place of women.

BARTHELME: Well, he speaks also of the replaceability of women. They are as multitudinous as plants.

BRANS: So "durability is not what we want." Jane is durable, but durability is not necessarily what we are—we'll go for a twenty-two-year-old.

BARTHELME: But, remember, Hogo's a bad guy.

BRANS: But he's a very realistic and—he's a very pragmatic guy too. He's obviously inherited the leadership after Bill has been hanged. I know you're leery of this, but is Hogo representative of—

BARTHELME: The triumph of evil?

BRANS: Or the triumph of the expedient.

BARTHELME: No. Somebody else has raised that point, and I think that the reader can imagine that the seven guys, who are now six, will in some sense change Hogo.

BRANS: Well, now, I didn't get that at all.

BARTHELME: Maybe it's not in there sufficiently clearly.

BRANS: They say, we had Hogo to show us how to hang Bill, and thank God we have Hogo. And they depart at the end in search of a new principle.

BARTHELME: That's true. But the Snow White principle now is no longer available to them.

BRANS: She's been revirginated. Risen into the sky. So they're going to go off in search of a new principle.

BARTHELME: I hope it's implied that that will also mean a new object of their devotion, a new Snow White, in a way.

BRANS: Sure, I think that is implied. I just thought they wouldn't have an effect on Hogo.

BARTHELME: Well, I think there's a sense in which they very likely will change him rather than having him change them.

BRANS: It's a more optimistic book, I suppose, than I had thought of it as being, if you regard being changed by the dwarfs as—

BARTHELME: They're not dwarfs. —I know, it's hard to say.

BRANS: Not dwarfs? I didn't realize that they weren't dwarfs. This really changes my whole view of the book.

BARTHELME: They are consistently spoken of as men. Of course that could be read as little men, but—

BRANS: I'll have to go off in search of new principles, to read *Snow White*.

BARTHELME: It's not my favorite book, by the way.

BRANS: I think it's terrific. And I chose it to read with students because I thought it would be fun for them. Undergraduates all love the sixties. They have aggrandized the sixties—the sixties are sort of what the Roaring Twenties used to be.

BARTHELME: I've noticed that, yes.

BRANS: So I thought it would work for them, and I

think it did. What is the new book about? What is *Ghosts* about?

BARTHELME: Oh, I'm not clear on that yet.

BRANS: I thought it was coming out very soon.

BARTHELME: Well, in theory, it's coming out next year. I'm inured to worrying about that book. It doesn't really matter whether it comes out next year or the year after, because there are no deadlines.

BRANS: Are you bouncing off of Ibsen in any way?

BARTHELME: No, I'm trying to avoid it. Indeed, that's a working title, and I'm not really clear whether I'll use it. It's just the way I identify it to myself. It may be that it seems presumptuous. On the other hand maybe it won't have any effect at all. I don't know. There's also an Ed Mc-Bain mystery I discovered called *Ghosts* published in 1979. It just happened—which I don't like. It's not that I don't like Ed McBain. I guess since it's in another genre, it would have no effect.

BRANS: Are there social forces that you would hold responsible for our loss of purity of language? The kind of garbage language that you're always making fun of? *Kinds,* I should say, because there are numerous parodies.

BARTHELME: Well, I think there are two devices that have clearly had an enormous impact on language. One is television. I don't wish to blame television for all the faults of the world, but it has had a vulgarizing effect. The other is the telephone, because we don't write letters anymore. I don't write letters—I don't even write business letters. I call up on the telephone. When people don't write letters, language deteriorates.

BRANS: Do you keep a journal?

BARTHELME: I keep a workbook with stray pieces of paper with things written on them. A kind of mulch pile.

BRANS: A student wanted me to ask you about another statement of Hogo's. Hogo says, "Our becoming is done." And the student offered the explanation that the society has become static and isn't changing.

BARTHELME: That was not the intention. It was rather a reference to the aging process. Both Hogo and Jane are older than the other people. Hogo is realizing that, or stating it.

BRANS: You're not attempting to show an essentially static society? I'm relieved because I don't think this society is static.

BARTHELME: No, I don't either.

BRANS: But you told the class that you don't expect to effect any social changes yourself. I wondered about that, because I didn't quite believe it.

BARTHELME: It is not a declaration of intent so much as a declaration of powerlessness. The effect that any individual writer is going to have in this time seems to me to be very, very minimal.

BRANS: You'd like to be able to do it, but you don't think—

BARTHELME: If I could clean up the world by writing about it, if I thought it could be done, I would do it, and I'd have everything tidied up within one generation, but I don't think I have that power. I mean it is really a declaration of powerlessness. Some small effect, possibly— nothing on the scale of what Tolstoy thought he was going to do, and in some measure did. I can't do a Tolstoy.

BRANS: A writer perhaps doesn't have a sense of his own power because he doesn't get an instant response, as a social reformer does.

BARTHELME: If I were a Marxist, say, I'd have a system which I believed would effect social change, and I would be morally bound to think that way and write that way, but I'm not a Marxist.

BRANS: But you have affected our perception of the world with your use of form. Was there a dramatic moment in which the form of a Barthelme short story emerged?

BARTHELME: Yes, but it was a ten-year moment.

BRANS: What were you trying to do those ten years? Were you trying to find some way—

BARTHELME: I was trying to write fiction that I myself thought was worth publishing—and I wrote a lot of garbage.

BRANS: But you've also said that you really admire the traditional forms of fiction. John Cheever, for instance.

BARTHELME: Of course I do. I'd be a fool not to.

BRANS: You were just trying to do what? To find your voice?

BARTHELME: I was trying to do something different. Well, I was trying to make art, and I didn't want to do it as Cheever does it, although I admire very much what Cheever does—but that's what Cheever does. I was trying to do something else. I suppose I was trying—in the crudest statement—I was trying to make fiction that was like certain kinds of modern painting. You know, tending toward the abstract. But it's really very dicey in fiction, because if you get too abstract it just looks like fog, for example.

BRANS: Words, after all, have referents. They mean something—colors don't.

BARTHELME: Not in the same way. So, the project is next to impossible, which is what makes it interesting. There's nothing so beautiful as having a very difficult problem. It gives purpose to life. And to work. I'm still worrying with it.

BRANS: Trying to create new forms. And essentially the first thing you have to do is get rid of the older forms.

BARTHELME: Well, not get rid of them. I don't think I've gotten rid of anything. People seem to regard it as a process of destruction in some sense, but I don't see why the two things can't coexist.

BRANS: But you are—in a story you do get rid of our traditional expectations in plot and characterization.

BARTHELME: I don't get rid of them in the sense that they're gone once and for all. I don't abolish anything.

BRANS: You're not wiping out anything already in the language.

BARTHELME: Just choosing to do different things. I believe that the way that's perceived has much to do with the tradition of—as each new movement of art comes along, the people involved traditionally issue manifestos, claiming that everything has been overturned, and a whole new order is extant. And what they are talking about, of course, is "Our Gang." Like the Futurists—they produced more manifestos than art, probably.

But I have issued no manifestos. Just doing my number. The sort of revolutionary rhetoric associated with art movements makes people assume that everybody is issuing manifestos. Or that the work itself is a manifesto.

BRANS: Right, sort of a gauntlet thrown down. Another problem in writing your fiction must be that you're dealing with a reader who has certain expectations about what fiction ought to do. So, short of creating a whole new generation of readers, and we don't seem to be doing that—

BARTHELME: I am glad to see you've got Joseph Campbell on your shelves—*The Hero with a Thousand Faces*. It's a book I give to my writing students—it's wonderful.

Have you read *The Masks of God*? That has some wonderful things in it too. And there's much of Jung that is useful to writers. Not in terms of psychoanalytic theory, but in terms of his interest in myth.

BRANS: Eudora Welty has said that in a short story there should be a kind of tension that runs all the way through. And she said that ideally one should write a short story in one sitting, but she wants that thread, that tautness that goes through it. I wonder if you would comment on what she said.

BARTHELME: I don't agree. I agree with her about the tension. But I disagree that it should be written in one sitting, because as a practical matter I don't think that that necessarily would produce the tension she's looking for, and I doubt very much that—

BRANS: No, she said she couldn't do that. She said there was a time when she always tried to get it down in one sitting.

BARTHELME: Well, Hemingway described writing two of his best stories the same day, and it probably happened. I forget which two stories he refers to. But I remember he says he got in bed with a bottle of brandy and began it after finishing the first one, and then he wrote the second one. They're very short, of course.

BRANS: Did you learn much from Hemingway?

BARTHELME: Oh, sure. Hemingway taught us all. First, wonderful things about rhythm, his sentence rhythms, and wonderful things about precision, and wonderful things about being concise. His example is very, very strong.

BRANS: I belong to that generation that rebelled against him. But when I started teaching him, I began to see how marvelously those books are crafted. Now, I teach *The Sun Also Rises* over and over.

BARTHELME: His best novel by far. Although I also like *A Farewell to Arms* and the stories—just beautiful. I certainly can't be said to write like Hemingway, but he certainly is an influence. There are a lot of influences that are not very apparent. Sabatini. And S. J. Perelman.

BRANS: You mentioned John Gardner earlier today. Where do you stand in the Gass-Gardner controversy regarding morality in fiction?

BARTHELME: With Gass. I think Gass is right.

BRANS: But don't you think Gass takes it too far in saying that fiction has nothing to do with morality?

BARTHELME: I don't think it's been taken far enough. At what point is it taken too far? Anyway, going too far is something I'm in favor of.

BRANS: Obviously. I guess I want something moral and beautiful to come out of fiction.

BARTHELME: I do believe that my every sentence trembles with morality. It's full of morality. But it's the morality of an attempt. It's not the morality of giving you precepts. To decide as Gardner would that my enterprise is immoral because it doesn't preach to you or elevate you in some dubious way— *On Moral Fiction* was clearly an attempt at a Saint Valentine's Day Massacre. That's what's so funny about it. It's so overt.

BRANS: I'll tell you why I think Gass goes too far. Because he makes all these statements about how fiction shouldn't have any morality in it, and yet I think I find a contradiction to what he says theoretically in his own fiction. I think *Omensetter's Luck* is an enormously moral book.

BARTHELME: Sure it is.

BRANS: But he apparently wants to make the point so clear that he will reject the plain evidence in his own fiction.

BARTHELME: No, I don't think he's overstating it simply to make a point. I think he believes what he says, and I also believe what he says. I think he's right. His position is the correct one.

BRANS: Even though he's writing moral fiction.

BARTHELME: Yes, but it's not moral so much in the way that Gardner conceives fiction as moral. It's the morality of art. And you're not going to persuade me that making art is not a highly moral act in itself. It's certainly difficult enough to qualify as a moral act.

BRANS: Do you know Gass?

BARTHELME: Yes, we're friends. I don't know him very well. He's a nice fellow.

BRANS: And you know Grace Paley?

BARTHELME: Oh, yes, she lives across the street. She's one of my best friends.

BRANS: She is a delight. She was wonderful when she came here. She had about twelve students following her around at all times.

BARTHELME: I believe it.

BRANS: What qualities do you admire in other writers? What do you look for?

BARTHELME: That's a general question. Many different things. I always look at another writer to see what he or she does well, because it's reassuring, refreshing, gives me something to admire. It imposes goals. For example, when Updike wrote *The Coup*—I haven't read the new one [*Rabbit Is Rich*] yet, although I have it—I was impressed with him all over again because of the richness of imagination and conception. Just being able to renew himself to that extent is wonderfully impressive. I've never really told him how much I liked the book. I guess I should.

BRANS: It's so totally unlike anything else he'd done.

BARTHELME: That's right, it was a departure.

BRANS: I was reading V. S. Pritchett the other day on the subject of *Rabbit Is Rich* and he said that he thought the best of them was *Rabbit Redux*.

I'd like to go back to that anathematization line from *Snow White*.

BARTHELME: It's a jaw-breaker, isn't it?

BRANS: "Anathematization of the world is not an adequate response to the world." You said that you wrote that because you began to feel some discontent with what you had done in the book. Do you think that in the later book, *The Dead Father,* and the stories that you have written, and the book that you're working on, do you think you've gone beyond cursing?

BARTHELME: I hope.

BRANS: Can you say how?

BARTHELME: It's hard to say precisely what you have done, because at some level you don't quite understand what you have done.

BRANS: You're not as angry?

BARTHELME: Yes, I guess that's probably it. Gass objected in *Fiction and the Figures of Life* to some lines in one of my earlier stories. The male character asks the female character, "Do you think this is a good life?" and she says, "No." And I think that got Bill Gass upset at me, a bit, because he felt it wrong to think that. And I wouldn't write those lines now, so I suspect he was right in being mad at me, to the extent he was mad.

BRANS: What has happened to make you think this is a good life?

BARTHELME: Well, as you're in the process of leaving it you begin to cherish it more. That's true.

BRANS: Don't say you're in the process of leaving it. I know when you were born.

BARTHELME: When you get to be fifty, you begin counting forward—you begin doing arithmetic.

BRANS: No, I don't like to think that approaching fifty equips me with wings or whatever is necessary to leave. I think I've begun to live. But maybe that's another way of saying the same thing.

BARTHELME: Yes—in one of the stories in *Great Days,* there is a quite clear statement to the effect that things become more exciting as there's less and less time. I think that's true.

BRANS: I felt I perceived a lot of anger in some of your earlier work.

BARTHELME: Probably true.

BRANS: I mentioned this to students, and they said, "Oh, he's not angry. How can anybody so funny be angry? You're mistaken in seeing anger."

BARTHELME: Joking very often conceals a lot of anger.

BRANS: Jokes are a kind of defense mechanism.

BARTHELME: That's true. Gregory Bateson has a great line in which he says, "Humor is the great alternative to psychosis." It's true.

BRANS: And what my mind immediately goes to is John Berryman's Henry poems, because there's so much dark humor in them. I sometimes attempt to teach some of his poems, and the students always think, This is not funny. But maybe, again, age is required to see it.

BARTHELME: Certainly true of some things. I mean, I like being this age. I don't want to be twenty again. It's not that I'm uncomfortable being this age, I'm enjoying it very much.

BRANS: Just that the days are dwindling down to a precious few?

BARTHELME: Yes, well, we're getting there.

BRANS: What do you think the proper response to the world is, then?

BARTHELME: Embracing it.

BRANS: Embracing the world. In fiction?

BARTHELME: In fiction and out of fiction, sure.

BRANS: How can you embrace the world in fiction when you write the sort of fiction that you're writing, which is not realistic fiction?

BARTHELME: But I take the position I am writing realistic fiction. Everybody's a realist. Every writer is offering a true account of the activities of the mind.

BRANS: Of mind, yes—but of body, no. You're not recording the minutiae of everyday life.

BARTHELME: Yes, I am. At the end of one of the stories in *Great Days* the two men are talking about the passage of time, and so on, and they begin reciting a list of beautiful things, and one guy says, "Like when you see a woman with red hair, I mean really red hair." And there's a list—and each detail is a real thing—an accurate report.

But I think the distinction between who's a realist and who's a surrealist and who's a superrealist is slightly specious. By definition, one can only offer the activity of the individual mind, however it's notated. It's all realism.

BRANS: It's your brand of realism.

BARTHELME: Yes.

BRANS: Realistically, are you hopeful about human life in the 1980s?

BARTHELME: Worried. Worried.

BRANS: What really scares me is the idea that people are talking about a safe bomb. Of course they've *been* talking about a safe bomb.

BARTHELME: That's madness. The doomsday clock has been set up a few notches, I gather. The way our present government is talking is absolutely mad.

BRANS: You said present government, but you've been railing at the government as long as I've been reading you.

BARTHELME: Well, I haven't seen a government I liked yet.

BRANS: I remember that you got off the plane for the Texas Institute of Letters dinner in 1979, and the first thing you said to us was, "What happened to the hydrogen bomb?" It was the weekend of Three Mile Island and you were apocalyptic. And I wondered if you have changed your—

BARTHELME: No, no, no. I think we are governed by some very strange people. What can you say to this century with the two great wars and all the other wars and the concentration camps? Sorry century.

BRANS: Do you think we might really destroy ourselves?

BARTHELME: Accidentally, sure. There's the ability.

BRANS: Then you were talking about writing. You said writing lasts.

BARTHELME: I said that I believe that writing will last as long as human beings last.

BRANS: Oh boy, the wind-chill factor is high at this point! You've faulted yourself for the lack of emotion in your fiction. Do you think you're becoming more able to express emotion?

BARTHELME: Yes, I think it's coming out now.

BRANS: Is the emotion that you want to express love?

BARTHELME: It's various—it's various. Not restricted to love or any particular emotion.

BRANS: Do you think that the vicissitudes of your personal life have anything to do with your ability to express—? I mean—I don't know anything about your personal life, but I'm just wondering if lowering of those defenses in your personal life makes you more willing to take chances.

BARTHELME: No, I think it's got more to do with being my present age.

BRANS: Are you trying something specifically different in your recent fiction?

BARTHELME: I've written a number of dialogues—stories.

BRANS: I've read the ones at the end of *Sixty Stories*.

BARTHELME: I may have written too many of them. I have more that I'm not satisfied with.

BRANS: What is interesting to you specifically about dialogue?

BARTHELME: It's stripped, allows essentials to be dealt with in a rather pure way.

BRANS: Essentials being—?

BARTHELME: I don't have to get people in and out of doors. I don't have to describe them. I don't have to put them in a landscape. I just deal with their voices.

BRANS: So the essentials—are their relationships?

BARTHELME: Yes. The dialogues really came from trying the dialogues between the two women in *The Dead Father*. That was the impulse. The dialogues in *The Dead Father* are really collections of non sequiturs, intended to give the novel another kind of voice, to provide a kind of counter-narration to the main narration. Then I got interested in doing them for their own sake, with a little more narrative introduced.

BRANS: Are you going to go from the dialogue to the monologue?

BARTHELME: I've done a monologue or two.

BRANS: Well, the monologues of the dead father.

BARTHELME: Yes, and also the story in the new book called "Aria," which is a woman's monologue.

BRANS: And "How I Write My Songs."

BARTHELME: A monologue of a kind. So, I don't know what I'm going to do next. We'll see. I gave a student an assignment a couple of weeks ago. She was having problems because she was writing a certain kind of thing, and it was too tentative—it was too jokey—too whimsical. So I tried to deprive her of her humor. The assignment was to write something on the highest possible level of abstraction—say four pages—to see what she got. And I gave her a couple of things to read: Ashbery's *Three Poems,* Robert Wilson's *Letter to Queen Victoria,* and I forget the third. Not so that she would do a pastiche of these, but so that she would get some feeling for what direction the assignment was going in.

She produced the most marvelous four pages—just marvelously inventive. It reminded me a little bit of Stein, at the top of her form. She was going along, reading it to the class, and at one point she reached down and tinkled a little bell.

BRANS: You seem to be caught up in teaching. Is there any connection between your writing and your teaching?

BARTHELME: When you've spent all these years sitting by yourself in a room, you like to get out in society once in a while—that's the original impulse. And I'm very fond of the students.

BRANS: Does your writing ever benefit from these exchanges with students, or is that such a private—?

BARTHELME: In the sense that you meet new people and see what their concerns are, you see what they're worried about, you see what they're enthusiastic about. It's just like any social situation where you can get rather close to people over time, get to know them to some extent. It's refreshing, in other words, as opposed to staying home and sitting in my room spoiling paper.

BRANS: Do you write on an Olivetti typewriter? (I know that's a corny question.)

BARTHELME: No, an old IBM Selectric.

BRANS: The Olivetti kept coming up in book after book, and I decided that either you had that kind of type-writer or it represented something to you.

BARTHELME: In New York, once, someone had perma-nently mounted in front of a store one of these flat Olivet-tis, on a stand, and it was there even at night when the store was closed. And they put a long piece of paper in it, and people used to type messages—and so you'd go to see what crazy things people had written on the Olivetti today.

BRANS: Oh, wonderful.

BARTHELME: That's in one of the stories. It's quoted in "The Shower of Gold." One of the Olivetti messages.

BRANS: Do you talk about your own work to your students?

BARTHELME: I talk sometimes about my own practices.

BRANS: Do you take one of your stories and show them how you did it?

BARTHELME: No. Occasionally I'll read something that has some pedagogic value. For example, there's a story called "Nothing," which I also use as an assignment. When somebody is stuck, I'll say, well, do me a piece that de-scribes "nothing." Sometimes if I give that to a whole class, when they're finished reading theirs, I'll read mine just to show how I dealt with it.

BRANS: That's an interesting assignment, especially for

people who say they have "nothing" to write about. It really has to come out of your own innards.

BARTHELME: Another story I did came from an assignment that I had given a class, which was to do a version of Mozart's *Abduction from the Seraglio.* I had set it up in such a way that they had to make certain changes in the situation, so I got interested in these, and I did it myself. So there is some back-and-forth effect of teaching.

And then students indirectly help with the problem of allusion, because you have to stop if you make an allusion to something and say, Will people remember this, or will they get it? I had to ask my younger brother the other day—I had Chill Wills in the story—Will everybody know who Chill Wills is? He assured me that they would. So, I try to use more allusions than perhaps every reader will get, so that there will be things that if he doesn't remember *this,* he will get *that.*

BRANS: Are the allusions connected?

BARTHELME: To each other?

BRANS: Yes.

BARTHELME: Yes, in the framework of the story. I like to pack it as closely as possible.

BRANS: You know, students always ask teachers of literature—I don't know if they ask teachers of writing this—after you've finished doing the job on the story, they'll say, Now, how much of that did he really put in there? And I have developed an answer, which is, Everything. Because I'm tired of implying that the critic is smarter than the writer, and so I just say, Give him the benefit of the doubt. He knew what he was doing. Do you think that's okay?

BARTHELME: Yes, it's true that a good piece will take on

added presences that were perhaps not specifically built into it. But because of the New Criticism, that intensely close reading, I think people did tend to read into pieces very often things that were not and should not be attributable to them.

BRANS: Sometimes I think writers today are very skittish about this in ways that maybe are detrimental to a proper appreciation of their writing. For example, Eudora Welty read a story called "Livvie," and in it there's an old black man, a very tightly curled character, everything is controlled by the clock. He's married to this young girl whose name is Livvie, a young black girl who just simply escapes with a young man. The students asked her about things it seemed to me—the young man was wearing a green suit, for example—and the old man has a black umbrella, which you know—is—

BARTHELME: Does the umbrella symbolize death, and the green symbolize hope? No, it's just a green suit.

BRANS: That's what she said. She said it's a green suit, it's a black umbrella. And I thought, You know, lady, you're not dealing with this quite straight. I can see why she did it, but at the same time it bothered me that she would take those precautions.

BARTHELME: Well, the way to protect yourself from that is not to make the suit green in the first place.

BRANS: Right. But the fun of reading it is in seeing that it really is all put together that way, and that it's not just telling a story but much more, something *made.*

Do you have an ideal reader, any particular person in mind when you write?

BARTHELME: Just ordinary folks like us.

photo by Nancy Crampton

D. M. THOMAS

The Grass Captain

THE AMERICAN PUBLICATION in 1981 of his
third novel, *The White Hotel,* brought unexpected
celebrity to D. M. Thomas, a handsome, quiet-
voiced, reticent Cornishman who had spent most of his
life in the predictable obscurity of provincial teaching. Until then Thomas was known primarily as a poet who had
edited three collections of poetry, had written eight others,
and had translated Russian verse. Neither of his two earlier
novels, *The Flute-Player* (1979) and *Birthstone* (1980), had
sold more than a few hundred copies. Upon its British
publication in January, *The White Hotel* too seemed des-
tined for only a small public.

But when the novel came out in the United States in
March of 1981, a torrent of critical acclaim lifted it first to
intellectual cult-book status and then to bestsellerdom. Already into its second printing before the official American
publication date, *The White Hotel* eventually sold some
100,000 copies in hardcover and almost two million in the
paperback reprint.

Thomas, poor as teachers often are, wrote the novel on the security of a year's severance pay when Hereford College, where he headed the English department, closed its doors in 1978. In subject matter and treatment, *The White Hotel* is anything but the usual stuff of pop fiction. The book tells the life story of Lisa Erdman, a Ukrainian singer treated for sexual hysteria by Sigmund Freud. In structure, the chapters range from Freud's letters, to Lisa's disturbing and sexually charged poetry, to a psychoanalytic case study of Lisa, to conventional narrative. Her character revealed against the background of the Nazi atrocities which climaxed in World War II, Lisa dies with thirty thousand other Jews at Babi Yar.

"I cried," Thomas has said, when he heard that Pocket Books had offered to pay $200,000 for the reprint rights to the book and another $150,000 for promotion, and that film rights had brought another $500,000. "Partly from sheer excitement, but also from guilt. It is a book about inconceivable suffering and it seemed to me almost immoral to make money from it."

Coping with his notoriety as its author was also inconceivable. In January of 1982, Thomas came to the United States to teach for a term at American University in Washington. There he found that he was a hot property: reporters had been calling the university to line up interviews for six weeks before he arrived. Two weeks into the term he resigned by wire and went home to Hereford where he could count on being "totally ignored."

"The writer should be an ordinary man," he told the baffled literati on both sides of the Atlantic. "I could not cope with being seen as some kind of media figure for the next three or four months."

Thomas began life in the most ordinary of circumstances. Born into a mining family in Cornwall in 1935, at
eighteen he entered the military for his two years of com-
pulsory service. Assigned to an army intelligence school
for translators of Russian, he developed an interest in Russian poetry which led eventually to his publishing translations of the work of Akhmatova, Yevtushenko, and Pushkin. On a scholarship he went to Oxford University,
receiving his B.A. with first-class honors in 1958 and his
M.A. three years later.

In the preface to *Selected Poems* (1983), Thomas observed that from the beginning of his career as a poet he
preferred his poems to have a narrative basis. He consid-
ers his novels, he went on to say, "poetry in the form of
prose fiction." *The Flute-Player,* which was written in four
months, won a fantasy-novel contest. A political and sexual fantasy which chronicles the heroic courage of artists
in a totalitarian state, it stemmed from his interest in the
lives of Russian writers under Stalin. Elena, "the flute-
player," a beautiful and good young musician who be-
friends other artists, is patterned in part after Anna Akhmatova. *Birthstone,* too, has a female protagonist, a young
Cornish woman named Jo who, like Lisa in *The White
Hotel,* is beset with psychological problems.

Though he still claims to be primarily a poet, in the
years since this interview Thomas has published a trilogy
in prose fiction on the theme of improvisation and inspiration, centering on an international poetry contest. *Ararat*
(1983), *Swallow* (1984), and *Sphinx* (1987), the three novels of the trilogy, are also the surrealistic and sensual blend
of poetry and prose, twentieth-century brutality, quirky
sex, and black humor which made *The White Hotel* such a

commercial and critical success. *Summit* (1988) is a fictional romp on the subject of superpower relations.

I met Thomas in March of 1982, when, after his hasty return to Hereford in January, he had come back to the States on a limited promotion tour for the paperback edition of *The White Hotel.* This interview took place in a small hotel room turned into an antechamber of hell by Thomas's cigarettes. A short stocky man with a shock of gray hair and bushy eyebrows, he was delighted to learn that I was interested in all of his work, not just in his bestseller. In spite of his incessant smoking, his voice was musical, with the faintest trace of a Cornish burr.

BRANS: Woman is a dominant figure in your poetry and in your novels. Do you think of yourself as a Muse poet?— of the kind that Robert Graves wrote about in *The White Goddess,* I mean.

THOMAS: Yes, I do, very much, though I don't go to the extent that Graves did in almost making a science out of it.

BRANS: Hardly anyone does.

THOMAS: I suspect he was spoofing a bit himself. But I surround myself with Muse figures when I write. Let's see, there's a bronze statuette which I found at Delphi of Leda and the Swan. The Leda is a very slim black girl, very tall, and the golden swan is wound around her. Then there's a framed poster of Anna Akhmatova on my left; she's looking at me constantly. I have a watercolor of a nude on my right, and a silver replica of a bronze by Donatello of the Madonna and Child. Certainly they all inspire me. My subject matter is, I think, love and eroticism, the relationship of the sexes. I feel that I am in touch with something, with some feminine principle, some anima, through my poetry, which is continued into my novels.

BRANS: I was thinking of a poem like "The Lady of Fetishes" and all the aspects of the feminine that you deal with there.

THOMAS: Yes, that poem really casts an ironic and light-hearted eye on the different ways men see women and women see women. Men do tend to generalize about women, of course. Fetishes are a very male prerogative, I think. Men substitute clothing or whatever for the woman, and women find this hard to understand. I think it means that men perhaps are able to symbolize more easily than women. Lou Andreas-Salomé, the great friend of Freud, wrote that women are much more rooted in reality and men have this gift for symbolism—which is maybe a compensation for their not being able to bear children. You probably disagree with this profoundly. It's quite old-fashioned in many ways, goes right against the feminists.

BRANS: Well, I don't know. I was thinking of what Addie Bundren says in Faulkner's *As I Lay Dying*. She's talking about the difference between herself and her husband Anse. She says Anse lives by words, but she lives by actions—she calls it "doing." The way she says it is beautiful, something like, "Words go straight up in a thin line, but how terribly doing goes along the earth, clinging to it." Isn't this what you mean?

THOMAS: Yes, men do symbolize and the woman in "The Lady of Fetishes" resents being invited to take on roles that men have chosen for her. She says, None of them is me. The feminine insistence on particulars.

BRANS: When you say "feminine," do you mean, literally, women, or a feminine impulse which might exist in men?

THOMAS: Literally women, but of course gender is a fluid thing, especially for writers. I'm very conscious of writing through a feminine side of myself. It's a spectrum, isn't it?—where largely those on one side are women and men mostly on the other, but they flow into each other.

BRANS: Would you say that your interest in the Muse and this poetic response to life comes out of your having been born and brought up in the Celtic country of Cornwall, so close to Wales—that sort of Welsh "calling up the spirits from the watery deeps," as Shakespeare put it?

THOMAS: I think it is a Celtic thing. The Celts are highly imaginative, an intuitive and in some ways a very feminine race. Not that they are women, of course, but that they have womanly qualities. Also, though Cornwall is a fairly bleak landscape, with stark cliffs and pounding sea and bleak moorlands, there are also incredibly lush river valleys. My ancestors were miners—tin and copper miners. In my study at Hereford, where I have all those Muse figures, I also have a plan of an old silver mine from Colombia. An uncle of mine was the manager, and he made a drawing of the levels of the mine.

BRANS: You mean the layers of the earth?

THOMAS: Exactly. What has been mined and what still remains to be explored. I find that very powerful too, the idea of going down into the womb of the earth. The Cornish actually call their mines by feminine names. "Wheal" is their name for mine, and it's "Wheal Charlotte," "Wheal Grace." They felt that when they went into the mines it was the mother.

This background is very important to me. I feel that I'm mining when I write. They had another term for someone who worked on the mines but didn't have the lousy job of actually going down. He was "the grass captain"—you

know, in charge and up on the grounds. So I regard myself really as a grass captain.

BRANS: Oh, that's lovely. You can mine but you don't
have to get your hands dirty. Isn't there an obvious association between you and D. H. Lawrence, who thought of
the mines and the miners in somewhat the same way?

THOMAS: That's true. In his case, the mother was the
spiritual, upward-seeking force, his father the dark down-
ward force, resisting rationality. Now my father is a very
intelligent man, though he didn't have the education.

He was educated through travel. He emigrated to California and later to Australia. I heard a story recently from
someone from my village. She remembered my grand-
father saying, "Look what going to America has done for
Harold. He can talk to the king now."

The Cornish always emigrate, so we always had this
feeling of flow, of letters from America or Africa or Australia. That's how my background differs from Lawrence's, of
course. His people were much more land-contained, more
engrossed and inward.

BRANS: Yes, but the physicality—

THOMAS: That our people have in common. The hearth
is the center, the Cornish range, the black grate which did
us for cooking as well as for heating the kitchen. And it
never quite burnt out. They could poke it up in the morning—it was glowing away all the time. But we were better
off than Lawrence. There was never quite the tin bath in
the kitchen or my mother saying, "I'll wash your back for
you," you know.

BRANS: Translating the work of another poet is a little
like going down into a mine, isn't it? Sort of an immersion
of oneself in the mind or the psyche of another person.
When you were talking about your translations of Akh-

matova earlier, I thought of John Berryman and his "Homage to Mistress Bradstreet." He talks about Anne Bradstreet in that poem as you did about Akhmatova—a love affair with someone you never met, in his case with someone who died three centuries earlier.

THOMAS: I had a similar affair with Emily Dickinson. I love her poetry and I found her life deeply interesting. Emily was another of those inspiring dead women. And of course it's also easier to love a dead person than a living one. There isn't the turmoil of things to quarrel about.

BRANS: Oh, yes, she creeps into *The Flute-Player*. But the Flute-Player is not Emily Dickinson.

THOMAS: No, she changes. One moment she is like Emily Dickinson, and the next she is slipping into Sylvia Plath.

BRANS: You have a poem about the marriage of John Keats and Emily Dickinson. Isn't that an unlikely match?

THOMAS: Well, I just felt that they were deprived, poor Emily being a spinster and poor Keats never living to marry Fanny. They were such sensual, such loving people. How nice if they could get married, at least in Paradise. And I thought that was a good title, "The Marriage of John Keats and Emily Dickinson in Paradise." I was almost tempted just to put the title down and leave it at that.

BRANS: You were talking about both Emily Dickinson and Sylvia Plath being aspects of the Flute-Player. Frequently in your poems also there is the necessity to choose between two very different women. In "After the Party," for example, there are a land-wife and a sea-wife who try to share the man and end up killing him off. Isn't that a grim picture of sexual love?

THOMAS: Sex is not all a cozy picture. Clearly the capacity of women to love, I think more fully than men, can also seem an engulfing, a threatening thing, as it does, say, in a doting mother. I suppose these two figures, the land-woman and the sea-woman, emerge in my consciousness from seeing the split which develops at adolescence between woman as the provider, the nourisher, the protectress, the comforter—sometimes the bully, but in the nicest possible way. And then, on the other hand, woman as the sexual creature, a woman who is not going to nourish and protect, but threaten, excite, stimulate, jangle the nerves, and even destroy. The vagina with teeth.

BRANS: Is the fear of that sexual creature actually a fear of loss of consciousness, of being completely absorbed by sex?

THOMAS: Yes, I think it is. Or being absorbed into one love and so dividing to protect oneself. I think of something Keats once said to his sister-in-law, the good woman who had married his brother George. He was telling her of a cruel girl that he had fallen for who probably inspired "La Belle Dame sans Merci." He said, "I would like to be ruined by her"—this cruel girl—"but saved by you"—his sister-in-law. There's the split again, you see.

We do have, or I do, I suppose, a desire for the intense experience of eroticism which is perhaps necessarily transient because of its intensity. But there's also the need for the continuous love. And out of all this comes the pulling apart the man in the poem feels.

If only these two women could be merged. If only you could find someone with whom you could live day by day and be mutually nourishing and supporting, and also have this incredible excitement, intoxication, and passion—that would be wonderful. But it's not easy to get those two together, obviously.

BRANS: The land-wife is the good mother?

THOMAS: The safe woman, yes. And the sea–wife is the threatening or disturbing one.

BRANS: The sea must have seemed tempting and dangerous to you growing up on the Cornish coast. Have you ever written directly about Cornwall?

THOMAS: My first novel, *Birthstone,* which you probably haven't read because it's not been published in the States. Actually it began really as a sort of game of a friend who is a poet and me. We were going to collaborate, and we sent each other chapters for a while. Then she copped out, and I took it over and changed it completely. I wrote the first draft, and then I had the idea for *The Flute-Player,* and I really had to write that.

So *Birthstone* came out second in England, but I've continued to like and enjoy it, perhaps because it is bound up with Cornwall and my family, and the mixture of security and danger we were talking about.

BRANS: But Lisa in *The White Hotel* fantasizes about a kind of sexual sharing which would make those two things possible simultaneously, doesn't she?

THOMAS: For Lisa it's just a brief outburst of eroticism, that sexual danger—a few days at a hotel that she would like to continue but they obviously aren't going to. But I see what you mean. In the dinner party scene, for example, when Lisa offers her milk–laden breasts to her lover and then to the old priest who happens to be sitting at the table also. And the young man says, "Do, please, it's too much for me."

Love is an inexhaustible lake, and we want to set up these little boundaries, but maybe we shouldn't. If we learned better how to get across those boundaries, then we perhaps wouldn't have the evils like Nazism which stem basically from repressions, from feelings of exclusiveness.

"We are exclusively Aryans as opposed to Jews," or "The woman is exclusively mine."

I don't mean to say I believe in simple sexual revolutions. I don't believe in any revolutions. But if only we eased up a little. And Lisa is not promiscuous, she's not. For most of her life she is not having sex at all. At one point she realizes with horror that she has slept with five men in her life, which is after all a fairly limited number. She is promiscuous in her fantasy world, in her dreams, as probably most people are.

BRANS: Do these dreams have anything to do with her natural generosity?

THOMAS: Perhaps. She dreams of an overflowing love while she stays at the hotel, but it ends. The hotel goes on, the nourishment continues, the chef keeps churning out the steaks, but the people keep moving in and out. They are not there permanently.

BRANS: What does the white hotel itself symbolize?

THOMAS: In the poem at the beginning that the book grew out of, there's that line, "He took me to a white lakeside hotel." I suppose I just saw the white hotel set in dark green fir trees against a lake, a very visual thing. It glistened, as this universe does, as the stars do, with no particular connotation of purity, a brilliant glowing thing with all its deadliness and with all its wonderful light.

The white hotel is ultimately a symbol of the universe, I suppose—of this great life itself, the feeling of its all-plenteousness and its destructiveness. But it's basically good. It's on the side of creation and nourishment rather than destruction.

BRANS: Is that why the people in Lisa's fantasy write testimonials in the guestbook when they leave?

THOMAS: Yes, I don't know if you have them in America, but in England we have guestbooks at hotels. "No-where better, back next year." "Food great." Not every-thing is perfect, of course, in any hotel—sixty percent good and forty percent bad. Like that line of Robert Frost: "I had a lover's quarrel with the world." And what else does he say? "Earth's the right place for love. I don't know where it's likely to go better."

BRANS: Is the white hotel also the mother's womb?

THOMAS: I think it's like any symbol as opposed to any allegory. Freud, who is Lisa's doctor in the novel, says it is the mother's womb, and he's not incorrect.

But it is also the body, the flesh, the white skin, which the spirit enters as a guest and then leaves. Akhmatova says in one of her poems, "We are brief guests of the earth." We come into the body and then leave it.

The hotel is also the world and it is—everything. Whether you can have a symbol of everything, I don't know, but that's what I was aiming for. To get within this fantasy a picture of life as I see it, with its bursts of joy, its beneficence, and its incomprehensible sorrows.

BRANS: Why is a woman as loving and even maternal as Lisa so afraid to have a child?

THOMAS: I decided in my mind that she would be a woman with powers of premonition, a highly sensitive woman, as hysterics traditionally are, like Cassandra and the Delphic oracle. She was aware of the threat of anti-Semitism, she had experienced it during her own child-hood, and she somehow knew in an intuitive way that she could not have a child because it would be curtains. And she was right, of course.

Her premonitory powers start waning when she reaches Russia. She doesn't predict that her husband will be ar-rested. That was a shock to her. The powers that she had when she was with Freud she tends to lose in Russia, for no other reason than that I decided she would.

BRANS: You seem to be fascinated with Russia, you've published a number of volumes of translations of Russian poetry, yet you say you have never been to Russia. So how has Russia influenced your own work?

THOMAS: I suppose the image of a totalitarian state that one has to struggle against I find very powerful—defining one's place in life through opposition. In a way that's easier to do than to live in a free but fairly uncaring society where the author is for the most part not thought very highly of. He's an extra entertainment like the sports page—you know, authors are just peripheral things really for most people here. Whereas in Russia, the few great writers who have survived with their integrity are great people and are recognized as such by their own countrymen. A greatness of soul.

I have two mental landscapes. One is Cornwall, a kind of hearth and oven, and Russia—what is Russia?—the spiritual counterpart of that physical world. It's like Yeats with his masks, Yeats as a very peaceable man having this thing about Japanese samurai with their swords—a flow towards the opposite. Living always in comfortable placid surroundings, I need that kind of harsh world in which to get to the roots of myself. It's a sort of spiritual battleground, an anti-Utopia. I don't really need to go there.

BRANS: Are you at all concerned about the literal Russia?

THOMAS: I am deeply concerned about Communism and its spread. It's an evil system with the destruction of the individual as its aim. I see Russia as some kind of laboratory where they've taken the theories that the West has cooked up and are actually working them out with live animals. There's something rather heroic about that, as there is in a highly dangerous laboratory where there are terrible microbes. It has a horrid fascination. But the risk is too great.

BRANS: Are there any other influences in your writing as strong as the Russian?

THOMAS: I don't think so. I think I've learned far more from the Russians, and particularly from translating the Russian poets, than I have from any individual English or American writer. I was thirty when I started translating Akhmatova, and she taught me quite quickly to simplify. My early poems, many of them, are too clever and too sophisticated. She taught me that you can be more powerful by being simpler.

When I started *The Flute-Player,* I had just been reading Turgenev's *The Torrents of Spring,* with that kind of sheer buoyant flow of narrative and lyrical matter without the clutter of too many details, both poetry and realism. I thought, That's the way I'd like to write. Of course, *Birthstone,* which is earlier, is full of a mixture of surrealism and realism and humor and darkness and black comedy— people like Joyce, Frost, and Yeats are obviously important too.

BRANS: I read someone who said that the one thing *The White Hotel* doesn't have is humor.

THOMAS: Well, I intended there to be some humor when I wrote it. For example, when the mad major is addressing the guests and saying, "Terrible things are happening, the elm leaves have turned red." And the German gets all white, and says, "How dare you disturb the ladies?" There surely one can see the humor.

BRANS: Why did you use Peter Kürten, a German mass murderer in the thirties, as a figure in the novel?

THOMAS: To me, he signifies the destructive and deathly side of sex. He was an actual historical figure, and his turn-on was drinking blood. He killed fourteen or fifteen women, a man or two, and children. And then after each murder, he would run off and set fire to a hayrick, as though the killing wasn't enough.

He was just pure evil, pure horror, and yet I have a little sympathy for him. I wonder what one does if one happens to be born a monster. One wonders. I mean, by the grace of God, I am turned on by very normal things, by a good-looking woman. But if one had these extreme sadistic impulses, how would you cope with them? As Freud said, sex is where the highest and the lowest are closest together.

BRANS: Yeats too. Remember that line Crazy Jane uses on the Bishop? — "Love has pitched his mansion in the place of excrement," I think it is.

THOMAS: The same emotions of excitement and pleasure are available to Romeo and Juliet when they go to bed together on their first night, and to Kürten when he starts thinking about blood and killing. Sex is the unifying feature. So Kürten in my book stands for that ultimate, deadly Thanatos, the other side of Eros. He's a personalization of the Holocaust. If you could sum up in one man the evil of the Holocaust, you'd choose someone like Peter Kürten.

BRANS: Was he executed?

THOMAS: Oh, yes. He belonged to the still liberal democratic regime in Germany at that time, 1930. They agonized over whether to kill him, to execute him. The guillotine was rusty, it hadn't been used for years, but because of overwhelming public opinion, they decided to execute him. Actually he wanted to die. He probably thought it was the supreme sexual pleasure to hear his own blood gush.

He turned himself in, you know. He wanted his wife to have the reward. They were sitting at dinner, and he said, "I am the monster of Düsseldorf. I'm handing myself over to you." She dropped her knife and fork. But she did turn him in.

Even the prosecutor said, "He's a nice man." You could imagine that ninety percent of him was a nice man. But then the Nazi commandants were perfectly decent family men, too. If Peter Kürten had lived, he would have been absolutely right for the Nazis.

BRANS: But if he couldn't help himself, do you think it was right to execute him?

THOMAS: Although I'm not a believer in capital punishment, I think it's a weakness even to worry about killing him. I'd just get rid of him like a dog with rabies.

The novel doesn't in the end take a comfortable liberal view of life at all. There's this ingrained evil, you might even call it original sin, and the only way that we can cope with it is to recognize it and bring this darkness into the light.

BRANS: Do you think of Kürten as being like Hitler with all his neuroses?

THOMAS: In a way. Maybe through misplaced tolerance and liberalism, Germany allowed Hitler to come into being. If they'd been a bit tougher, maybe they'd have stopped Hitler too. You know, the strange thing is that before Kürten turned himself in, the names of *nine hundred thousand* other people were given to the police as being possible mass murderers, possible Peter Kürtens. You can see what people in Germany before the war thought of their neighbors, their husbands. There must have been a lot of evil around.

BRANS: I understand dozens of women wrote to him in prison, some threatening dire punishment and torture, and others wanting to go to bed with him or to marry him. How do you explain his attraction for women?

THOMAS: It's a thrill. You might also ask why people want to buy the Pocket Book edition of *The White Hotel* that has the Nazi storm trooper with a bayonet on it. People are attracted to evil. Maybe it's forgivable. They're living out some kind of fantasy—the extreme thrill of being in danger from a man like Kürten—as a sexual terminal.

In reality, of course, they wouldn't go along with it. If he wrote back and said, "I'm free and I'm coming around tomorrow at five o'clock," they'd change their minds. What is so terrifying is that there were apparently normal people who just by the impetus of the Nazis unleashed the same terrible forces. The ignorant loutish camp guard at the end of the book who impales Lisa on the bayonet has been brutalized by the scenario which was set up by the Nazis. He's one of the nine hundred thousand surrogate Peter Kürtens still around.

BRANS: The characters in your poems and novels are, like your father, always taking journeys, especially train journeys. Any special reason?

THOMAS: I really don't know. I'm very fond of train journeys. I like the sense of adventure, whom you're going to meet and talk to, even though I'm very reticent and usually don't say a word, and get offended if someone tries to talk to me. But there's always the possibility of meeting someone. This is tied in with Russian literature, the way so many Russian novels have scenes at railway stations, like the one in *Anna Karenina*. And *Dr. Zhivago,* that wonderful journey across the plains with the snow coming down.

BRANS: Your family was very much on the road too. I was surprised when you said that your sister was lonely and homesick after she married and moved to Australia, and so your whole family just picked up and went to Australia. I think of only the idle rich as doing that sort of thing.

THOMAS: Oh, but at that time you could emigrate to Australia with ease. We paid ten pounds each and I was free, for a kind of hotel stay, a whole month of travel by sea, just when I was reaching puberty. It was very important in my life.

BRANS: How did you pass the time?

THOMAS: I used to haunt the ship's library. I picked up adult books for the first time. There was one called *My Son, My Son* which had an erotic scene of a man with a young woman. He pulls the belt from her robe and it falls open and her breasts are exposed. That for me was—well, the curves of the breast were like the curved sea. And it haunted me. I used to go back day after day and find it and read it again.

BRANS: Are the journeys sexual in themselves?

THOMAS: I think so. It's that I may meet the stranger who will be the Muse and who will fuse the two women that we talked about earlier. I remember going back to Oxford once as a student. It was an overnight journey, which is very erotic anyway because of sleeping on the train. Well, there was this young woman. I was very shy and we never talked at all until right at the end. Then we came into Reading, and she went to her compartment and said she was going to sleep. I got off the train, and she leaned out of the window, and said, "I wish you were coming with me." And I almost leapt in again.

BRANS: Perhaps you should have; you shouldn't have missed the opportunity. She may have been the one.

THOMAS: Instead I let it creep into a poem I wrote called "The House of Dreams," where a woman leans out of the window and says, "I wish you were coming with me."

BRANS: You've talked about your father and your sister. I haven't heard you say much about your mother.

THOMAS: My sister is ten years older than I am, and because she was a nubile, attractive young woman when I was pubescent, in a way she replaced the mother at the time. But I've written actually quite a lot of poems about my mother.

BRANS: I know. But mostly in her old age, when you're visiting her and she's ill.

THOMAS: That's right. But there are poems about her earlier—"The Honeymoon Voyage." There again is a journey. She and my father married and left for America on the same day.

BRANS: Are you like her at all?

THOMAS: My mother once said in her old age, about me, "We've got nothing in common except that I'm his mother." That really was a very wise thing to say, and there was no resentment in it. It was simply true. I mean, we really didn't have anything in common. I had more in common with my father, in terms of character and interests. She was nonliterate. She never read anything except Biblical texts.

BRANS: Was she stern?

THOMAS: No, entirely loving and rather smothering, and always very worried about me because I was a late child. I used to visit her as an old woman and there was really nothing we had to talk about. But a feeling of love— we knew we loved each other. As I say in "The Journey," "We are journeyers together, Whatever else we are."

BRANS: There's something healthy about that. Americans try to be everything to their children. Friends. I'm not sure our children need us for friends, but we impose all these awkward roles on ourselves.

THOMAS: I think all parents screw up their children in some way. I've done it with mine, I'm sure. But that's the way it is. Even if you're a perfect parent, then your children feel they could never live up to that with their own children. If you're too loving, you smother them. If you're cruel, you—

BRANS: There's no way to win.

THOMAS: No way to win, but you know in the white hotel the balance is very much in favor of goodness and beneficence, and I bless their existence.

BRANS: Are you optimistic about human life, even with the possibility of atomic destruction?

THOMAS: Basically optimistic, though I recognize the essentially evil forces and I have none of the sociological jargon that tries to play them down. I don't believe in "the perfectibility of man" and so on. I'm like Mandelstam, who wept at the word *progress.*

But I still feel that the forces of light are a little stronger than the forces of darkness. I write as a thank-you gift for life, and I would hope to add to the forces of light.

BRANS: And you embody these forces in women, in Lisa and in Elena, the girl in *The Flute-Player.*

THOMAS: Yes, Lisa is the Rose of Sharon, the soul, the bride, the daughter of Jerusalem. And Elena is of course the Muse.

BRANS: Is that why she plays the flute?

THOMAS: Yes, it suddenly occurred to me that the Muse traditionally did play a flute. You see, I didn't have the title at that stage at all. I never intended her to learn to play the flute. She doesn't know she is the Muse, she doesn't know what her purpose in life is, but she becomes this figure. At the end she has survived a terrible time, she is training to be a kindergarten teacher, and new things keep coming in.

So she decides to learn to play the flute. That heightens her identity.

And of course it gave me the title, which was nice. Once you have the title of a work, it's a sign that maybe it's okay.

BRANS: The flute gives you a point of identification with the story too, because you are playing her song in the book you wrote.

THOMAS: Yes, and at the end I appear, diffidently. And when I come in, I'm not sure whether she is really saying, "Oh God, an interruption," or "Yes, you are welcome."

BRANS: You could be the person from Porlock or the bemused poet.

THOMAS: Yes. Is she going to play the flute for me? I don't know. And you can never tell how long she is going to play for you. There's always the anxiety that she will turn away and not favor you.

The only attitude that you can take is one of humility before her. Don't force her. Just stay available. It's not like a carpenter who can be reasonably confident that he can go on making tables and furniture until he is old. As a writer you can't predict that. You just have to rely on a continuation of grace. Here's hoping.

Using What You're Given

THROUGHOUT A WRITING CAREER that began seriously when she was sixteen, Margaret Atwood has received numerous awards and several honorary degrees. She is best known as the author of six novels, *The Edible Woman* (1970), *Surfacing* (1972), *Lady Oracle* (1973), *Life Before Man* (1979), *Bodily Harm* (1981), and *The Handmaid's Tale* (1986), as well as a dizzying number of television plays, children's books, short stories, critical works, and volumes of poetry.

Born in 1939 in Ottawa, Ontario, Atwood has become the high priestess of Canadian literature. She studied English literature with the distinguished myth critic Northrop Frye at the University of Toronto. After graduate work at Harvard, she returned to Canada, where she worked as an editor and board member of a Canadian publishing house. She serves as co-chair of the Canadian Center of PEN International. Her landmark *Survival: A Thematic Guide to Canadian Literature* (1972) triggered a controversy with its thesis that Canadians are willing victims but survivors, a description that can also be applied to a number of her fictional characters.

Anything but provincial in its concerns, however, Atwood's fiction has been published in more than fifteen countries. She herself has traveled extensively, has taught in the United States, and has lived in England, West Berlin, and Iran, with a stay in Afghanistan just six weeks before the war broke out. Currently she lives in Toronto with the novelist Graeme Gibson and their daughter Jess.

Atwood has an uncanny knack for writing novels that anticipate the popular preoccupations of her public. Feminists seized upon her second novel, *The Edible Woman,* for example, as a "product of the movement," though, as she has pointed out, it was written before the women's movement began. *Bodily Harm,* in which a young female reporter recovering from a mastectomy becomes a political prisoner in a Third World setting, mirrors the personal and political tensions of the eighties.

She has explained this political and personal prescience as concomitant to the act of writing. In the introduction to her volume of critical essays *Second Words* (1982), she says, "When you begin to write you're in love with the language, with the act of creation, with yourself partly; but as you go on, the writing—if you follow it—will take you places you never intended to go and show you things you would never otherwise have seen. I began as a profoundly apolitical writer, but then I began to do what all novelists and some poets do: I began to describe the world around me."

Or the world of the hovering future. It was with her sixth novel, *The Handmaid's Tale,* which was published four years after the interview here, that Atwood sprang into greatest prominence. An anti-Utopian novel literate yet provocative enough to bridge the gulf between serious and commercial fiction, *The Handmaid's Tale* is a detailed narrative of what life might be like in the United States if a coup were staged by the Moral Majority. Atwood has long insisted that all human relationships involve, to use the title of one of her poetry collections, "power politics" or, as she told me, "who gets to do what to whom." Even her poems have been called, by the critic Helen Vendler, "guided missiles" with "deadly force" which "pierce the mind and leave a wound." This militancy is most apparent in *The Handmaid's Tale,* which succeeds brilliantly on several levels: fantasy, psychological study, page-turning thriller, and feminist and political tract with a sense of humor about itself. Like the author herself, it is an intriguing combination of elements which logically should, but somehow do not, cancel each other out.

The vision in Atwood's work, with its emphasis on power and survival, is grounded in her childhood experience. Her almost scientific observation of the world runs in the family; her mother, father, and brother are all scientists. Her unsentimental respect for the natural environment, as well as her independence of judgment, may be products of the pattern of family life. Every year from April to November her family lived in the wilderness of Quebec, where her father, a forest entomologist, did research for the government. Margaret, who was eleven before she attended a full year of school, "grew up in and out of the bush." This forest experience is particularly important in *Surfacing,* in which the heroine returns to a state of nature to recover her suppressed past and to her barbarous self in order to achieve psychic wholeness.

Atwood's understanding of natural cycles may also explain her emphasis on the power to survive. "The Atwood message," Melvin Maddocks wrote in 1970, "is beyond formulated pessimism. It has the rhythmic cycling of hope and despair natural to life itself."

Margaret Atwood is an attractive woman, with lively blue eyes and an aureole of dark curly hair. Her manner is authoritative, even adversarial, and her responses come with a semantic precision. Before this interview, she and I had gone to lunch with a feminist group on campus, so I thought I was on safe ground with my opening question. That I was not was both the challenge and the value of this interview.

BRANS: Are you a feminist writer?

ATWOOD: "Feminist" is now one of the all-purpose words. It really can mean anything from people who think men should be pushed off cliffs to people who think it's okay for women to read and write. All those could be called feminist positions. Thinking that it's okay for women to read and write would be a radically feminist position in Afghanistan. So what do you mean?

BRANS: Let me try again. What I meant by asking that question was whether you consciously espouse a feminist position in your writing.

ATWOOD: I don't think that any novelist is inherently that kind of a creature. Novelists work from observation of life. A lot of the things that one observes as a novelist looking at life indicate that women are not treated equally. But that comes from observation. It doesn't come from ideology. I started writing in 1956. There wasn't any women's movement during my writing life until 1970. That's fourteen years of writing.

Now, on the other hand, and you have to try to define this very clearly, I'm not one of those women who would say, "Well, I made it, therefore anybody should be able to do it, and what are they whining about." That's not the point.

Nor am I against the women's movement. I think it's been a very good thing and I was happy to see it. But that's very different from saying that what you write is embodying somebody's party line. It isn't. And none of the women writers that I know, including ones who are regularly defined as feminists, would say that they are embodying somebody's party line. It's not how they see what they're doing.

BRANS: You have gotten crossways of some feminist groups, particularly with *Surfacing,* where a woman character wants to undo the effects of an abortion.

ATWOOD: To me that is just what that character would do. The abortion was coerced—it was forced. That's not an anti-abortion stand. It's an anti-coercion stand. I don't think even women who are in favor of freedom of choice would say that abortion is a good thing that should be forced on everyone. And if they've read the book, which you sometimes feel these people don't do, or that they don't know how to read, that is what they would see. That the negative effects that happen to her are connected with the fact that the thing is forced on her by the circumstances.

BRANS: What does pregnancy mean in your writing? There are so many places, for example in *Life Before Man,* and then the little story called "Giving Birth," where pregnancy seems to mean something profound and various.

ATWOOD: Well, girls can have babies and boys can't. The fact has been noticed by more people than me. In the story "Giving Birth," giving birth is wonderful for the woman from whose point of view the story is told, but she mentions this other shadow figure for whom it's not wonderful, it's awful. I think one of the things that the story says is that there is no word for forced pregnancy in the language. We don't have that concept, although the fact itself exists. So, there again, I wouldn't say that pregnancy is wonderful for everybody. We know that it isn't. It can be wonderful for a person who wants to do it. But you could say that of every act in life.

BRANS: What about a girl like Lasha, for example, in *Life Before Man,* who becomes pregnant in order to prove a point?

ATWOOD: Once upon a time a lot more women than we would like to admit got pregnant to prove a point. In fact they got pregnant to get married. Remember shotgun weddings?

BRANS: Sure. But were they really calculated?

ATWOOD: They could be very calculated. I'm sure that still happens. I don't think it's tip-top for the children who are involved.

BRANS: It's a tremendous gamble. I could never understand a girl getting pregnant in order to get somebody to marry her, because suppose he just refused, or went to Texas.

ATWOOD: Many have done it. It would depend on the social attitudes of the community that you were trying it in. But certainly that was a time-honored technique.

BRANS: Yes. But Lasha doesn't have that in mind.

ATWOOD: No, no. She's tired of being put down for not being a mother. You can't say that pregnancy is one thing. It's many things, like making love. I mean, it's not just one thing that ought to have one meaning. It's one of those profoundly meaningful human activities which can be very multifaceted and resonant and can have a very positive meaning for some people and a very negative meaning for others.

BRANS: Which is the point of the extra woman in "Giving Birth."

ATWOOD: Remember that I'm old enough to remember the time when women were told that they had to get pregnant and have babies in order to "fulfill their femininity." And I didn't like that either. Nor do I like women being told that they oughtn't to get pregnant, they can't get pregnant—that it's anti-feminist to get pregnant. I don't like that line either.

BRANS: So you're really defining your feminism for me, I think, right now.

ATWOOD: Yes, I'm defining my feminism as human equality and freedom of choice.

BRANS: What do you think an ideal relationship between a man and a woman would be?

ATWOOD: A happy one.

BRANS: Thanks a lot, Margaret. I was thinking of "Power Politics."

ATWOOD: That talks about all different kinds of ways in which it isn't happy. You often define a positive by defining negatives.

BRANS: I think what I like most in "Power Politics" is the wit. It is the sharpest and wittiest poem—and there's a lot of anger in it, and frustration because of the impossibility of communicating.

ATWOOD: But there again, that doesn't rule out the opposite pole. I'll read some love poems in the reading tonight, to show it can be done. I'm not a pessimist. People sometimes read the stuff and think, Oh, this is a pessimist.

BRANS: Anyone who thinks that should read "There Is

Only One of Everything." I love that poem, and it is a love poem—wonderful. But it's not only a love poem, it's also a poem about observing the world, and the particularities of the world, I guess.

What about your particular origins? What effect has being Canadian had on your writing? That's a terrible, big question, I know.

ATWOOD: There's a funny poem in Canada called "Recipe for a Canadian Novel" in which it's recommended that one take two beavers, add one Mountie and some snow, and stir. I'm not in favor of anybody consciously trying to be the great anything, but every writer writes out of his or her own background.

I give you William Faulkner as an example. There's a genre of writing that we call "Southern Ontario Gothic," which is something like Southern Gothic. The South has often had problems making itself felt as something other than a region. It so often just gets called regional, doesn't it?—whereas in fact Southern writers are doing what all writers do. They're writing out of what they know.

BRANS: Right.

ATWOOD: There's a story you'll appreciate. At Harvard, when I first met our mutual friend Charles Matthews, who as you know is from Mississippi, I said, "Oh, I so much admire William Faulkner. He was so inventive, and he made up all these funny and grotesque things." And Charles drawled, "He didn't make anything up. He just wrote it all down."

That just proves my point. That's what writers do, and Canadian writers are no different from other writers in that respect. They write about what they know. Some of what they know is Canadian. When they travel, or when they think in other terms, then the terms become larger.

But the base, the way of thinking, remains Canadian, just as for the Southern writer the way of thinking remains Southern. So to me it's not a question which is particular to Canada. It's a question that's about all writing and all writers.

BRANS: And how to transcend region somehow?

ATWOOD: I don't think that you transcend region, any more than a plant transcends earth. I think that you come out of something, and you can then branch out in all different kinds of directions, but that doesn't mean cutting yourself off from your roots and from your earth.

To me an effective writer is one who can make what he or she is writing about understandable and moving to someone who has never been there. All good writing has that kind of transcendence. It doesn't mean becoming something called "international." There is no such thing.

BRANS: No. Makes sense. So you don't think then that there are national literary qualities, even though you wrote a book about Canadian literature.

ATWOOD: I think that in any transaction involving a book there's the writer, there's the book, and there's the reader. Now, the writer can write the book and make it as good a book as he or she can, and it can be a pretty good book. That doesn't mean that the reader is going to understand it, unless the reader has receiving apparatus that's equal to the product.

I'll give you an American example: *Moby Dick*. *Moby Dick* was not recognized as a great American classic until the 1920s. When it was first published it was rejected by the American reading public, which at that time was divided into camps, the Anglophiles, who wanted it to be like English writing (it wasn't), and young Americans who were looking for the great American genius, but didn't think it was Melville. Those are the two groups that reviewed the book. It sank like a stone. Melville died a broken and disappointed man, and *Moby Dick* did not come into its own until seventy years later. So that's what I mean when I say that the receiving apparatus has to be there as well.

And I write for readers. I write for people who like to read books. They don't have to be Canadian readers. They don't have to be American readers. They don't have to be Indian readers, although some of them are. I'm translated into fourteen languages by now, and I'm sure that some of the people reading those books don't get all the references in them, because they're not familiar with the setting.

I don't get all the references in William Faulkner either. That doesn't mean I don't enjoy the books, or can't understand them. You can pick a lot of things up from context, even though you may not understand that it was that particular family in Oxford, Mississippi, that was being talked about.

BRANS: But as an educated reader you still would have this human rapport with the book.

ATWOOD: An educated reader has a rapport with all books, depending on taste to a certain extent. But an educated reader would never *not* read a book because it wasn't by somebody from his hometown, right? Or because the person was a different color, or because the person was a woman or a man.

I've had women say to me that they just don't read books by men anymore. I think that's shocking. I've had that said to me by several people within the last couple of weeks.

BRANS: In that case, then, you would cut yourself off from the whole literary tradition in English?

ATWOOD: If you're a reader, that's what you're doing to yourself.

BRANS: Let me ask you this. If some women have difficulty reading books written by men, can't even bring themselves to do it, do you have any difficulties in portraying a character of the opposite sex in your writing?

ATWOOD: It's a little bit harder.

BRANS: What sorts of problems?

ATWOOD: The same problem I would have portraying an English person, or somebody that was just enough different from me that I'd have to do the research. So, with men—it depends on what kind of men you're doing, of course, but just to give you an example, writing *Life Before Man* I showed the manuscript to a man (I showed the manuscript of *Bodily Harm* to a West Indian, and that was helpful, too) because I wanted to just have a read on the details, the accuracy of the details. He caught me in one major mistake, which a man would never have made. He said you cannot shave a beard off with an electric razor. It doesn't work.

BRANS: You have to use something—

ATWOOD: You have to use a straight razor. An electric razor will just get all clogged up if you're trying to shave long hairs with it. It's only suitable for shaving stubble.

BRANS: That's fascinating.

ATWOOD: Little things like that. I think men have often written women characters, and sometimes they slipped up on those kinds of details. Unless they go and do the research on how you put on panty hose, they aren't going to know.

BRANS: But you don't think there's anything—intrinsically different in the mind of a man and a woman?

ATWOOD: Sure, lots of things are different. But I know a lot of men. I talk to a lot of men. They're not foreigners. They really can be conversed with.

BRANS: You wouldn't agree with the poem by Adrienne Rich, "Trying to Talk to a Man," where she says you're talking across vast distances in a desert area.

ATWOOD: You're still talking, and of course it depends partly what you're talking about and what your attitude is and who the man is. That does make a difference. I don't think that all men are the same, any more than I think that all women are the same. And there is such a thing as an intelligent, cultivated, well-read, and sensitive man.

I find it just absurd these days that I'm having to stick up for men. I find that such an absurd position to be put in.

BRANS: To have to tell a woman that she should go and read a book by a man.

ATWOOD: It's ridiculous. I've been doing the other thing for years, I mean telling men that they ought to read books by women. Here I am suddenly, feeling, out of a sense of fairness, that I have to say not all men are pigs, some of them write good books.

BRANS: Do you get attacked when you have a character like Nate, for example, in *Life Before Man* who's sort of wimpy, as a man?

ATWOOD: I don't think he's that wimpy.

BRANS: You don't? You don't think he's just dreadfully wishy-washy and too—?

ATWOOD: He's having trouble making decisions, but that's a decision that a lot of men have trouble making, namely whether to leave their kids because their marriage is rotten, or whether to stay with the marriage for the sake of the kids. Any man leaving kids and a wife is going to have residual guilt feelings which he's going to have to work out and expiate and get rid of. And Nate is observed at the time during which he's caught in that process, but it doesn't mean he's a wimpy man.

BRANS: Well, I'm glad to have you defend him, because—

ATWOOD: There again, people, even women, expect men to be better than they are, and better than women. Now, notice what you did. You came after me for Nate, who's actually the nicest person in the book. You didn't come after me for—

BRANS: You think he's nicer than Lasha is.

ATWOOD: Yes, he's lots nicer. Now Lasha is a wimp. Nobody ever mentions her because she's a girl—girls are expected to be wimps. Nobody ever attacks Lasha for being unrealistic and wimpish and so on, because they expect girls to be like that.

BRANS: I just thought she was a child.

ATWOOD: Yes, but nobody ever comes after me for that. Hardly ever at all has anybody ever said that. Nobody comes after me for Elizabeth being a bitch.

BRANS: I would have come after you for that.

ATWOOD: Next? It's always Nate. And I think the truth about that is that people expect men to be supermen. Even women—even feminists—take points off them when they aren't. They don't take equal points off the women for having failings, because women are expected to be imperfect.

BRANS: I thought of Elizabeth as having a bad childhood, and of Lasha as being young, and so I was willing—you're right. That was prejudiced of me.

ATWOOD: Women are supposed to be imperfect, but they're also expected to be supermoms, so you can't win, either way.

BRANS: In that book, what did you have in mind about

the dinosaurs? Do you think that we've lost something by becoming overly civilized?

ATWOOD: I don't like to close my symbolisms.

BRANS: But you were suggesting something about a sort of purity of action and motive in the dinosaurs?

ATWOOD: No, they're Lasha's escape fantasy, among other things, but I don't like to explain and pin down things that I've put in my books. They have multiple meanings. One of the meanings is that all kids love dinosaurs and I was no exception.

BRANS: Question—you have such diversity. All of the novels are very different from each other—there's really no such thing as a Margaret Atwood novel. Then of course there's your poetry, which is quite different from the fiction. Do you consciously put on different hats? Do you set out, say, to write a comedy of manners, or just to do a particular kind of thing, let's say with *The Edible Woman* or *Lady Oracle*?

ATWOOD: Yes, both of those, definitely.

BRANS: Were you working for a genre, or did you start with an image that lent itself to that sort of treatment?

ATWOOD: I start out with an image and the book develops around that. Yes, I always start with images, and the tone of the book comes later.

BRANS: How about sitting down to write poems and sitting down to write fiction?

ATWOOD: I'm not a theoretical writer—I'm not a programmatic writer in any way. I don't set out little things for myself that I'm going to do next.

BRANS: Like poems from two o'clock to three. Nothing like that.

ATWOOD: No, I usually write a lot. A book of poems that you'll actually read is usually distilled from at least twice that much writing. It only becomes apparent to me toward the end of that process what the form is that's going to emerge from it.

BRANS: Do you do the same thing with fiction? Do you write vast amounts, more—?

ATWOOD: I write vast amounts. I try to get through the first draft quite quickly, and then I see what it is, and then I work on it and revise it. I'm not one of those people who puts it down on filing cards first and then writes out a filing card a day. I can't work like that.

BRANS: You're so caught up with the transformation/metamorphosis/rebirth idea. Does that have anything to do with your having studied with Northrop Frye? Did he shape your thinking?

ATWOOD: No, I think it has to do with the fact that my father was a biologist. I had the kind of reading childhood that Norie Frye would advocate. But he hadn't advocated it while I was having it. In other words, I read very early *Grimm's Fairy Tales,* Greek mythology, I was familiar with the Bible, and so on and so forth. Norie Frye didn't enter my life until the third year of university, when I had already been writing for four or five years.

BRANS: You started when you were sixteen? I read somewhere nineteen.

ATWOOD: That's when I started publishing, nineteen or twenty. No, I started in high school, and my first poetry was a lot like Shelley and Byron, because that's what I had been reading. But I think that the interest in those topics comes much more from having had really a biological training rather than a training in writing.

BRANS: That doesn't come in any way from your sex—your thinking of yourself as a giver of life, or—?

ATWOOD: I wasn't of the generation taught to think of

themselves as women. We weren't taught anything much about women at all except those kinds of things you read about in the novels of the fifties. We picked up from the culture pointy brassieres and what not to do after the formal, and all of that kind of folklore.

Canada was so backward that we weren't even taught Freudianized psychology. We weren't even told that we had to have babies to be fulfilled, and that we had to be passive to be feminine. That was the United States that was going in for that.

So, in fact, I came from a family that believed that I should go on to college—that would have been appalled if I got married too early. So, that whole set of attitudes that you had to marry the football player was not part of my thing at all.

My interest in metamorphosis may have come from *Grimm's Fairy Tales*. People are always having rebirths there. The culture is permeated with rebirth symbolism. It's Christian, among other things. And it's an idea that is very much around. If I were in India, they would say, "Do you believe in metamorphosis? Do you believe in metempsychosis, do you believe in the transmigration of souls?" But it seems to have been a concept in one form or another that has been run through the sausage machine by many different human cultures.

BRANS: But it's clearly so central to you.

ATWOOD: It's central to me, but it's also central to lots of other people as well. I also think it's central to any novel. Usually in a novel the central character changes. That's one of the things that happen in novels—the person learns something, or they become something more, or they become something less, but they always change. They're not the same at the end as they were at the beginning.

If you did write a novel in which they were exactly the same, you would probably find it either terribly experimental or terribly boring or possibly both.

BRANS: It seems to me that all of your novels are affirmative in some way.

ATWOOD: Thank you.

BRANS: I'm not sure that other readers would think of them as affirmative.

ATWOOD: Some do, some don't. It depends on the degree of sophistication of the reader, it seems.

BRANS: I was struggling very hard with *Bodily Harm,* because it did seem to me, with the political satire—

ATWOOD: You made it through to the last page, though.

BRANS: But on the last page I found this rather guarded affirmation, because she's "paying attention." That was a phrase that you used, which to my mind is a very affirmative statement. And then something like, She's flying. Her luck is holding her up. So, though it seemed to me that of all the books that you have written this would on the surface be the least affirmative, yet—

ATWOOD: I think it's actually the most affirmative, because you can only measure affirmation in terms of what it's set against. I mean, having hope for the human race in India is a really different thing from having hope for the human race in Texas. In Texas you don't have to deal with massive poverty and people dying in the street and starvation and beggary and so forth. It's easy to be optimistic here.

BRANS: I was thinking too of her personal trauma, because of the loss of the breast, which seems to be—

ATWOOD: That happens to a quarter of all women over the age of forty. That's what the statistic is right now, so people better begin to deal with it.

But part of what the novel does is, it sets our way of thinking, which is an affluent way of thinking—you know, we can afford to worry about our personal health and our fitness and our personal romances and what we're eating and whether we're fashionable, and whether we look good, and personal change and growth and all of those things we read about in women's magazines. That's in the forefront of our lives.

Move that to a country in which most people don't have a job and—

BRANS: Don't have the luxury of thinking that way—

ATWOOD: They don't think that way at all. They think about what's coming tomorrow.

BRANS: People are concerned with more fundamental questions.

ATWOOD: But once you don't have to be concerned with that, then you can embroider, and we do a lot of embroidering in our society.

BRANS: Why are Americans often so hateful in your books?

ATWOOD: I don't like American foreign policy, in many instances. But neither do a lot of Americans.

BRANS: No, I don't like American foreign policy.

ATWOOD: Nor do I confuse individual people with decisions made by governments. I think it's wrong to do so.

BRANS: But, for example, in *Surfacing,* when the Americans come in and they're so clearly the enemy, or the CIA in *Bodily Harm.*

ATWOOD: All that stuff is realistic. It's not made up and it's not my attitude. I'm just writing it down. People sit around in bars and discuss who the CIA is this month.

BRANS: Are you serious?

ATWOOD: Absolutely.

BRANS: You see, I didn't read *Surfacing* at all on that level. I thought the Americans were a symbol.

ATWOOD: No, no. No, no, no, no.

BRANS: You see, that's where being Canadian, or knowing about Canada, would probably help.

ATWOOD: I was just writing about people's conversations. That's how people talk about the Americans, at least some people. But you notice that the guy who talks about them that way the most is also the most spurious person in the book. And the people that he thinks are Americans actually turn out to be Canadian, so you have to watch that kind of playing around.

BRANS: And in *Bodily Harm* it's the CIA.

ATWOOD: Yes, in *Bodily Harm* people really do sit around in bars, and say, Well, you know So-and-So was the CIA, but they've moved. And who is it now? Well, I hear they're using locals. And there's a lot of speculation as to just who the CIA is, and the CIA is known for knowing who's doing the drugs, but not being concerned about turning them in, because that's not what they're interested in. They're only interested in the political stuff.

BRANS: And if they leave them alone they can find out more?

ATWOOD: And if they leave them alone they can find out more, that's right. But in fact a lot of people doing the drugs are Americans as well.

BRANS: Do you have a specific political position?

ATWOOD: Politics, for me, is everything that involves who gets to do what to whom. That's politics. It's not just elections and what people say they are. You know, little labels they put on themselves. And it certainly isn't self-righteous puritanism of the left, which you get lots of, or self-righteous puritanism of the right, I hasten to add.

Politics really has to do with how people order their societies. Whom power is ascribed to, who is considered to have power. A lot of power is ascription—people have power because we think they have power, and that's all that politics is. And politics also has to do with what kind of conversations you have with people, and what you feel free to say to someone—what you don't feel free to say. Whether you feel free during a staff meeting to get up and challenge what the chairman has just said. All of those things.

BRANS: Those are political situations?

ATWOOD: But they're also social situations, and they're also observable situations, and they're also part of everything that a novelist looks at. Jane Austen is a political writer for me. She's talking about how to get what you want.

BRANS: You don't belong to a political party? Not any political party?

ATWOOD: Not any political party. I belong to Amnesty International, which concerns itself with torture and political imprisonment. I belong to the Canadian Civil Liberties Union.

BRANS: So you maintain then a kind of writer's immunity.

ATWOOD: Nobody's immune. I don't endorse political candidates.

BRANS: But in your books you don't—you're not attitudinizing at all? You're simply showing the world as you see it and sense it and feel it?

ATWOOD: Let me just think about that. I don't think people are morally neutral, okay? But that does not have anything to do with labels. That is, if you call somebody a democrat—if they say they're in favor of democracy, you then have to find out what they're actually really in favor of by asking them a number of specific questions. Only then do you find out what's under that. If somebody says they're socialist, well, same thing. You have to ask a whole bunch of different questions to find out what they really mean by that. The same with feminist.

And what you're really trying to put your finger on is, How will this person behave in this situation or that situation? Is this going to be somebody who's going to vote for burning witches, is it going to be somebody who's going to vote for fair trial, or is it going to be somebody who's going to vote for shooting people—lining them up against a wall and shooting them? Those are the things you need to note.

BRANS: And those are not the things that you learn by looking at a label.

ATWOOD: You don't learn those by looking at a label. People use labels for their own purposes—either to put on other people so they can line them up against the wall and shoot them, or to put on themselves to make themselves feel good, or whatever, you know. So, that's why I took you through the mulberry bushes when you asked me about feminism. It's a label.

BRANS: And again about politics.

ATWOOD: That's right. I think when you say "political writer" you usually mean either somebody who writes about doings in the White House or somebody who has a particular ax to grind, in that they think everybody should vote for So-and-So, or that the world should be such and such a place, and that this is the way to get it. I don't have any surefire recipes like that. I am, of course, somebody who would vote, as I did recently in the Toronto election, in favor of an East/West nuclear arms freeze. That to me isn't even politics—it's survival.

BRANS: It's universal survival, yes, I agree.

ATWOOD: I think all kinds of people who don't ordinarily pay any attention to politics at all are coming out for that one.

BRANS: You've been writing for so long. Apparently it's a very great need for you to write.

ATWOOD: It's very enjoyable for me to write. It's a pleasure. I bet you've never heard a writer say that before.

BRANS: Writers say various things, but for a lot of them I think it is sort of a torment—but a necessary torment.

ATWOOD: Don't ever believe that. If they didn't enjoy it on some level, they wouldn't be doing it.

BRANS: What do you think you accomplish for other people with your writing?

ATWOOD: It's not my business. That's their business. They are the receivers. They are in charge of their own equipment.

BRANS: So you simply do it out of a love for it.

ATWOOD: Partly. I don't rule out communication and so on. Reading a book is, according to the neurophysiologists, almost the equivalent of having the experience, on a synaptical level, [the level of] what happens in your head. In fact, you could think of a human being as an enormous computer that you can run programs through. But if you think of a book as an experience—as almost the equivalent of having the experience—you're going to feel some sense of responsibility as to what kinds of experiences you're going to put people through. You're not going to put them through a lot of blood and gore for nothing, at least

I'm not. I don't write pretty books, I know that. They aren't pretty.

BRANS: But they're better than pretty, they're beautiful. There's a beauty of structure, and beauty of language.

ATWOOD: But they're not sweet.

BRANS: No, but the world is not a very sweet place.

ATWOOD: Well, that's what I feel. On the other hand, I don't think it's an armpit either.

BRANS: No. And always, in your books, there's this sense of making do. You have a phrase that runs throughout your poetry and your novels. Something like, It's your life and you're stuck with it. You have to make do.

ATWOOD: That's a fairly negative way of saying it.

BRANS: I never read that as a negative line. It just seemed right to me.

ATWOOD: That is a negative line. But there's another way of putting it, which is this: Some people, by "freedom," mean freedom to do whatever they want to, without any limitation whatsoever. That isn't the pack of cards that we're dealt. We are dealt a limited pack. So I would see freedom more as the power to use what you're given in the best way that you can. It doesn't mean that you're given everything. You aren't. Nobody is.

Book Burning

E RSKINE CALDWELL was born in 1903 on what he described as "an isolated farm deep in the piney-woods country of the red clay hills" of Georgia; he died of lung cancer in April of 1987 in Paradise Valley, Arizona. During his life, he wrote more than fifty books. His best-known, *Tobacco Road* (1932) and *God's Little Acre* (1933), over the next fifty years together sold seventeen million copies, to become two of the biggest sellers of all time. *Tobacco Road* was adapted for the stage and, in 1933, began a Broadway run that lasted for seven and a half consecutive years, bringing the author two thousand dollars a week in royalties.

If Caldwell was a financial success, he was also one of America's most banned and censored writers. Though he received good reviews for *Tobacco Road* and *God's Little Acre,* and for several of the other novels, like *Journeyman* (1933), *Trouble in July* (1940), and *Tragic Ground* (1944), which were part of a ten-novel "Southern cyclorama," fifty years ago his books shocked the sensibility of the country. Their frank portrayal of sex, violence, poverty, bigotry, and cupidity among the poor whites of the South and the direct language which the author put into the mouths of such characters as Jeeter and Ty Ty made Caldwell what one critic has called "the South's literary bad boy." He was denounced as an immoral writer from the pulpits of fundamentalist churches, and in bookstores and libraries his books were banned.

Politically, Caldwell's graphic descriptions of the dying agricultural world he grew up in riled conservatives because they called attention to the plight of the sharecroppers, mill hands, and others at the bottom of the country's economic ladder. As a proletarian novelist, he was suspected of Communist sympathies, and he did in fact win a large following in the Soviet Union. His work remained popular abroad long after it had fallen into obscurity in the United States.

Nor was Caldwell taken up by scholars. After the initial flurry, academic critics came to regard his work as merely popular or salacious, unworthy of serious regard. After a short story prize from the *Yale Review* in 1933, Caldwell never won another major literary award. He was not elected to the American Academy of Arts and Letters until 1983, when he was eighty years old.

Nevertheless, he never lost faith in the value of what he had done, which he insisted throughout, as he insists in this interview, was simply to tell the truth about the world as he saw it. "I write to let life express itself," he told me. The international appeal of his books he attributed to his ability to strike "the elemental" in human experience. The son of a Presbyterian minister in the rural South, Caldwell often accompanied his father on pastoral visits, and, for a time, he also drove a country doctor on his rounds. With his second wife, the photographer Margaret Bourke-White, he again roamed the rural byways, producing the remarkable collaboration *You Have Seen Their Faces* (1937).

The poetic resonance under the stark scenes and simple language of his best work is indicated by the ongoing controversy as to whether Caldwell is a comic or a tragic writer. He is, of course, both. In his sterile landscapes, among people brought tragically low by poverty and their own ignorance, even the manipulative greed, the explosive anger, and above all the irrepressible sexuality are welcome signs of the life that comedy celebrates.

Caldwell not only saw poverty up close at an impressionable age; he knew it from firsthand experience. During his early life, he worked at various times as a mill laborer, cotton picker, cook, waiter, cabdriver, farmhand, soda jerk, bodyguard, and stagehand. He attended college briefly but left to become a reporter on an Atlanta paper, at a salary of twenty-five dollars a week. Later, for seven years he worked as an unpaid caretaker on a farm in Maine, raising his own food, while he tried to succeed as a full-time writer.

In an autobiography, *Call It Experience* (1951), he recalls his first big financial break in the world of letters. After numerous efforts, he succeeded in selling two short stories to Maxwell Perkins at Scribner's. Perkins volunteered to pay "two-fifty" for both of them.

"Two-fifty?" Caldwell replied hesitantly. "I don't know. I thought maybe I'd receive a little more than that." So Perkins raised his price to "three-fifty."

Grudgingly Caldwell accepted. "I thought I'd get a little more than three dollars and a half, though," he said, "for *both* of them." He was elated when Perkins revealed that the "three-fifty" he was bidding was "three hundred and fifty."

Virginia Fletcher, his fourth wife and the illustrator for several of his books, was present in the hotel room in Dallas during our 1983 interview. Caldwell, a tall, spare, impressive man with a craggy face, proudly referred to her as "my editor." As the interview began, the two teased each other lightly about their meeting and marriage almost thirty years earlier. On the subject of his work, however, Caldwell held the floor, and spoke with matter-of-fact conviction and authority about the world in his books.

BRANS: I think I'll start by telling *you* a story. When I was about thirteen, I was reading some of your books—you know, had them in bed with me and was reading them under the covers with a flashlight the way kids do. My mother, who is a very respectable little Mississippi lady, came in and discovered them. And she said, "Honey, you just can't read these books. Now this is what we do with books like that." And she took them away from me and out to the backyard. For some reason there was a fire going under the outdoor wash pot—I guess it was wash day or something. She put them in the fire and she burned them.

CALDWELL: I've heard of that going on all my life. You had a good beginning in life. You were censored, weren't you?

BRANS: I was censored and you were censored. Of course I couldn't wait to get out and get other copies and hide them a little more carefully this time. I wanted to find out what she was so shocked about. But how does that make you feel? You must have had stories like this told to you for years.

CALDWELL: Well, you see, when I was a novice, I didn't know any better than to write the way I perceived something to be or the way I imagined something to be. So to have someone criticize or prohibit what I had written was outside my understanding. I could not understand how anyone would presume to censor what I wrote. How could anyone declare such and such a book or passage was not to be read or that what I had seen or imagined was not to be observed?

My own family was very respectable, too, but they were very liberal-minded, you might say, and they had never forbidden me to read anything. They never forced me to read anything either. My father was a minister, but he never suggested that I read the Bible. He left everything to me to determine myself, to form my own opinions and ideas. So I had no inhibitions about anything. The fact that a book was censored was outside of my ken. I couldn't understand it, so I just accepted that it was so, and continued doing what I was doing.

BRANS: Were your parents supportive when you began writing?

CALDWELL: I suppose so. I've often thought they figured out that I wasn't qualified to do anything else. They saw that I couldn't be a lawyer or a doctor or anything, so they let me go my own way to see if I could find my path in the world. At least that's the way I looked at it. I was never advised about what to do, so I just assumed that I was on my own and I remained that way.

My father was a little bent toward journalism and writing himself. In addition to his sermons, he would occasionally get a request for an essay or something from the local newspaper. So I kind of grew up with the idea that writing was my calling.

BRANS: What did you write first?

CALDWELL: I got my first writing job with a weekly newspaper in the small town where we lived in Georgia. I was writing social notes from all the communities around. Then when I went into professional journalism as a reporter, I started out writing obituaries.

BRANS: That used to be how all reporters started, I think.

CALDWELL: There's no better way to learn to write. I learned something, I don't know what. I just became interested in people's behavior, their actions.

But journalism is a very strict field because when you report something you have to have the facts completely known and provable. I began feeling that there's more to writing than fact, so that started me into the world of fiction. I wanted to make facts myself rather than accept someone else's facts.

As a writer, I sort of fall between two schools, journalism and fiction. I still have the inclination every once in a while to write a fact piece, something like an observation about travel, say. But then I'll have a feeling that I want to invent something, create something, like fiction.

BRANS: Are you ever tempted to invent something when you're supposed to be writing fact?

CALDWELL: There's a dividing line between journalism and fiction. You can slide in either direction just a shadow, but I try to be factual and accurate when I'm writing nonfiction. But when I'm writing fiction, I don't want to be factual and accurate. I want to invent something that does not exist and has not existed before, something that has never existed in the world. In order to do that, you have to make it more real than reality itself.

BRANS: You mean exaggerated. Is that what you're talking about?

CALDWELL: In fiction, you exaggerate and then you take away. You have to add something to your skeleton and then take something away from your skeleton.

BRANS: What do you mean, take something away?

CALDWELL: If you were writing a description of this room, for example, and you were a very good observer, you'd say there are four drawers in the table, and another drawer over on the side, and another drawer down below. If you do that continuously, you'll overburden the story being factual. So you say, there are many drawers in the table. To me that would be adequate.

Or I would say something like, "The room was oppressive," or "When I walked into the room, I felt oppressed. I felt that I wanted to get out of there as soon as I could." And to me that would describe the room better than saying a light bulb here, a curtain there, and all that. Or I might have a pistol ready for you in one of those drawers. Somebody might commit suicide just by opening that door. You never know what's going to happen when you try to invent something. It's limitless, completely limitless.

BRANS: I'm thinking about the car in *Tobacco Road*. You describe the breakdown of the car in pretty great detail. And you keep on doing this.

But when you keep on describing the breakdown of the car so carefully, bit by bit, over and over, after a while it's not just a car anymore.

CALDWELL: It becomes an individual car.

BRANS: Yes, it becomes an individual car. But it was even more than that to me when I read that book. The car is all the things that these poor people can't handle and don't know what to do with, you know.

CALDWELL: Well, of course that's nice in writing fiction. It makes your imagination run as a reader because I think the reader can read more into a story than the author himself can put into it. Because the reader has a different state of mind, he has different experiences, he has different social status and education. All those things interact with the reader's comprehension of the story. And it may surprise the writer to have this found in his story. He didn't know it was there.

BRANS: Are you telling me it was just a car to you? You're putting me on a little bit, I think. Let me ask you this. You've attracted such vast numbers of readers. Millions of copies of your books have been sold all over the world. How do you feel about the kind of influence that you must realize you have?

CALDWELL: That's something to speculate about—readers in a different culture and a different civilization, from China and Japan and the Soviet Union and Bulgaria. Each must have a different concept of what he is reading. His imagination must sometimes stop at a certain point. A man in Bulgaria cannot conceive, for example, that working people in America can have a new car, a brand-new car with shiny paint and everything, because he himself in a deprived economic state can never expect to have any kind of a car. He rides a bus or walks. It's hard for him to understand a man who's maybe a carpenter in America, and this man in Bulgaria is a carpenter. He can't understand.

And the American can't understand how a man in Bulgaria could put up with living in a mud hut, for example. Why doesn't he build a wooden house or a brick house? Why is he living in a mud house? So you have to consider that readers in different environments are going to have different conceptions of what the world is like.

But what I try to write is the elemental. I try to write a simple story about simple people. I think readers in any environment will be able to understand the events that are happening and what these people are like. I have more readers in translations than I do American readers, I suppose. The fact is, in my opinion—not knowing any better—maybe what I've been trying to do is what everybody should try to do. That is, to appeal to the whole world and give them ways to understand each other.

BRANS: You think all writers would be universal if they make the stories true to the elemental facts of human nature, as you try to do?

CALDWELL: But I couldn't tell someone else how to do it. I couldn't even explain how I do it. I just write the way I do because that's the way I am.

BRANS: You don't think of yourself as a regional writer then.

CALDWELL: I admire regional writing. And my life has been, as a writer, more confined to the Southern states: Georgia, Alabama, Florida, Virginia, and the Carolinas. That's where I've lived my life, and that's what I've written about. You might call that regionalism. The only difficulty about regionalism now is the fact that it really doesn't exist anymore, what with radio, television, motion pictures, and so on. Everybody tries to talk like Walter Cronkite or Dan Rather. We have all become slaves to this new universal Americanism.

BRANS: The whole country's becoming sort of homogenized? I was going to ask you how you think the South has changed, and that—

CALDWELL: Well, the South, the real South, was an agricultural empire, with agriculture influencing every aspect of life. So when the last back fields of that agricultural empire became urbanized and mechanized— In my state of Georgia, very rarely can you find anything of that old agricultural world.

Cotton picking by hand, for example. The average modern person today could not understand how you could go out and pick cotton all day by leaning over and pulling— They can't understand it.

BRANS: But you did it.

CALDWELL: I did it. I grew up in what I consider a transition period. As a very young person picking cotton, I had a short sack that didn't touch the ground. It was slung on your shoulder with straps, and the bottom of the bag didn't touch the ground. Therefore you had to fill your bag and carry it to a wagon more frequently. Then later, I observed that bags became ten to fifteen feet long, and you could drag them along the whole row. You wouldn't have to empty that bag until just before lunch or after lunch or whatever.

BRANS: Years ago you did a series of four pieces on conditions in the South, in Georgia, for the *New York Post.* And there was a terrible outcry on the part of Georgians about what you said.

CALDWELL: Well, of course, life existed there as it always had. But the agricultural empire was crumbling and breaking up at that time and people were becoming more educated. And so they'd look at the conditions of that life as being a little bit different than they should be. The tradition was changing and people did not want to admit that the past had been such an unpleasant existence for the poor people, black or white. When they had to recognize that these poor people that I wrote about were the remnants of their agricultural system, they became very embarrassed. They wanted to deny that this poverty existed. That was my understanding of the resentment that came about.

BRANS: You really didn't make any of that up, even the two babies who were suckling the old dog? That was the worst thing. The mother was sick in bed and there was this dog lying by the side of the fireplace—

CALDWELL: I've lived in that neighborhood, you see. No, I didn't make anything like that up. Where I lived at that time was eastern Georgia in the Savannah River valley, sandhill country near Augusta. In the back country out from Augusta these conditions existed, but the people in Augusta itself had no comprehension of what was happening ten, twenty, or thirty miles away. They had never been there, and when this was called to their attention they could not believe it. They said, You must be making that up.

BRANS: Exactly my reaction. It's just hard to believe.

CALDWELL: The poverty that I observed when I was growing up was so very real that it was an unbelievable experience. I remember very well. When I was about twelve, my mother became very perturbed because, oh, maybe three or four miles from the small town we lived in, there was a region where people were living in incredible poverty and illness. Some of these people got the habit of coming into town on certain days, Friday or Saturday, for example, to beg. They seemed to congregate and sort of form a procession, and they'd come into town to beg.

Before long they found out that my father was very soft-hearted and that he lived in the house across the street from the church. They would come and sit on our porch, maybe eight of them at a time, some with babies, some with sick members of the family, some with sores on their faces. I remember one woman with a cancerous sore that was as big as a coffee cup. Her whole cheek was— My father said it was a cancer and he tried to get a doctor to treat it, but the doctor wouldn't do it.

Anyway, these people would come and sit on the porch. We had a veranda around that house and they would sit on the steps or lie down on the porch and just hold out a hand. They wouldn't say very much. They'd just hold out a hand like that. My mother gave everything we had to the poor things, till she just said, "We can't do it any-more." She told my father, "You've got to make these people go somewhere else for a while. We just can't stand giving them any more." I don't know what happened. Gradually the people disappeared. I think most of them died. I don't know how they could have gotten away any other way.

People who were sick then were really sick, because, you see, there was no treatment—no welfare, no medical treatment, like there is now. When a person had a cancer on their face, it stayed there. I remember very well a man who had a goiter on his neck that was about the size of a football. You can imagine how big—think about holding a football up against your neck. Well, this thing just grew there. I remember seeing it for several years.

There were those who would try to help these people. I suppose my father was one of them. He had no money or anything, but he begged medical assistance for them and gave them old clothes and food. But a person with a big cancer sore or a goiter oftentimes just had to live with it. It was just a fact of life. He accepted it.

BRANS: Do you think that sort of thing is still around, and we are just protected from seeing it?

CALDWELL: It's just everywhere, to some extent. When I was growing up, it was just about as bad as it could get, I imagine. I couldn't imagine anything worse.

BRANS: Of course, when you live in a small place everybody sees almost everything and that makes a difference. In cities we segregate ourselves so. What do you think is the worst thing you have ever seen?

CALDWELL: The worst thing I've ever seen? Cruelty is the worst. I don't know if the cruel things that come to my mind are worse than the illnesses I've been describing, but they seem worse to me.

BRANS: Like what?

CALDWELL: In those days, the chain gang was sort of a standard operation. People now could not comprehend what a chain gang is. If they saw men dressed in stripes and all chained to each other, working on the roads or in the fields, they could not understand what was going on. If you told them about it, they would think this must be some fantasy that you dreamed up. But when I was living in Georgia, I really used to associate with certain people on the chain gang, so I know.

One black boy, for example, used to work for my mother as a yard boy. He was about, oh, twelve or fourteen years old. He'd go out and sand the yard, rake up the leaves, cut down the weeds for my mother in the backyard. I got to know him very well. He was put on a chain gang because somebody accused him of stealing—a knife,

I think it was, or something. So he was put on a chain gang. And I would go out and see him on Sundays when the chain gang was not working. They took Sundays off.

They had a little encampment down the road from the town that we lived in. I would go to see the boy and he would shine shoes for a nickel. I would give him five cents to shine my shoes and he would give me the five cents back and say, "Go buy me a bottle of shoe polish so I can shine some more shoes." So, you see, I got to know that whole situation very well.

We would talk, and he would tell me, in a low voice so that none of the guards could hear him, about somebody being beaten to death last night or last week.

BRANS: By the guards?

CALDWELL: Yes. "They just beat him to death," he'd say. But he wouldn't speak out loud. He just sort of whispered to me.

And I remember other things. The cruelty to mules, for example, was so bad to me that I didn't understand how it could exist. Before modernization, before road machinery and trucks and things like that to work on the highways, they used mules. Now, nobody knows what a mule is today. They've only seen one in a picture. But in those days, all the hard physical labor was done by mules and black people. And I remember very well my father taking me out to see some roadwork going on. They were filling a big fill, going to build a bridge across a river or creek, and he took me out and showed me the construction activity.

They were scooping up the dirt with the mule team. The mule team might be six or eight, I guess, in a tandem. They'd drag this heavy scoop of dirt up and dump it over to make the fill. This was hard, hard work for the mules. They were overworked and underfed, and in the hot weather some of these mules would die of heat, just die right in the harness.

And the driver would unhook their traces, junk the carcass and cover it up with dirt, and that was the burial of the mules in the highway. To me that was a cruel thing to do, literally to work those mules to death. Even as a little boy I knew something was wrong and my father told me, "They are not given enough food or even enough water. They are overheated, they are overworked, and they die."

Mules were cheap. It cost nothing to buy a mule, ten or twelve dollars, and nothing to raise a mule. Now that's cruelty to me, whether it's to a human or to an animal.

BRANS: You still get angry when you think about it.

CALDWELL: I can remember these things. They made such an impression upon me. And I saw them. They were not just hearsay.

BRANS: Do you think these people who did that—were they cruel or were they just ignorant?

CALDWELL: Certain feelings did not exist for them because they had been raised that way, I suppose. They often had the same attitude to the Negro. The black person was considered not as a human anyway, but just another animal like the mule. So it made no difference whether it was a mule or a black man that they wanted to get rid of for some reason or another. They would beat him up and cover him up with dirt and go ahead.

BRANS: It's like your line in *Tobacco Road*: "Niggers *will* get killed." As if it's just a kind of stubborn perversity of black people.

Mark Twain has a line sort of like that in *Huck Finn*. After a riverboat accident, some woman asks, "Did anybody get hurt?" And the answer is, "No'm. Killed a nigger." It's exactly your point: "Niggers *will* get killed."

I can tell your father meant a lot to you. If he was a preacher, why are you so rough on the preachers in your stories?

CALDWELL: I think my father was apprehensive about the morals of preachers anyway. I don't think he quite believed that they were strictly religious, that they lived the way themselves that they preached to other people. So he used to take me to various churches—the foot washers, the Holy Rollers, the ones speaking in tongues. He was not embarrassed by the fact that religion had been used as it was, but he thought it was something you should know. He didn't think you should take life blindly; you should know what goes on around you.

BRANS: Do you think all those preachers who go into the foot washing and the tongues and all that, the radio evangelists I'd put in that camp too—do you think any of them believe what they are saying?

CALDWELL: I don't know. I don't know what thoughts are in a preacher's mind and why he does certain things. I think more than anything else some of them just don't know any better. They just accept the fact that religion is a good thing to have. They think, It makes me feel good, and I believe in God, so I want to be sure to go to heaven when I die. To me, that's the concept of these people who preach religion. They are really just ignorant about what the future is going to be.

BRANS: What do you mean? What do you think the future is going to be?

CALDWELL: I'm an agnostic. I don't have any great feelings about the hereafter. I don't even want to be buried; I want to be cremated. I'm not going to rise up, I know, so why be buried? Why not get it over with the next day?

BRANS: Do you think that religion does a disservice to people in that it makes them focus on expectations of things that they can't have and keeps them happy in a world where they ought not to be happy?

CALDWELL: Religion is sort of a cough syrup with alcohol in it. It tastes good, it's sweet, it might even relieve your cough a little bit. You finish one bottle and you want another, but you won't admit that it's the alcohol in it that is making you feel good.

I don't know what people who believe in religion really feel deep down. Some people have the feeling they want to be on the safe side, I think: "Just in case there is a heaven, I want to go there. So I'm not going to deny that there is one."

BRANS: The academic critic Kenneth Burke wrote an essay about you in which he said that your principal theme was something he called "balked religiosity." I guess what he meant was frustrated religious impulses. What do you think about that? I think for example of the people who look through the crack in the fence in *Journeyman*. That's wonderfully comic, of course, but clearly they're looking for something that isn't quite of this world. At least they're trying to get a view of life that normal twenty-twenty vision doesn't give them.

CALDWELL: I don't really know what prompted that invention. I can try to explain myself, but I don't know whether I could convince you.

BRANS: I promise I'll believe anything you tell me.

CALDWELL: Well, these people were sitting around in the barn or the shed. Nothing was happening, but they could *imagine* that something was happening out there in the field or the woods or wherever.

And then you stop and think about it. People do take the telescope up on top of a building just to see as far as they can see. They want to see what is happening way over on the next hillside or on the river over there. So if you got up on top of a building with a high-powered telescope, you could see a lot of things there that you would not see here. So that would sort of widen your field of life. You might be attracted to what these people were doing over here. Maybe they're just doing some laundry and hanging it on the clothesline, but you wouldn't know that just by sitting here without a telescope. So it might be a diversion. It might be a sight that you would not otherwise see.

Looking through the crack is sort of a substitute for looking at stars, for example, looking at the North Star and all the planets all around the world. It's not so much what they see. These people sitting down here see something across the street or down the road. What matters is not what the people see, but the character, the scene, the action.

BRANS: That's beautiful. It's the desire to enlarge your horizons, to get a wider view of life. I like your version better than Kenneth Burke's mouthful of words.

Also, looking through the crack is a way of framing what you see. Framing it makes it special, separates it from everything else. I like that.

There's an interesting attitude toward religion in *God's Little Acre*. There's Ty Ty trying to outguess God or something by moving the acre as the spirit moves him. But of course Ty Ty doesn't have any genuine desire to give God the tithe, God's acre.

CALDWELL: No, that's just a residue of his past, I suppose. He probably grew up with parents who were religious. When Ty Ty came along and had a little skepticism, he had held on to the idea of tithing to some extent, but he didn't really believe in it. He was just in a transition period.

Instead of religious feelings, he has fearful feelings. You know religion can make you fearful of a lot of things: "The devil is going to get you if you don't watch out." You have it at some point and it's going to linger with you as long as you live.

BRANS: He does have reverent feelings, almost religious feelings, for his daughter-in-law. He's completely in awe of her beauty, of all that she represents.

CALDWELL: Yes, I guess she became a goddess to take the place of a living god. Dealing with a goddess is much more pleasant that dealing with God.

BRANS: What about Will Thompson in the same book? Does he have some of the divine in him?

CALDWELL: There's good and bad in life. Every person has a little bit of good and a little bit of evil in him. I think Will had more good. Instead of being primarily an evil person, he was basically a moral person. He had a feeling for other people, and he wanted to be helpful to the people around him, so he took the liberty of being a leader.

BRANS: What is it in him that the women in the book respond to?

CALDWELL: He was a man of good nature. He probably had some bad in his character, might have been a dishonest person and be stealing something from me the next day. But the good was stronger, and he was aggressive about his good feelings. You have your villains and your heroes, and I would consider him a hero.

BRANS: You sound as if Will is a real person whom you don't know completely even though he's your creation! How do you get to know these characters in your books?

Apparently you don't start out (or in this case even end up) with a complete picture of them.

CALDWELL: They have to invent themselves as they go along. Once they get started, there's no limit to what they can do and be. Some might be good, some might be evil, but I have no control over them once they get started.

BRANS: No control over them?

CALDWELL: To be true to these people you invent, you have to let them have a say. Their influence determines their nature and determines their actions. You can see these people. There they are. They're not going to just sit there and do nothing. They're going to do something. What is their nature? Their nature is to do.

We were talking about Will Thompson. His nature was to do something good for people. So I would have no control over him. In other words, I wouldn't want him to exist if he could not exhibit his feelings as he did.

BRANS: But how does he make those feelings known to you?

CALDWELL: Unconsciously, I think, a writer can observe someone else and know that person's feeling. I'm just a conveyor. I'm the person who carries it along. I'm not influencing the character. I don't want to influence him because then he would be like me. I want him to be like he is, his own self, not what I conceive. If I try to make him conform to my standards of living or my understanding of human nature, he would be false, he would be unrealistic. I have to let these people be themselves.

So I don't know what they're going to do. I don't. When I start to write a story, I don't know how it is going to end. I don't want to know. If I knew, I would be too bored to write it.

If I knew how it was going to end, I would have to have a plot. Everybody knows what a plot is, all right. I don't know what a plot is. A plot would make all these things conform to get to the end that I have already conceived. But I don't want to end up *there*. I want to start *here* and see what is going to happen. I never did know how anything was going to end. It just reaches a point of conclusion, and that's it.

BRANS: All of a sudden you realize that it's done.

CALDWELL: It's done. You can't go any farther. The people have already expressed themselves. You cannot add anything to it, and you don't want to take anything away.

You certainly don't want an editor to come along and strike out this or that. So you have to be real selfish. Editors have to earn a living by editing, but I don't want to have anything to do with them. I want to be my own editor.

And I don't care what a reader wants. I wouldn't write pornography to be sensational in order to get published. Pornography doesn't interest me at all. The facts of life interest me, whatever they are. I can understand the beauty of life, the openness of life. I just want life to express itself regardless of what the publisher wants or what the reader wants. Then if a reader likes what I've done, fine. If he doesn't like it, let him go find another book.

BRANS: Do you think you're a better person because you've been writing all these years? Has writing changed you?

CALDWELL: I've always been what I am.

BRANS: Do you think art serves any sort of moral purpose? What would you say to those, like my mother, who find your books shocking?

CALDWELL: Morals are just customs. Customs change, so morals change. The writer goes beyond the reality of today and invents something that might be the reality of tomorrow.

In nonfiction there is no beyond, but in fiction there is. Fiction is not a photograph. In fiction, you conceive a new world, invent a new life, invent a new person. He's never existed before. He's never been born. This is his first life. Writing is just an extension of life itself. And life itself is shocking.

IRIS MURDOCH

Virtuous Dogs and a Unicorn

"**N**O OTHER CONTEMPORARY British novelist seems to me of her eminence," the respected critic Harold Bloom wrote of Iris Murdoch, citing her "formidable combination of intellectual drive and storytelling exuberance." Exuberance indeed: the occasion for Bloom's words was the appearance of *The Good Apprentice* (1986), Murdoch's twenty-second novel in thirty-two years. Since then she has published another, *The Book and the Brotherhood* (1988).

Her exuberant flow of stories is equalled only by her intellectual energy. During her years of novel-writing, interspersed with several plays and a book of poetry, Murdoch has also published four books of moral philosophy. The novels, which show fallible human beings trying to live the good life as Murdoch defines it, take up where the formal philosophy leaves off. "A moral philosophy," Murdoch has written, "should be inhabited." She populates hers with the creatures of her fiction. First a word about her philosophy and then a word about her creatures.

photo by Mark Gerson

The philosophy came into existence in the forties under the influence of Sartre, the subject of her first book, *Sartre, Romantic Rationalist* (1953). Born in 1919 in Dublin of Anglo-Irish parents, Murdoch grew up in England and studied classics at Oxford, taking a first in 1942. She joined the civil service, and while posted in Belgium met Sartre. Soon after, she returned to England to study philosophy at Cambridge under Wittgenstein. In 1948, she began to teach philosophy, first at Oxford, then at the Royal College of Art in London, but retired in 1968 to devote herself to writing. However, she continued to write philosophical studies: *The Sovereignty of Good* (1971), *The Fire and the Sun: Why Plato Banished the Artists* (1977), and *Acastos: Two Platonic Dialogues* (1987).

Chance is an important element in her philosophy, which combines Platonic idealism and Sartrean existentialism. The critic John Bayley, whom Iris Murdoch married in 1956, has said that he glanced out of the window of his Oxford study one day to see her cycling by and knew at once that they would be married. As in a Murdoch novel, an accidental glance altered the course of two lives. So with all human life, according to Murdoch, which, as she sees it, has no meaning, direction, or destiny beyond itself. "We are simply here." On our own in a world where anything can happen, anytime, to anyone, we must teach ourselves freedom and virtue. That process gives moral shape to life in an amoral, contingent universe.

Freedom comes when we see the world clearly as it is, not as we would like it to be—in other words, when we acknowledge the power of chance in our lives. *Virtue* comes when we see other people clearly in their unique particularity rather than as extensions of our own wishes or fears, and when we respect their separate reality, "the otherness of others." Both freedom and virtue then depend upon "unselving," displacing the self that distorts perception of the world and of others. Love, the highest form of virtue, thus the most selfless regard one can have for another, must always be imperfect but striving toward perfection.

The novels in which Murdoch embodies these concepts create a contemporary social cosmos which is British, intellectual and artistic, upper middle-class. She subjects her secure, leisured, civilized characters to a sudden and heady dose of the contingent and inexplicable. Then she follows the characters in a more or less complete examination of the whole of their lives.

For example, in *The Nice and the Good* (1968) a Whitehall civil servant shoots himself, a suicide which leads a dozen of his personal and public connections to a complete reconsideration of their own apparently happy circumstances. More recently, in the opening scene of *The Good Apprentice,* a college student, Edward Baltram, tricks his friend Mark into taking a psychedelic drug, and then, seeing Mark happily asleep after a good "trip," leaves the room for several hours. When he returns, Mark has thrown himself out of the window and lies dead on the pavement below. The death, officially declared an accident, becomes the catalyst through which Edward, the "good apprentice," learns to accept the contingency of a pointless and uncaring universe, to recognize the unpredictability of others, and to love beyond the demands of ego.

Often the *coup de foudre* comes not through death but through sex. Bloom calls Murdoch "a major student of Eros," "an original and endlessly provocative theorist of the tragicomedy of sexual love, with its peculiar hell of jealousy and self-hatred." In her fiction men and women alike are powerless in the grip of erotic passion, which makes them absurd or miserable but also has the beneficent effect of making them open to moral improvement. Through the bizarre entanglements of the characters in *A Severed Head* (1961), one of her most popular novels, Martin Lynch-Gibbon comes to respect "the dark gods," the primitive forces under civilization which erupt in adultery, incest, violence, and threats of castration and suicide. Charles Arrowby in *The Sea, The Sea* (1978), determined to have a woman he has not seen in several decades, kidnaps her. Facing up to the turmoil created by his folly, Charles sets out more knowledgeably upon "the demon-ridden pilgrimage of human life."

Victims of such blows of chance can comfort themselves that they have been lifted out of "the net," as Murdoch calls it, the artificial structure of complacency or routine they have built into their lives to guard against the terrors of disorder. As pleasant as these structures are, they do harm by preventing the clear-sighted perception of the human condition and of other people. Language itself can be a net, as it is for Hilary Burde in *A Word Child* (1975). Having escaped a perilous childhood by his gift for language, the adult Hilary mistakenly expects the world and other people to behave as consistently as the rules of grammar. Like Bradley Pearson, the novelist in *The Black Prince* (1973) who falls tumultuously in love with a girl forty years his junior, or Miles, the poet in *Bruno's Dream* (1969), Hilary must learn to accept the chaos of life without the use of a net of words.

The novel is, as Murdoch has said, "about people's treatment of each other," so it can aid in the necessary and ongoing process of "unselving," for the writer as well as for the reader. In *Under the Net* (1954), Jake frees himself from "the net" of self-regard by a rebirth of imagination as a writer. But writing will not, of course, free Jake from chance; his new life begins with a litter of kittens in which two are Siamese and two are tabby. "I don't know why it is," Jake exclaims. "It's just one of the wonders of the world."

Before my first trip to England, during the summer of 1982, I wrote Iris Murdoch for an interview. "I'm sorry!" she replied. "But I am sure you will be in England again before too long, & then do write again."

The nicest possible brush-off, I thought, but the following summer I tried again. This time I got a tentative yes. "Maybe you could telephone me when you are in England." And she sent me not one but two numbers, one in her little Oxfordshire village, Steeple Aston, the other in London.

As soon as I got over jet lag, I called the Steeple Aston number. A gentle male voice told me that Miss Murdoch was in London. I dialed the London number and got the lady herself. Oh, yes, she remembered. Could I possibly call her in Steeple Aston later in the week, say about 8:15 on Friday morning? Then she would know more.

I could and did. She couldn't promise me anything, but would I mind terribly phoning her in London the middle of the following week, say about 1:30 Wednesday afternoon? I wouldn't and did. Same song, second verse. The gentle male voice would re-direct me, or Murdoch herself, in the nicest possible way, would make vague promises for very precise times, like 7:30 on Thursday morning or 12:20 on Tuesday.

This went on for five weeks. I felt guilty, but I didn't stop calling. She didn't seem to want me to stop, and I even decided she might be hurt if I stopped. Along about the third week, I began to find the whole thing as amusing as some elaborate philosophical muddle in an Iris Murdoch novel.

But time was running out, so I leveled. "Please just say," I told her, "if you don't want to see me. All you have to do is say no."

A silence. Then, "Oh, no, I certainly couldn't do that," she said. Another silence. "Could you come out to Steeple Aston on Thursday?" Oh, yes. "But how will you get here?" A friend will drive me.

Very well then. "Be here at 11:30 Thursday morning." A pause. "No, make that 11:40."

I won't tell you how we got lost on her directions—another philosophical muddle—and found the place only when a very persnickety lady working in her yard directed us to "the untidiest garden in the village, you cawn't miss it, it's a disgrace."

I won't tell you how we found it thirty minutes late, and after a long time Murdoch came to the door, and she had forgotten all about our appointment.

I will tell you that it was worth it to me, as I sat in the comfortable, cluttered sitting room, balancing a small glass of sherry on my knee and struggling with the tape recorder, taking in the chessboard and the painting of perhaps Perseus and the books overflowing the shelves and stacked on the floor and Iris Murdoch herself, a small round woman with kind brown eyes and disheveled gray hair over a head full of mysteries. It was worth it to me, and I hope to you.

BRANS: I went to the Tate yesterday, and saw the Gainsborough portrait of the Pomeranian bitch and puppy, I suppose you're familiar with it. Seeing it made me think of

Zed, the little Pomeranian in *The Philosopher's Pupil,* and the goodness that he exhibits in the book. His tact, for example. He pretends to like water, pretends to like swimming. I began to think of all the other dogs in your books—Mingo, for example, and the big Alsatian in *Under the Net.* I wondered why these dogs often seem to be a lot better than some of your people.

MURDOCH: Yes, they're virtuous dogs. There's a very virtuous dog in *An Accidental Man,* that black Labrador which Charlotte acquires. I think dogs are often figures of virtue. Of course, there are bad dogs too. There are bad dogs in *The Sacred and Profane Love Machine,* you remember, who pursue and attack—they're like the hounds of Actaeon. They attack the hero at one point. Dogs are very different from cats in that they can be images of human virtue. They are like us.

BRANS: Is there any significance to the fact that Zed is so tiny?

MURDOCH: I don't normally portray my characters from life, but in the case of Zed, he is actually copied from an individual dog I know, the dog of a friend. But his being very small is of course part of the drama. The dog is a character in the book and interacts with the other characters. He is a very important figure.

BRANS: So that he's much more vulnerable because he's small, and you're much more frightened for him?

MURDOCH: Yes, indeed. He is fragile.

BRANS: His size doesn't have anything to do with the shrinking of virtue?

MURDOCH: Nothing like that!

BRANS: Good. I thought I might be overreading. Do you think Americans react differently to your work from the British, or read you differently?

MURDOCH: I don't know enough to say. What do you think?

BRANS: An American friend told me recently that he thinks a lot of Americans read you for a certification of what they consider to be the social and intellectual superiority of the British, and that in a way it's satisfying to them to find this superiority in book after book that you write.

MURDOCH: I think some people—but this wouldn't be only Americans by any means—might read my books because there is a kind of assertion of old-fashioned values or the reality of virtue. Of course this also annoys other people who regard it as something not proper to be said.

BRANS: Not proper for aesthetics' sake, I suppose.

MURDOCH: There's positive critical warfare on this subject between the "old-fashioned" critics and writers, and those who want fiction to deny the traditional idea of character and the traditional notions of absolute guilt or the reality of virtue, which they regard as "bourgeois" or "religious" in some unacceptable sense. These are partly very deep matters and partly things to do with immediate style and what attracts people to a book.

BRANS: For some people, if a writer doesn't espouse the highest morality he or she knows, doesn't attempt to write morally, that writer is writing badly. I guess that's the kind of position that Tolstoy took when he wanted to destroy Anna Karenina, for example. Where do you stand?

MURDOCH: A writer cannot avoid having some sort of moral position, and attempting to be nonmoral is in a way a moral position, an artificial one. I think that a novelist, a storyteller, naturally portrays his own moral judgments. But these very judgments are not just a small area of human discourse; they're almost the whole of it. We are always making value judgments, or exhibiting by what we say some sort of evaluation, and storytellers dealing with persons must constantly be doing this. It's Tolstoy's great apprehension of the whole moral scheme which makes his novels great, not his artificial, censorious feeling that he had to burn *Anna Karenina*; that's an incidental thing. But the moral perception and depth of the writer is something very important. It's a kind of realism—seeing what the world really is, and not making it into a fantasy.

BRANS: In *The Sovereignty of Good*, you say that ordinary people do not, "unless corrupted by philosophy," believe that they create values by their choices. They think that some things are really better than others and that they may get it wrong—make the wrong choices. I wanted to ask you about this phrase, "unless corrupted by philosophy." How do you think philosophy can corrupt? I thought you might be thinking of pragmatism and "whatever works is good"—a very American attitude, I suppose.

MURDOCH: That would be one example certainly, but I was talking more of various kinds of existentialist philosophy and Oxford philosophy, which attempted to explain value judgments as emotive statements or arbitrary acts of will. This has distorted moral philosophy in recent years by suggesting that one has got to make a sharp decision between fact and value; and if something isn't factual, in the sense of scientific fact, and so presentable in some way, it belongs to a shadowy world, of private will or emotion, so that moral attitudes would simply be private emotional attitudes of one sort or another. There are refined versions of this which suggest that moral statements are really commands—that through moral language we attempt to influence people and alter the world.

BRANS: So philosophy corrupts by making moral decisions simply a matter of preference or taste?

MURDOCH: Yes, you can just choose. You then just choose your attitude, and there's nothing behind it. Now it's perfectly true that one cannot prove that moral statements are right in the sense that one can prove ordinary matters of fact or science. But this is true of a whole world of value, of art for instance. And the fact that you can't "prove" a painting or a book doesn't mean that it isn't in some sense true or significantly connected with reality. It seems to me obvious that morality is connected with truth, with rejection of egoistic fantasy, and with apprehension of what's real; that the ability and the wish to tell the truth are a very fundamental part of morals. Morality is connected with the real world in innumerable ways, and is something that goes on all the time. It isn't a kind of special activity that you suddenly take up.

BRANS: To follow your idea that ordinary persons and even dogs can readily be exemplars of virtue, let me ask this: Do you think, as Tolstoy seemed to imply with his peasants and children, that behaving rightly, behaving correctly, is easier for simple characters? Are there levels of sophistication, let's say, that make behaving correctly, doing good, more difficult for some than for others?

MURDOCH: Well, I think that some people are blessed with happy, friendly temperaments. I think that what Freud says about these things is roughly true; one is influenced by one's history, one's early life, so that some people are calm, some people are excitable or easy to anger, by temperament.

The question of sophistication is another one, a complicated one, and I don't think I hold any special view on that. A simple person can be either good or bad, and obviously a sophisticated person could be either good or bad. I think that goodness at every level of sophistication demands the ability to face life and be truthful, and the ability to be honest and faithful and loving, and the ability to give help. Facing life honestly is important at every level of sophistication.

BRANS: Without illusions or fantasies.

MURDOCH: Yes, I think "fantasies" is the name of a very important tendency to protect oneself by imagining that things are other than they are.

BRANS: But aren't we all damaged too by others' fantasies about us?

MURDOCH: That could be the case too. People often like to build up other people through fantasy or destroy them through giving them pictures of themselves which are false.

BRANS: I once had a good friend who kept telling me what I was like.

MURDOCH: Yes, this can be very damaging. I mean, people sometimes, as it were, damage the being of other people, as if they were actually scratching it away.

BRANS: I felt myself stripped of the freedom to change, to try to be better.

Suppose I were to come to you as a child would come to a parent or a disciple to a guru, and say to you, I want above all things to be good. What would you say? What would be your instinctive response to that?

MURDOCH: I'd want to find out something about the question. It would matter whether or not you were in some kind of tangle. I mean, if this was an immediate thing, then one might want to talk about that, particularly about truthfulness.

BRANS: Suppose I just wanted a beautiful life—"I want my life to be good."

MURDOCH: There are many aspects. I think getting hold

of work which is good, which you want to do, which you think you can do well, and which you feel does something for yourself and perhaps for other people is important.

But then of course everyone is a victim of circumstances. That's what's so tragic in our country and even in your country—people can't find work. Why isn't some statesman brave enough to grasp this problem and say, "Well, look, there isn't going to be work in the future. We've got to try and see how we live in a society where people can't all work"?

But I think work is good and if you can find a work which connects you with the world and allows you to use your talents, I think this is quite a large part of the good life. But there are all sorts of ways whereby our natural selfishness can be checked. I mean, if one has a religious belief—do you have one?

BRANS: My beliefs are vague and undefined.

MURDOCH: How were you brought up?

BRANS: In a fundamentalist religion, scared of hell for years, nightmares about hell.

MURDOCH: You must have felt you'd gotten out of something when you broke free. It's an awful thing to bring up young people like this. But if one has religion, if one is in any sense at home there even as a lapsed believer, this probably can help, because one has the idea of how to pray. Not in the sense of asking God to do these things, but in the sense of retiring from the world into a different dimension. Actually anyone can do this. I think meditation is important. I would like meditation to be taught in schools, the ability just to be quiet, and to see what is worthless, to distinguish between what's important and what isn't important.

BRANS: You've written a lot about selflessness, about

getting rid of the self in order to love the world, in order even to see the world. You define humility as getting rid of the self. All of this makes me think that you might intend a specifically Christian vision in your work. Let me turn the tables. Do you have a religion?

MURDOCH: Oh, yes, I believe in religion, in the sense in which a Buddhist believes in religion. My background, as it happens, is Christian. But I don't believe in God and I don't believe in the supernatural aspect of religion, I don't believe in life after death, or heaven or anything.

BRANS: How can it be religion if you strip it of the supernatural?

MURDOCH: Ah, but religion is everywhere, religion is breathing. It's connected with the deep aspect of one's life at every moment, how one lives it all the time, and with truth and love and all these things we've been talking about. I mean, this is what any sophisticated Buddhist or Hindu would say; he doesn't believe in God, or heaven. Though obviously in any religion there's imagery which is understood by different people in different ways.

Some hold very literalistic beliefs about God, but many people can't hold such beliefs now. It's too contrary to their own perceptions of truth and reality. But this doesn't mean that they can't be religious. I became a Marxist when I was young, and I thought I had given up religion. Then I gave up Marxism, though it's very enlightening to have been a Marxist. But I thought when I gave up believing in God that religion was gone out of my life. Then I realized that this wasn't so after all. Religion is still there, even if one holds no supernatural or dogmatic belief.

BRANS: You said you prayed. To whom do you pray?

MURDOCH: I don't exactly pray to anyone. I retire into myself, perhaps have a conversation between the higher self and the lower self or something of that sort. It sounds rather pompous. But all I mean is an ability to withdraw from immediate concerns and to be quiet and to experience the reality of what's good in some way. But one is doing this all the time, through beautiful things, through art, through music, and of course very much through other people, apprehending their reality and their goodness or wanting to help them and so on.

BRANS: Yes, you've written about these stairsteps to the good, art, relationships with people—

MURDOCH: Intellectual studies also. Any religious replacement such as some sort of craft or study or work—

BRANS: Which imposes a discipline on the life, is that the idea?

MURDOCH: Yes, if you don't have ordinary work, try to learn something, learn another language for instance. Of course it's all very well to say this to people, but people have such terrible troubles. At least one can picture perhaps a society where people don't have ordinary work but are always learning something.

BRANS: I almost instinctively reject that; maybe it's the American in me. I feel terribly sorry for people without work.

MURDOCH: Well, exactly, yes, if one assumes that we can come back to full employment in Western society. But I don't think we can. We've never had *full* employment here in England, and everything to do with modern technology suggests that computers will take over all sorts of jobs which they can do more efficiently than we can. People feel very concerned with this. I'm not an expert, but it looks to me as if it is all going to be very difficult.

BRANS: So we'll have all these energies that aren't being used unless we think up a way to use them.

MURDOCH: Yes, people get demoralized. I think education helps enormously, and so one must spend more money on education. People can be taught how to learn, and can learn to enjoy things which are worthy, like art, and creation, and helping other people, and can use their energy in this way.

BRANS: In a number of your books you have women who are more or less imprisoned by the expectations of the men in their lives. I'm thinking of Hannah in *The Unicorn,* who's both idolized and imprisoned; of Dorina in *An Accidental Man,* with Austin's adoration of her which really serves to keep her separate from him and to keep her enclosed; and of Crystal in *The Word Child,* whose brother's definitions of her entrap or imprison her. There do seem to be a number of them, and I wondered if it were deliberate on your part for some reason.

MURDOCH: I don't think it's deliberate. The three women you mentioned are very different from each other. Crystal seems to be a sort of redemptive sufferer, who gives herself over to love for her brother, and I don't think that she feels trapped.

BRANS: But the reader feels that she is trapped, and that this man is not really worth her attention and her love.

MURDOCH: All the same, she is right to love him and that love makes her happy. Dorina is more of a victim, more of a wispy figure without very much strength. And Hannah is entirely different because the whole story has an allegorical aspect, and it's much more official and less logical. Hannah is a figure who is either spiritual or demonic. The spiritual and the demonic are very close together. She's seen either as a kind of noble victim or as a sort of *la belle dame sans merci,* a *femme fatale.* She doesn't know herself really, and it's not clear which she is. She's a power figure as well, with a great deal of effect on all these people, and they in turn build her up. It's like a case you mentioned earlier of somebody's fantasy building somebody else up into something which perhaps they are or are not.

BRANS: But she is trapped, because Effingham realizes that he could have sprung her, but he chooses not to.

MURDOCH: Yes, partly because he's afraid of the consequences, partly because he likes her to be there shut up and sort of kept a prisoner for him.

BRANS: There, you see. And in *The Sea, The Sea,* remember, Charles kidnaps Hartley and shuts her up.

MURDOCH: That's a much more realistic situation. Charles is suffering from a delusion that the first love is the great one and that people don't change.

BRANS: You said there's something to what Freud said about early experiences. Does that mean that you're somewhat in agreement with Charles?

MURDOCH: Oh, no, I think Charles is making a mistake, but it's a natural mistake. I mean it's not totally absurd. He feels so sure that this thing meant so much to both of them at the time that it must retain its meaning for her as well as for him. But then, he fails to do what a more sensible person would do, having looked at the situation to drop it.

BRANS: And this is what you mean by not facing reality, his inability to imagine that she feels differently.

MURDOCH: And his arrogance too, because he's so grand, he can't help feeling, How much she must regret that she didn't marry Grand Me, and that she married this absolute nonentity.

BRANS: And it would have been such a good thing—

MURDOCH: She would have had such a happy life!

BRANS: But actually, as she tells him quite frankly, he would have been too grand for her. She would have been hopelessly out of things.

MURDOCH: She might have had some regrets sometimes, but on the whole I think not.

BRANS: Do you think that people can ever serve as solutions for other people? Often in the books I've mentioned men will offer themselves as solutions for these women, and of course the reverse is true. Several women in various books, like Hilda in *The Nice and the Good,* think of themselves as solutions for these muddled males who clearly need to have their socks washed and their sitting rooms tidied.

MURDOCH: Yes, I think that people do solve each other's problems. In happy marriages people do that and in long friendships one's supported by other people all the time. I mean this can go wrong, but it can go right as well. That's quite often what one's looking for, someone to love one and be with one in some permanent way.

BRANS: So that's a way of coming to a sense of reality about the world?

MURDOCH: I think so, though of course any love relationship can be full of delusions. You may wish a person to be what he really is not, but a long relationship then becomes more truthful.

BRANS: We were talking about the discipline of art and work. What's the connection, do you think, between discipline and visions? I'm thinking of that glorious vision that Effingham has when he is sinking in the swamp in *The Unicorn.* He imagines himself dead, and he says that if *he* were to die, what was left was everything else, and this vision shakes him and enlightens him. Do ordinary people get visions like this? How do these visions relate to life as it has to be lived in the discipline of the day?

MURDOCH: In the case of Effingham, he has a truthful vision of the world without the self, but of course he cannot sustain it, it disappears from him.

BRANS: And the same thing happens to Cato in *Henry and Cato*. He's had these visions of goodness and he's gotten increasingly separated from them.

MURDOCH: Yes, though with Cato, it's more connected with religion and with a sort of orderly life. But it's something very odd for Effie. I don't know how often people have such visions, but I think they do come in one way or another to people, through art or other people, sometimes rather suddenly or remarkably and other times more gradually.

And then one drifts away from the vision, but it can also remain as something that you remember, like having a good dream. Sometimes in a dream something extraordinarily real can happen.

BRANS: Your books are full of dreams. I once heard a psychiatrist remark that a criminal who doesn't dream can be regarded as beyond redemption.

MURDOCH: What we invent in dreams is astonishing. Sometimes there are very beautiful symbols in dreams. Religion is a kind of formalization of such matters. We have all sorts of ways of experiencing things which are pure and sort of out of the world. But then anything can become like that. In certain states of mind we see things as full of grace.

BRANS: Do you believe that grace touches your life?

MURDOCH: Oh, yes, though again not in the dogmatic, supernatural sense. But I think that there are forces of good that you suddenly can find, streams flowing toward you, whatever the metaphor would be. Yes. And I think sometimes people try for a long time in a rather dull way to do what they think is right, and then they're suddenly rewarded or cheered up. Some sort of vision holds the world together, I think, and this is part of the subject matter of literature.

BRANS: There's Lisa, that wonderful girl in *Bruno's Dream,* who's going to give herself over to the starving millions in India. Then all of a sudden at the end of the book you see her in a sports car and she's married and she's cut her hair and she's bought clothes. Was this a kind of grace? I was surprised that Lisa didn't have to live the rest of her life in suffering poverty to be good. No one reading that book could have predicted what would happen to Lisa.

MURDOCH: I dare say she might have chosen a much nobler life if she'd gone off to India, and in some sense a better life. But I think happiness is important too. That's part of this thing about finding work and finding the right place for yourself in the world. One has a right, even a duty, to be happy. For some people, happiness is part of organizing a good life. Making other people happy is part of that, but very often making other people happy is a happiness of one's own. Lisa's end has something to do with Danby. Danby is the happy hedonist. He makes happiness for other people too.

BRANS: Is she reciprocating when she marries him and lives in a way that will make him happy?

MURDOCH: I think she is infected by his particular kind of life energy, which he's been lucky in.

BRANS: I was terribly thrilled that you allowed them to have this happy ending.

MURDOCH: Yes, I'm glad you felt that. I liked it too. I was fond of Danby and I think it was probably a good thing.

BRANS: Another one of your characters with a shocking contradiction for me was Tallis Brown. Here is this supremely good man, and I was horrified when I read the description of his house. It's so dirty! Julius King comes in and cleans up for him, and he has to scrape the kitchen floor because there's this sticky substance all over it, and the dirty milk bottles in which various things are growing, and really just this sort of horrifying filth.

MURDOCH: I must say, I don't mind filth as much as you do.

BRANS: But his was an exaggeration of filth. Why, for such a good man?

MURDOCH: That book too has an allegorical background. Tallis is not only a good man, he should be seen as a high incarnation, a holy man, something like Christ, arriving in the world. And it's symbolic of the situation that nowadays the holy man is sort of shaky, hopeless, muddled, he hasn't got a place. Somebody else has to clean up his kitchen and so on.

And the person who cleans it is Julius, the prince of darkness. Julius should be thought of as the devil. The conflict between the two is really what the book is about. They recognize each other as two spiritual beings, of opposing kinds, though Julius doesn't recognize Tallis at once. And Julius has been in a concentration camp, so perhaps the devil suffers too.

But, then, all this is part of the struggle between good and evil that lies behind ordinary life. Because of course at the same time they are ordinary characters. One doesn't have to know these things to read the book and understand the drama.

BRANS: Your books are so full of meaning. Would you be disappointed if people only read them for the exciting, suspenseful stories they tell?

MURDOCH: I would like the reader to see everything in the book. But I'm glad if people like those stories. It gives me pleasure, because stories are a very good way, you know, of getting away from one's troubles. Now let's have a drink.

Games of the Extremes

"My fictions are, by and large, experimental constructions," William Gass has commented. "That is, I try to make things out of words the way a sculptor might make a statue out of stone. Readers will therefore find very little in the way of character or story in my stories." The most ardent of "art for art's sake" aestheticians, Gass, a writer, philosopher, and university professor, nevertheless reached a wide audience with his first novel and has maintained a steady readership with the two volumes of fiction and four volumes of essays he has published since.

Actually, in Gass's mind the distinctions between fiction and nonfiction have little credibility when applied to his work. "I think of myself as a writer of prose rather than a novelist, critic, or storyteller, and I am principally interested in the problems of style," he has said. And it is true that his essays are a lot closer to his fiction than they are to conventional nonfiction, and that both his fiction and his nonfiction sound like poetry.

photo by Nancy Crampton

Born in North Dakota in 1924 and brought up in Ohio, Gass decided at the age of eight or so to become a writer, and accordingly "read whatever came to hand," from detective stories and books about bees to biographies of Napoleon and *Thus Spake Zarathustra*. After three years in the Navy during World War II, he took a degree in philosophy in 1947 from Kenyon College, where he audited several classes of the Fugitive poet John Crowe Ransom. Ransom's New Criticism, a theory of aesthetics that stresses the independence of a literary text from any extratextual consideration, converged with Gass's own leanings toward formalism in writing.

From Kenyon, Gass went to graduate school in philosophy at Cornell, where he specialized in the philosophy of language and wrote a dissertation on "A Philosophical Investigation of Metaphor." "I love metaphor the way some people love junk food," he has said. Receiving his doctorate in philosophy in 1954, Gass taught at Wooster College and at Purdue University. Since 1969, he has been a professor of philosophy at Washington University in St. Louis.

A high point of his years of graduate study at Cornell was a seminar conducted by the philosopher Ludwig Wittgenstein which Gass later described as "the most important intellectual experience" of his life. Wittgenstein views philosophy as an activity to be pursued for its own sake, apart from content. Another high was a growing familiarity with the work of Gertrude Stein. As Wittgenstein was interested in the process of philosophy rather than a fixed philosophical system, Stein was similarly interested in the process of writing, especially in the sound and significance of single words and repeated sentences, rather than the lifelike content of literature. From these influences and others, particularly the textual insularity of Ransom, Gass came to conceive of fiction as a construction made of metaphor, with no relevance to the world outside the book and no obligation to be "lifelike."

The central figure of *Omensetter's Luck* (1966), Gass's first and most conventional book of fiction, is the Reverend Jethro Furber, a "verber with fervor," a man whose whole life is lived in language. Set in conflict with Furber in the structure of the book is the almost silent Omensetter. The reader watches while Furber builds a structure made entirely of language, which has no counterpart in any reality except Furber's madly verbing mind, for the purpose of destroying Omensetter. Difficult though the book is, it was unanimously praised. "The fever is in the words on the page," one critic wrote.

In the Heart of the Heart of the Country (1968) is a collection of two novellas and three short stories. The title story has autobiographical elements, but Gass has insisted that the narrator, a poet "in retirement from love," has "a mind with severe limitations" and "a psyche whose feelings are full of self-pity." Gass tries to get inside this character, as he tries to get inside the adolescent Jorge who is the narrator of "The Pederson Kid," the longest story in the collection, and as he tries to do in his fiction generally. Both in *Heart* and in a second book of short stories, *The First Winter of My Married Life* (1979), Gass is more interested in the way his often damaged narrators tell the stories than in the content of the stories they tell. Because the concern of his work is with the process of its own creation, because his fiction takes itself as its own subject, critics have dubbed Gass a writer of "metafiction."

Willie Masters' Lonesome Wife (1971) has been called by the author an "essay-novella." The form of the story is an interior monologue of Babs, the wife, once a stripper and a whore, which takes place while she is having sex with a lover. A collage of divergent elements—authorial asides, little essays interspersed at random, parodies, footnotes—breaks up the narrative and makes for what Gass refers to as an experience in art. "You have fallen into art," *Willie Masters'* concludes, "—return to life."

On Being Blue: A Philosophical Inquiry (1976) is like a long Symbolist poem, in which every association with the word "blue" is explored through the use of image and metaphor. The "inquiry" concludes with an analysis of the blue, or sexual, content of literature, in which Gass theorizes that erotic fiction uses language "like a lover" to seduce the reader.

Gass has written three additional books of essays, *Fiction and the Figures of Life* (1970), *The World within the Word* (1978), and *Habitations of the Word* (1985), in all of which he defends his theory that the artist has no obligations to morality or to life, but should concern himself only with beauty of form and language. For *Habitations,* Gass received a National Book Critics Circle award. He has also received a Guggenheim Fellowship.

This interview took place on a rainy Sunday afternoon in Dallas in the fall of 1984. Gass is a round-faced man, with longish straight gray hair, and dark eyes. Exhilarated but surprised at the frankness with which he spoke of the loss of the *Omensetter* manuscript, I remember afterward running into the room where my husband sat reading, setting up the tape player, and demanding, "Put your book away. You've got to listen to this!"

BRANS: I've been reading you a long time, you know—since *Omensetter's Luck* came out in 1966. I read you before I even knew you had a literary theory.

GASS: Good!

BRANS: I wondered how you feel about being wedded to this theory, being known as the apostle of aestheticism.

GASS: People insist on it, but I don't think I really have a theory. A bunch of attitudes and opinions, maybe, but I've never written any general justification, any clear-cut, organized theory. I just take up little problems here and there, and anyway that's a separate activity.

BRANS: From your writing fiction?

GASS: Yes, in the sense that I don't think about it when I'm writing fiction. I'm not interested in trying to write according to some doctrine. When I'm writing fiction, it's very intuitive, so that what happens, or what I do, or how it gets organized, is pretty much a process of discovery, not a process of using some doctrine that you can somehow fit everything into.

BRANS: I'm relieved. I really loved *Omensetter's Luck,* but then I tried to fit your theory that art is nothing but form to the book, and it just didn't work. No matter how often your essays say that art and morality don't mix, I keep seeing morality, moral positions, in *Omensetter.*

GASS: A lot of people feel that way, but it doesn't bother me. I mean, I'm not concerned with it that much. I think partly it has to do simply with the connotations of a formalist position. But that's a mistake in understanding the word "formal." It's not formal in the sense of stripped or regular or anything of the sort. I am a romantic writer with a formalist theory. So that gives people problems.

BRANS: And it gives you a lot of room too, doesn't it? Your great rival on the whole issue of art and morality for years was John Gardner, of course. I'm curious—were you and Gardner friends before he died?

GASS: Yes. We couldn't have been close because we never lived close enough to one another. But we were friends for a long time, first through correspondence. And then when he moved from California to southern Illinois, I visited him on his farm there. Then we saw each other more often when I was at Washington University. We were friends for about twenty-five or thirty years.

BRANS: So the fact that you disagreed on this fairly vital subject didn't turn you off?

GASS: No, it didn't bother me. In fact, it was one of the bases of our friendship. We used to have wonderful arguments at three o'clock in the morning, in the kitchen over a bottle of bourbon. They were much better than the official arguments that took place.

BRANS: Did you shout at each other?

GASS: Sure. But—John was a very good-humored man, very kind and generous.

BRANS: That wasn't a very good-humored book he wrote, *On Moral Fiction.*

GASS: No, it wasn't. People didn't get over it easily, either because they didn't know John well enough or didn't know the situation. John wrote that under difficult circumstances. Part of the time he was ill with cancer. Then part of it was written early, before he had published much.

It was a kind of funny coming together of resentments when he was not well known and of the effects of this illness.

I think a lot of writers also felt that, since they weren't used to having John as a critic, he somehow turned on the writing group because he was attacking so many people, of such different sorts. I have found an enormous amount of dislike of John, even from writers who weren't mentioned who were mad because they weren't. So you can't win.

BRANS: In interviews, I often ask writers where they place themselves in this controversy between you and Gardner—on the side of art for art's sake with you, or on the side of moral art with Gardner. John Cheever, for example, put himself on Gardner's side, as you would expect, but he wasn't too happy about having Gardner as his spokesman.

GASS: Most people, I would think, would lean in John's direction rather than in mine, but his book didn't help his cause. People didn't like its peevishness.

BRANS: That's a good word. Well, how do you like having placed yourself against the attitudes of Cheever, say, and Saul Bellow and Iris Murdoch?

GASS: I feel very good about it, as a matter of fact. Though I admire those writers. They're very accomplished. I know Iris, and we've argued about this. I've never really discussed it with Bellow, but I admire his work very much—on my grounds.

BRANS: You have some similarities. He has the same infatuation with language that you have.

GASS: Sure. And I don't care what position his book appears to espouse, or what the characters argue, as long as they fit into the book. What's disturbing to many of the writers like John is that they want something more than that. If I just keep what they want to say *in the book,* then I'm not allowing them to say it. But I just say, "All right, in *here,* that's what goes on."

The problem with the "moral" position comes when people start to theorize about it. Cheever, for example, had feelings of this sort, but he wouldn't erect a theory. Consequently, his attitude toward other writers could be very generous. Whereas, if you start erecting a theory, that theory then pretty soon is going to lead you into the Tolstoy problem. You're going to have to start kicking out too many people. And I don't have to do that. I can find formal value in a short story by John Cheever. I think that's why he's a good writer.

So I think that my theory, if you want to call it that, allows more people than the other one, so that's an advantage. I also don't, because of the kind of thing it is, take the theory so seriously. I mean, I don't, as I said before, approach reading somebody else's work with a doctrine in mind. I just read it, and I either like it or I don't like it. I'm either moved or I'm not. Then sometimes I have to find reasons. But most of the time I haven't bothered to do that. It would be a pretty sad life if you went around trying to figure out reasons why you like people—similarly for books, paintings, and so on. But when one is in that business, one is forced to do it.

BRANS: I guess what bothers me about what I would call your extremism in, say, "Fiction and the Figures of Life," is that you imply that we are never changed by books.

GASS: Oh, we are changed, but not in any way the book could have foreseen. It isn't as if it is a cause and effect relationship. Here's an example I like to use: People are changed by other people. But the person that comes into other people's lives and changes them isn't like a hatchet falling;

it is simply quite different each time, from person to person. Nor can a person who has that effect—well, it would be very odd if you had a child who was brought up to have a certain effect on everybody. Books have powerful effects certainly, we all know from experience, but the effects are very hard to measure.

I don't think of the effect so very much as a change of mind; sometimes books act as a kind of crystallization. You are ready to think a certain thing, or feel a certain way, or move in a certain way, and a book comes along and just does it for you. But by and large they become companions. They influence you because what is in them is incredibly valuable. But, again, not I think in the same sort of obvious way in which you fall in love with somebody and therefore take up all their opinions. That would be bad.

So I feel that although those changes are there, they are multiple and unpredictable, and certainly can't be traced to the author's intention or any specific thing. What's often a common denominator, whatever a book's opinion or attitudes, is that a book, because it's an example of excellence, may enshrine those attitudes. I can move from one writer to another and be moved by both, be changed by reading both. Then I look at the books and see they are quite different in every respect, including in their opinions.

BRANS: To what extent are the heroes in your novels you?

GASS: Well, they're me in the sense that I think them up. They reflect some things of mine, but it's a mix. For example, the hero of *The Tunnel* is a not-nice person. He's a historian of the Nazi period, and he's got a lot of fascism in him. He doesn't go around murdering people; he's not wicked in that sense. But he's not good; there's a quality to his mind which I think isn't that of a hero. So I have to draw on a lot of things which are opposite to what I approve of—anti-Semitism, bigotries of other sorts. And if your book is going to have any dramatic power, you've got to give all the sides. Otherwise your book has no strength; it's just paper. Bellow is very good at this, maybe because he's an intellectual. He finds ideas powerful and he likes to get inside them, even if they are ideas he disagrees with.

BRANS: This is true of you too.

GASS: I hope so, I hope so. It's partly the teaching business, where you get used to getting inside of another system of ideas and arguing it.

BRANS: I remember a sentence in an essay you wrote, "Fiction is the ultimate act of voyeurism." That seems to be what you're talking about in writing about this man with the Nazi mind. But don't you feel fearful really? Somewhere else you say that the job of the writer is to take over the reader's consciousness. Suppose you really took over someone's consciousness with a powerful portrayal of this fascist.

GASS: But that indicts the reader. If a person accepts these things, then he is that sort of person in a way.

BRANS: What do you mean?

GASS: I mean one of the strategies of the book is not to present this character as unattractive. We use this technique in philosophy too. You lead a student to an argument which seems innocent and as long as it seems innocent the student assents to it. And then he suddenly sees that all kinds of ideas which he holds must fall if he is going to accept this argument. You thus produce in the student the realization that he has been led into a trap.

I do this in the book a lot. I make the narrator attract you at certain times. Then you turn the corner and you see where that attraction leads. But if you were feeling the attraction, it must be that you have some of the same thing yourself.

BRANS: You've been caught in the net. That's exciting!

GASS: Yes, I want the readers to find themselves saying, "Hmmmm," realizing that what they are assenting to is not benign.

BRANS: Are you about finished with *The Tunnel?* I know you've been working on it for ten years or so.

GASS: Almost. There are lots of problems with it because it is visually, typographically, full of maneuvers which I hope won't be just gimmicks.

BRANS: Like the things you did in *Willie Masters' Lonesome Wife?*

GASS: Even more of them.

BRANS: I have to tell you I threw that book across the room. I had to go and pick it up and say, Well, okay, I'll do it. Then I liked it very much. But a book like that makes such a demand of the reader.

GASS: *The Tunnel* won't be that hard at the beginning, but it's going to be a very demanding book. And it changes tone and style a great deal from section to section and even within sections. I can't imagine that most people will want to wade through it.

BRANS: Then maybe no one will be tempted to steal the manuscript. Is it true that someone stole the only copy of the manuscript of *Omensetter's Luck?*

GASS: Yes, I was working on the last chapter—you know how short that chapter is—and had the manuscript on the desk in my office at Purdue. I went off to teach a class, and when I came back it was gone, just like that.

BRANS: And you hadn't made any copies?

GASS: I had notes, but that was the only copy. My editor, afterward, kept insisting all the time, "Are you making copies? You send me material, *I'll* keep the copies."

BRANS: But the thief couldn't have possibly brought the book out!

GASS: No, no, no, he tried to redo it as a play. That's how we learned who it was, though I had suspicions. I couldn't prove anything. Then he tried to change it around. He changed Omensetter to Hopewell, and he wrote this sort of play, and he showed it to some people who recognized it.

BRANS: Did you prosecute?

GASS: No, the man left the country. He had done those things before, and gotten away with it.

BRANS: You mean literally stolen other manuscripts?

GASS: Yes, from several people. He pretended he was putting together a collection of essays on [Nathanael] West, got someone to write a West piece, then stole it and published it under his own name. He had stolen something else from me in almost the same way. He told me he was collecting a volume of essays on Katherine Anne Porter for a publisher. And indeed I think this may have been a legitimate project at one time. He had written his dissertation on her, knew her, showed her my manuscript—I have copies of their correspondence about it.

Then several years later, I happened upon an essay, and it was mine, almost word for word but not quite, under his name. Katherine Anne had complained about certain things I had said in the essay, and he changed a few things to soften it from her point of view, but that is about all he changed. The piece has been anthologized several times.

BRANS: Was he certifiably loony?

GASS: Well, he was, I think, a very sick man. He was strange. He was very bright. He could be very personable. But he just had a compulsion—he was an orphan, if anything he ever told me was true.

BRANS: I'm surprised you can keep from writing about this.

GASS: Well, I think I may be able to sometime, but my feelings were so strong at one time that I just couldn't manage anything. I mean, I couldn't talk about it even. Then one day six or seven years later I was driving down the street on the edge of the campus and I saw him on the sidewalk. I steered the car right at him—but it wasn't he. I stopped, and I was absolutely terrified and shaken, because I would have killed him.

BRANS: You would have run right over him.

GASS: That's right. My feelings were that strong, and I suppose they still are. That unconscious hatred must be very great. It was a bad time.

BRANS: Did anything good come out of that, do you think?

GASS: Yes, it did. I rewrote the book. Then I went to Urbana as a visiting teacher, and I put the book aside, feeling relieved that I'd been able to recover it. Several months later I got it out and looked at it, and I realized it was no good, I had to start all over again. That was the worst part. A whole lot of psychological energy went into facing that. It just seemed that I'd undergone this ordeal for nothing. Nevertheless it was good in the long run, because I got some distance, and I learned a lot from the whole experience.

BRANS: That you might not have learned otherwise?

GASS: Maybe, or not so soon anyway. It just takes me a long time to get things right, if I'm going to get them right at all, and a lot of distance. That's one reason it's taken me so long to write *The Tunnel.* But everything is that way, even an essay. Rejections have almost invariably been an occasion for me to get very angry and furiously redo everything, and just as invariably there's an immense improvement, and I see it would have been really too bad if I had published the earlier version. Not that I'm giving the people who wouldn't print them any credit! I don't think that at all. But the delays, the impediments—

BRANS: It would be bad for you to rush into print.

GASS: Yes. I've learned that. So now, if something doesn't happen, I make it happen. I slow things down.

BRANS: What about a writer's connection between fiction and politics? I remember your addressing this in your review of Barthelme's *Unnatural Practices.*

GASS: I admired the work. It's very well done, and it's nice, and it's fun. His writing is very much socially oriented. There's a strong satiric, critical bent in everything he's doing. I probably feel just as strongly about what's going on in the country as he does, but I'm not an activist. During the sixties I was very active, but I was active because I was asked by people and sort of dragged into the situation. And even now, no one's less interested in literary politics than I am, and yet I'm in these meetings, I do a great deal. But once again it's being asked and feeling finally that you are obliged to say yes. Similarly I've done some speechmaking and written a few things on nuclear disarmament, but always at an invitation. But I'm not really an activist. I don't work in groups. I don't like groups.

BRANS: Philosophers and writers usually don't, do they? Which matters most to you, philosophy or literature?

GASS: For me they're very similar. Philosophers create systems of ideas and relationships of meaning, very much as poets and novelists work. Philosophical systems are often to be valued as fictions, because very frequently they are quite hopelessly wrong. But they're still beautiful, and you can enter them, and you can see the world this way if you wish.

BRANS: But you have to suspend disbelief.

GASS: Yes, but of course that's what one does when one reads a novel too. You work with that world, you accept its premises. But in philosophy the point comes when you say, "Yes, but is this so?" And then you treat it not as a fiction, but as an alleged assertion about the world. Then come the fights and you start to poke holes in it and find it inadequate.

BRANS: Philosophy is supposed to be a search for the truth and fiction isn't.

GASS: But in class, you see, you're not entirely just searching for truth. You're trying to make clear to people what a certain system is and what it's like and why it goes the way it goes. Then while you're doing that, you're playing that you're in the system, you're following it. And that part of the teaching process is a literary one—you're playing with the system.

BRANS: Just as you teach a novel by getting into it, no matter how extreme its characters are, and saying, "What's going on here? Why does he do this? Why does Gass make him do this?"

GASS: Sure, and while you're doing that, it's a similar activity. It's just that it works at a different level. In philosophy you're presumably talking about the world, but you're talking about it at a level of abstraction and law and generality, with very few concrete things—those are mainly the illustrations and usually misleading and bad ones. A novelist works with concrete things all the time, but the implications, the principles, are always there. So in that sense the two activities are very companionable.

There are, however, sharp differences. Coherence and rigor and clarity are good words in both fields, but they mean different things in each. A novel's aim is to be beautiful in this most general sense, and the aim of a philosophical system is to be true.

BRANS: How can you not want to bring those two together though? Put the truth that you discovered in philosophy—

GASS: Because I think the philosophical theories that do that are wrong. I think that Plato was mistaken. Because he subordinates everything to the Good. There are some philosophers who don't, like Kant, who argues that the Good, the True, and the Beautiful, if you use the old trinity, are very distinct things. Now they can *appear* together, be intermixed in objects, that's certainly true, but they're different qualities, differently determined. I am convinced of that. That's one of the places of course where I argued with John.

BRANS: And with Iris Murdoch. She has a phrase, "the corruption of philosophy." She argues that philosophy *keeps* us from knowing right from wrong.

GASS: Yes, she wants to say that with philosophy we've banished good and evil, and she wants to make those metaphysical categories again. Which is another philosophical enterprise, of course, though it's not the prevailing mode. And again, she's wrong, but it works wonderfully for fiction. She should think that way. Her fiction's wonderful.

BRANS: What is "good" for you? What is the greatest good?

GASS: I really don't think there is one. I'm mostly skeptical about philosophical issues.

BRANS: Not human kindness, not the act of writing, not creativity?

GASS: I think those are good, but I don't think there is such a thing as the greatest good. There are arguments in Kant that good will is the only unqualifiedly good thing.

BRANS: Is that love?

GASS: No. It means being ready to subordinate your intentions to the categorical imperative, which is really a notion of treating everyone as an end in himself. I have some difficulties with that because it's hard to make clear what's involved, but no one should ever be treated as a mere means. That leads to a hatred of all kinds of coercion. I certainly have that. I don't even give to the United Way, because I feel it's a coercive solicitation and not a free one.

But freedom from coercion is only one of the good things. There's Aristotle's self-realization, to realize your essential capacities and so on. But I wouldn't want to do what Aristotle does, say "This is it!" Because all these things are important. Utilitarians are quite wrong about most things, but I do think that human society should be dedicated to the maximizing of freedom—not the greatest happiness for the greatest number, but the greatest freedom for the greatest number of people.

But all this is an ordinary way of looking at things: to speak about moral values in terms of the intrinsic value of the individual, political values in terms of freedom, and personal values in terms of Aristotelian realization. It's just not very exciting.

BRANS: So it's more fun to write about the guy in *The Tunnel*?

GASS: Of course, to get out to the edge of experience. I love to play the games of the extremes, but when it comes to the actual, I recognize all the problems, and I don't want to be anything like that.

BRANS: Why is sex your central metaphor? Or would you agree that it is?

GASS: It's not sex, it's the language of sex. That is, there's very little sexuality in my work, but there are a lot of sexual words. I have very few steamy sexual scenes, if any. The metaphor is fundamental, sure. But my interest in that subject and my use of a character's sexuality are almost invariably either symptomatic or metaphorical, whereas for a great number of writers sex is the direct subject.

BRANS: Symptomatic?

GASS: Yes, symptomatic of some larger quality in the character that isn't directly sexual at all—dominance, power, or what might be called the verbal sexualization of the mind.

BRANS: Wait a minute, let me run that by again.

GASS: It's the sort of thing you get in a character like Jethro Furber when the language becomes so eroticized that—

BRANS: Oh, yes, he's making love with words.

GASS: Yes, and everything that comes into him falls into a nest of images that transforms it in that way.

BRANS: But you could have used another set of—

GASS: Oh, I could have. Well, no, I don't think I could have, because I certainly think that, with respect to creativity, the sexual images are basic.

BRANS: I'm being very fancy, but I wondered if your using them had something to do with the generation of the fictional world.

GASS: It's basic, but again it always operates at a symbolic metaphorical level.

BRANS: I'm not really accusing you of having a dirty mind or anything like that.

GASS: Oh, I do have. However, on the whole, it's not the direct object of my interest. It's light I will throw on that object that's a sexual light. I think it has to do with my conviction that language becomes the object it displaces— not just for sexual impulses, but for everything.

BRANS: So that everything can be experienced in language.

GASS: What happens for a writer frequently is that what you can't control in the world becomes moved on to the page where you can. And not only control but express: things you couldn't express in the world you can express on the page. Or you can try out, so that the words then become more real than their objects.

BRANS: Which is what happens to Furber; he completely forgets that Omensetter is a real person, and he has to be recalled to that at the end.

GASS: That's right. That happens with my characters all the time.

BRANS: There's a sort of androgyny in one of your stories, "The Order of Insects." That's a really wonderful story. Is what this woman, this narrator, sees in the roaches the order that you see through your stories? She has the artist's mentality?

GASS: Yes, sure, she's seeing the world as an artist, trapped in a world which does not allow her to have that kind of consciousness.

BRANS: She's not supposed to think that roaches are beautiful. They're the enemy of the housewife.

GASS: So the moment you do, you have stepped quite outside the whole role, of course. That's the sign. It's not a feminist piece, I guess.

BRANS: It's so close to what Sylvia Plath does in her work—I'm thinking of her as the archetypal contemporary female writer. It really is an act of voyeurism that you can see the contradictions of the two roles of housewife and artist.

GASS: Well, one feels that it isn't hard to put yourself in that kind of role, because in a sense you are in that kind of role yourself.

BRANS: Who's this "you"?

GASS: Most people. One of the great enemies of an artistic life is distraction—the impediments of every day, standard responses, and all the rest. Everybody has them. It doesn't matter what you're doing.

BRANS: So that for her to make an unstandardized response like seeing the roaches as beautiful . . . But they're dead! If you could only see the live roaches.

GASS: No, they're always dead.

BRANS: So they're only beautiful to her when they're dead. That's chilling. Is art full of dead roaches?

GASS: It's only when . . . It's hard to inspect a roach when it's alive.

BRANS: What do you mean when you end *On Being Blue* by saying it's for all those people who live in the country of the blue? Who lives there?

GASS: It's the James story ["The Next Time"]. It's not a terribly good story, but I like the moral of it.

BRANS: Now there you are, you see! *You* even talk about the morality of fiction!

GASS: But it isn't a terribly good story. It's about a man who decides to write a popular success. And he fails, and it's a masterpiece. He says, Oh, well, the next time I'll really get a winner. And he fails again, of course—it's just another wonderful book.

And so at the end he resigns himself and says, All right, I'll just have to live in the country of the blue. That's the realm of the purified and uncorrupted imagination, not the commercial. So my book is in a sense addressed to all of those who live in that place.

Beasts of the People

AN OLD-FASHIONED NOVELIST with a modern consciousness, the British writer Margaret Drabble has been called by the *New York Times* "the novelist people will turn to a hundred years from now to find out how things were, the person who will have done for late twentieth-century London what Dickens did for Victorian London." The subject matter of Drabble's ten novels is today's world, the exploration and analysis of ordinary, contemporary human experiences.

Stylistically, too, her books, in their narrative power and comprehensible point of view, can be read by those being hurried along by life. In her craft, Drabble has rejected self-conscious experimentation or literary solipsism. "I don't want to write an experimental novel," she has said, "to be read by people in fifty years, who will say, Oh, well, yes, she foresaw what was coming. I'm just not interested."

Drabble applies her observant eye, her acute understanding, and her storytelling skills to a central theme in all

her work: the necessary reconciliation of opposites. Like Virginia Woolf, whom she admires, she frequently brings her disparate and warring characters together at social events, like Clarissa Dalloway's party or the dinner in *To the Lighthouse,* where for a brief moment, with luck, their differences are forgotten. "Of such moments," Woolf wrote, "the thing is made that endures."

Born in Yorkshire, in 1939, to Judge John Frederick Drabble and his wife Marie, Margaret Drabble was the second of four children. (Her older sister is A. S. Byatt, a noted novelist and literary critic.) Upon graduation with a double first from Cambridge, where she was active in theater, she married the actor Clive Swift. With Swift, she spent a year as a member of the Royal Shakespeare Company. She and Swift had three children, and were divorced in 1975. In 1982, she married the biographer Michael Holroyd, but they maintain, she has said, "separate worlds," living in houses about five miles apart, which she calls "an ideal arrangement."

If she likes a certain opposition in her life, opposites inhabit her fiction also. Her first three novels, *A Summer Bird-Cage* (1962), *The Garrick Year* (1964), and *The Millstone* (1965), explore what has been termed "the brain and breast dichotomy." Drabble wrote all three while pregnant with her three children. Each of the protagonists is female, young, pretty, and smart—"high-powered girls," Drabble has called them. Two are Oxbridge graduates, like Drabble herself. All must face a conflict between the ambition to succeed in the world and the instinct to marry or have children.

Another Drabble opposition is the individual will against the forces of circumstance, which is also the theme of her fine biography, *Arnold Bennett* (1974). The strictures of a joyless, provincial home in *Jerusalem the Golden* (1967), the overwhelming passion of an extramarital affair in *The Waterfall* (1969), and the guilt of inherited wealth in *The Needle's Eye* (1972) are circumstances against which the heroines pit their wills, with mixed success. Drabble herself has remarked of Rose Vassiliou in the last book, "Whatever she did, she was going to lose." On the other hand, Frances Wingate in *The Realms of Gold* (1975), a grown-up "high-powered girl," embodies the successful will and achieves a happy ending against a counterpoint of disasters for other, more passive, characters.

In her last three novels, Drabble enlarges her canvas to show the importance of community in the face of a disintegrating social order. Using a male persona in *The Ice Age* (1977), she analyzes England's economic depression through the tribulations suffered by a group of men and women of various ages, attitudes, and backgrounds, who survive by managing to function in concert. In *The Middle Ground* (1980), Kate Armstrong at forty-one contemplates herself and her life against the decay of urban London. Torn between self-sacrifice and self-interest, she aims in her mid-life for the middle ground: simply to be "a nice woman." Three such "nice women" and their interwoven stories are viewed against the last quarter-century of English history in *The Radiant Way* (1987), which Drabble had not published at the time of this interview.

Margaret Drabble has had a diverse literary career, both as writer and as editor. From 1979 to 1984, she devoted herself to an epic task: *The New Oxford Companion to English Literature* (1985), a one-volume reference work first published in 1932 which had never before been totally revised. Drabble added such writers as Doris Lessing, Edna O'Brien, and Angus Wilson, and her sister, A. S. Byatt, but modestly—and mistakenly—did not add Margaret Drabble.

Just as her work on *The Companion* came out of a strong sense of duty to English letters and culture, that same sense of duty brought Drabble and Michael Holroyd to Dallas in March 1986 on a tour to raise funds for the restoration of Charleston, the Sussex farmhouse which once belonged to Virginia Woolf's sister, Vanessa Bell. Drabble had, I thought as I watched her cross the lobby of the new hotel where she and Holroyd were housed, the look of a young page, with her bangs and helmet of brown hair, her wide, intelligent face, and her keen humorous blue eyes. I remarked that the hotel was as unlike the simplicity of Charleston as one could imagine, but "I rather like it," she said democratically.

Neither of us liked the noise in the lobby, however. So we moved upstairs to the room which she was, yes, sharing with Michael Holroyd and which he cheerfully vacated for our conversation.

BRANS: As a writer you certainly have exercised a lot of options in your work—novels; books on other writers, including your biography of Arnold Bennett; travel books; journalism and essays; and most recently, the huge *New Oxford Companion to English Literature*. Did you set out with a plan to be as diversified a writer as you could be, or were you just picking daisies, and you altered your path as you saw a bright daisy somewhere?

DRABBLE: Very much seeing a bright daisy, or being offered a possibility. I think I really started off with the view that one ought to say yes to almost everything that was suggested and to see if you could do it. And sometimes you found that you couldn't do it. I can't write plays, for example. I've tried once or twice. I've been invited to do plays, and I've found I just don't like doing it very much.

Now I'm lecturing on Bloomsbury because I discovered that I did quite enjoy lecturing. The first few were agony, but after that I felt that it was a very good way of seeing people. And similarly with journalism and articles. "Say yes and see what happens" has been my philosophy.

BRANS: If you say no, you always wonder—

DRABBLE: Then you never know. I think at some point you don't want to do something because you've tried it and didn't enjoy it. I don't enjoy after-dinner speaking, where people have dinner and then you're supposed to get up and speak. They're somnolent, the whole scene is wrong, and I don't enjoy that.

BRANS: Do you want a serious group of people?

DRABBLE: That, or an unserious group that you can relax with genuinely, at another time of day. I don't like the dressing, the dinner jackets, that sort of thing. But then again, I'm none the worse for having tried, am I?

BRANS: Kate in *The Middle Ground* like you has a preponderance of choices, even though she goes through agonies of indecision throughout the whole novel. At the end she's having a party, and she has to decide what to wear. I wondered why her last decision in the book is so stereotypically feminine. Why clothes in particular?

DRABBLE: She can't find what she looks like, that's it. One could look at it another way, which is, far from having planned first what she looks like at her party, which is what other women do, she hasn't bothered to think about it at all. Therefore she's not at all interested in clothes. She's less interested than most women, who plan their wardrobe and get a special dress for the party.

Kate has taken some interest in the party. She's bought flowers. She has worried about what people are going to eat and whether there's going to be enough of it, and whether the people will get on with each other. But at the last minute, which doesn't show very much interest, she gets around to thinking what she'll wear.

So in a way it's a double thing. Choosing what to wear is not very high on her list of priorities, but when it gets to that point, it represents a certain amount of panic about her public appearance, about a relatively unimportant aspect of it, but nevertheless one she has to make her mind up about. And she is in a very indecisive state.

It also has to do with age. I think that a lot of women find at a certain age in their lives that they don't know what they look like, or can't decide what kind of older person to be. And she's obviously never decided. So it represented a fairly trivial indecision, but a kind of indecision that a lot of women spend a lot of time on, and she tends not to.

BRANS: And then there was something wrong with everything. The black dress is too tight, the caftan is not fresh—

DRABBLE: Oh, of course. There would be, because she would never have had the time or bothered to go and buy a new dress. I was thinking also of her indecision about how to make salad dressing. She has never made her mind up quite about how to make a salad dressing, what kind of mustard to use and so forth. It's really a reflection on the fact, isn't it, that her personality hasn't crystallized, hasn't settled.

BRANS: And there's the way she can't fix on a single man. Earlier in the book there's the catalogue of men, the men that she sees. And there's something wrong with each of the men. There are always things wrong with all the choices she can make.

DRABBLE: There are things wrong with most choices.

BRANS: I wondered if maybe you were showing that all choices are really compromises, that "the middle ground" is in part a matter of compromising.

DRABBLE: I do really believe that. I don't think that there is such a thing as the perfect dress or the perfect man or the perfect marriage or the perfect child. But I also do believe that it's very important to retain flexibility and the ability to adapt, which I think she has done in a way.

BRANS: Oh, very much. That's what the reader sees in the conclusion of the book, this openness and adaptability that Kate has toward life.

One of the most interesting characters about clothes is Philippa in *Jerusalem the Golden,* who's different from Kate. Clothes are important to Philippa, a way for her of making up for the pains of the world, the only thing that matters. But her vanity, if that's the right word, doesn't extend to her house, which she's unconcerned with even though it's downright shabby.

DRABBLE: Philippa was based partly on someone I knew whom I found quite fascinatingly contradictory, and I think it was an early revelation to me of how people have areas of their lives which they take very seriously and other areas which they totally neglect. A friend pointed out to me that I have no interest at all in the front steps up to my house. I mean, I consider that the public domain. If they're a mess, that's the street's fault, it's the local authorities' fault. Other people would extend their protectiveness down the steps, and some even extend it over the pavement. And I find that very interesting, the point at which one cuts off.

For women this is a very significant point, because a woman who decides that everything in her life is going to be neat and orderly is fighting a losing battle. She has also made many possibilities impossible for her, because it is so time-consuming. She has decided to conquer a domain that is really illimitable and pointless. And I suppose I looked upon Philippa as an extreme example of someone who had chosen one rather than the other, and who didn't care about it, someone who deliberately wasn't a perfect woman.

BRANS: She was interesting to me because she was enigmatic. I wanted another story about her.

DRABBLE: She comes up in *The Middle Ground*. What's she doing there? I can't remember.

BRANS: She and Gabriel are divorced, and Gabriel has remarried.

DRABBLE: And, oh, yes, she's become a Roman Catholic convert. And there's some gossip about her in the novel [*The Radiant Way*] I'm working on now, but no one knows for sure what she is really up to. I think she has a very intense inner life, which reveals itself in peculiar ways. I find her a very intriguing person, just as one finds people in life intriguing.

BRANS: Of all of Kate's choices, the most difficult is the one between having an abortion and bearing an imperfect child. For her, and for many women, that's an almost impossible decision.

DRABBLE: But she actually makes the positive choice about that.

BRANS: The abortion? I consider it a positive choice.

DRABBLE: Yes, so do I.

BRANS: But you do have a number of women in your novels who have these imperfect children to whom they're very much bound—for example, Alison Murray in *The Ice Age,* for whom you say there's no future because she's all bound up with Molly.

DRABBLE: Yes, her future is all involved with death. I'm very interested in the fact that maternal devotion is so consuming, and I suppose Kate knowingly therefore rejects what seems to her perhaps the indulgence of children. I don't think Alison would have had the child if she had known. I believe myself very strongly in the right not to have an imperfect child. I admire the devotion of those who manage to bring them up so well, but I don't think one should knowingly choose it, any more than one should knowingly choose to injure a child—knowingly choose to bring into the world a child with a very imperfect life.

BRANS: Then there's Rosamund in *The Millstone,* who has a damaged child, but who—well, she knows the child is vulnerable and damaged but the child is infinitely valuable to her and therefore to the reader. Because she learns to love through the child. So it's almost as if you're giving the reverse side of the coin through her. Alison is trapped by her child, but Rosamund is liberated by hers.

DRABBLE: Yes, I think children do have this double power. And even though Alison is trapped by the child, she has also gained a great deal of knowledge, her life is more profound, it's simply that there's not really much way forward for her. But this is life. And I suppose it's also true that twenty or thirty years earlier she might have been liberated too, but she's a little old for it.

BRANS: I read somewhere that you admire Saul Bellow. Your books remind me of Bellow's, you know, in their combination of high morality and the density of experience.

DRABBLE: I must say, I very greatly admire him. I started reading his things when I left university, and I've been a great admirer of his, that combination of thought and daily life.

BRANS: Another combination you share is the realism of the nineteenth-century novel with the irresoluteness of the twentieth. I'm thinking of the "unsatisfactory" endings for which you and Bellow have both been criticized, the complaint that your books don't end, they just stop.

DRABBLE: Well, I think I'm in very good company. But then that's it. Until one writes the final chapter of one's own life, one can hardly, in my view, arbitrarily finish other people's lives in a novel. But of course one can end a novel with a death. I admire certain novelists who have done that—Zola, for example, who usually ends with a very dramatic ending, or Hardy, whom I also greatly admire. But it's not—to me life seems more continuous. I can actually conceive of the possibility of writing an ending when I'm older, when I've had more experience of the turns.

BRANS: You're very conscious then of the stages of your own life, of the different ages? Your books certainly seem to be.

DRABBLE: Yes, I think they've developed in a fairly obvious, orthodox way.

BRANS: Wasn't it very daring of you, though, to write the first couple of books in the first person? Did you feel that this was the natural way to write them?

DRABBLE: Entirely, yes. Of course, I didn't really think much at the time about getting them published. I just wrote them for fun and to give myself something to do. And it didn't seem daring at all. It seemed natural. It seemed more daring in a way to turn to the third person, which I did with a certain sense of effort.

BRANS: You thought you were playing God more obviously?

DRABBLE: Yes. Technically, writing in the third person is much more difficult, or I find it so. I find writing in the first person very easy, which is why I'm not interested in doing it. I feel in a way I enjoy it too much. It's rather an indulgence.

But it's not so much playing God with the third person. It's more that the narrative becomes automatically more complex, and the numbers of characters and points of view become self-multiplying. And controlling them— well, one feels that one isn't godlike enough; one can't control them adequately. Whereas with the first person one can control the point of view totally.

BRANS: You don't feel that there's something solipsistic or closed in about first-person narrative?

DRABBLE: I do, yes, and that's why I didn't wish to go on doing it. But it seemed a very natural form when I was twenty-one, and I think a lot of very young people do find it very much easier, because you avoid a lot.

BRANS: The first-person narrative is great fun for the reader, but the difficulty comes when the reader tries to decide what's the author and what's the character, making distinctions that I think a reader often feels unqualified to make.

DRABBLE: You're speaking as a trained reader. I think the naive reader doesn't have these problems necessarily. The naive reader can read a first-person narrative—

BRANS: And assume it's Margaret Drabble?

DRABBLE: Or assume it isn't, without worrying very

much about it. Whereas the more conscious one is of narrative form, the more these questions raise themselves.

BRANS: At the end of *The Middle Ground,* you say—and this is another Bellow-like statement—that really all we can do is to learn to·care for one another within the society that we have. Can you point to methods whereby we learn to care for one another that you are intent on showing in your books?

DRABBLE: I suppose I tend to have used most frequently the model of parent-child relationships, because I think that obviously is where a lot of people learn to love; the child learns to love the parent and the parent learns to love the child. But I think one can also learn to love one's fellow man. There's the friendship, for example, between Hugo and Kate in *The Middle Ground,* which is a kind of pairing.

BRANS: And this friendship develops in spite of their dissimilarity. I remember that she looks at him at a certain point, and though she loves him very much, she realizes that she will never comprehend him and he will never comprehend her. There's a kind of strangeness beneath their intimacy. Do you think this essential strangeness is a part of all human relationships, or just the relationship between the sexes?

DRABBLE: I think there are ways that are shortcuts through it. There are intimacies, such as parent-child, or erotic relationships, which give one an illusion or reality of very close understanding. I think with an erotic understanding, it's usually transient. What is satisfactory about the parent-child relationship is that if it's good, it's permanent. Some kinds of friendship can be permanent.

But, as with Hugo and Kate, one has to learn the limitations of this very close friendship. One learns that it's not subsuming or total, the understanding. And, in fact, if I'm right in remembering this, *The Realms of Gold* ends with the realization of Frances Wingate that she actually doesn't understand her cousin David Ollerenshaw. Though she likes him very much, she is utterly astonished, she who prides herself rather on knowing what people are like, when she goes to his flat and finds that it's not at all what she had expected.

I like the idea that one can't know people wholly, but one can value them for what they are and they continue to surprise. And that is a way of caring, taking them for what they are and being continually intrigued by them. I find this very much in friendship, not male-female friendships, but female-female friendships, the fact that one's women friends can go on surprising one, interesting one, compelling one's love and irritation over decades. I find that very, very good and reassuring about human nature.

BRANS: I think one of the most damaging things we can do to one another is to decide that we know another person absolutely—

DRABBLE: Yes, to place them definitely—

BRANS: In a way we strip them of freedom.

DRABBLE: Yes, I agree. I agree. I think that happens in bad marriages where people think they know everything about the other person and can't stand their repeating themselves yet again.

BRANS: For example, the marriage of Janet in *The Realms of Gold*—that terrible, terrible marriage. It really was painful to read.

You use a phrase in *The Middle Ground* which I like very much, but which is mysterious to me: "the brief illusions of parenthood." Do you mean illusions similar to those we just spoke of in some friendships or bad marriages, the illusions that we have that we understand and control our children?

DRABBLE: Yes, one does have a lot of illusions about babies—

BRANS: And about our own power.

DRABBLE: I find it much more satisfactory with my own children when I have thought that I control them and they go off and do utterly different things.

BRANS: We spoke of the friendship between Kate and Hugo. But the friendship between Kate and Evelyn is perhaps even closer. They file things away during the day to tell each other, for example. Do you consider that an unusual friendship between women?

DRABBLE: No, I think it's very common actually. A lot of women have a close woman friend, one or two close women friends, friendships that survive a great deal of friction from the outside world.

BRANS: Although they were completely different, their approaches to life were totally different, there was almost total acceptance of each by the other in a way you don't show very often in male-female relationships.

DRABBLE: Yes, male-female relationships in fiction are more tense, don't you think? One of the good things about women's friendships, I think, is that when they have survived a decade or two they can survive almost anything. That's very good. I think my mother had a couple of friends whom she'd known from college days, and they went on almost to the end, although they were very different, entirely different people, but they were intensely loyal. It was very touching.

BRANS: But isn't it remarkable especially that Kate and Evelyn can even share a man, Evelyn's husband Ted?

DRABBLE: It's not all that unusual actually. I mean, we're

here to celebrate Bloomsbury, and the Bloomsbury group was perpetually doing that—I mean to a remarkable degree. They didn't believe in sexual jealousy. Sexual jealousy is a terrible thing, but it's not as permanent as it appears to be while you're in the grip of it. Nor is erotic passion as permanent as it appears to be. Eroticism and jealousy, which I believe to be very intimately connected, tend to blast their way through two or three years of your life and the other friendships survive beyond them. I think that's a common experience. It's just that society tells us we ought not to feel this way, that we ought not to speak to people again and so on. And Bloomsbury was very strong on that.

BRANS: In view of the controversy during their lifetime between Virginia Woolf and Arnold Bennett, it's remarkable that you seem to have allied yourself with each of them.

DRABBLE: Yes, it is very strange, that. I think that obviously in their own time one can see how that animosity appeared to exist between them. But in fact they had a great deal in common as writers, and they both of them reflect something in me that I don't think is a contradiction or a conflict. It's just two parts of my own upbringing and self and interests.

BRANS: In your biography of Bennett, you remark on an "odd similarity" between the two of them, and go on to say that both of them describe "the little movements of the spirit in its daily routine" and "the inner dramas of ordinary events." Would you consider that a fair description of the action in your books also?

DRABBLE: I'm very interested in the events of daily life, but I suppose I'm increasingly interested in the way in which our small daily lives, our inner lives, are colored by the social climate in which we live. Ideally one would like to get all of this in a book—the social climate, the direction of the country, the culture of the country, and the inner moments which are a response to that.

BRANS: You say of Bennett in summary that he was "generous rather than mean, tolerant rather than intolerant, cheerful rather than depressed, modest rather than vain." Are generosity, tolerance, cheerfulness, and modesty the qualities you most admire yourself, or simply the qualities most in evidence in Bennett?

DRABBLE: They're certainly qualities that I greatly admire. That's why I admire him; there was so much stacked against him as a person that could have made him bitter. And he wasn't. I think it was very much a triumph of character over circumstances. I continue to admire people who make the best of their circumstances and who don't blame others for what has gone wrong. They play the hand that's dealt to them very well.

I think it's true that we're dealt a hand of cards. We don't have total control and free will, but there are elements of control. We can play the hand badly, lose, then blame other people, give up early. And then I think also that generosity about one's colleagues is something that I've always admired.

BRANS: Bennett certainly had that.

DRABBLE: He was remarkably generous and helpful and supportive.

BRANS: I suppose that's why Woolf's essay ["Mr. Bennett and Mrs. Brown"], in which she lambasts him, seems so meanspirited really.

DRABBLE: Virginia Woolf was tempted into meanness a great deal. I still think, in spite of my conversion to Bloomsbury, that there was something uncomprehending in their attitude toward the lower middle classes. Certainly when they were younger—they matured as people too—but when they were younger they didn't wish to understand. They liked to make jokes about the way others dressed and so on.

BRANS: You are generous in crediting other writers. At the end of the last book, Evelyn is reading Emily Dickinson, and Kate is preparing to give a party à la Virginia Woolf—in case we miss the tribute, Kate's daughter is even doing a paper on *Mrs. Dalloway*. And on a trip to the museum Kate feels "cultured" and "virtuous," she says, like an Iris Murdoch character.

You know, Murdoch has said that even dogs can be innocent exemplars of virtue in her books. What about the dogs in your stories? You lean rather heavily toward Alsatians, I've noticed. There's the Alsatian who pisses on her skirt, when Kate is feeling depressed. And there's that wonderful scene in *The Ice Age* of the Alsatian walking down the middle of the highway, with his whole side ripped off, but he's moving steadily along toward his goal. I don't know exactly what an Alsatian looks like, I'm afraid. Why do they figure so prominently in your fiction?

DRABBLE: I think Alsatians are very interesting symbols for me. Unlike Iris Murdoch's view of the dog as innocent or virtuous, Alsatians are not an innocent dog. In England, Alsatians represent the police state.

BRANS: Then that makes the Alsatian in *The Ice Age* a sinister figure! I never saw him that way.

DRABBLE: No, because that is the innocent Alsatian, the innocent wolf, the undomesticated. What we've done in England and in Europe too is to train the Alsatian for police work, to teach him to catch people and to sniff things out. They've very fierce dogs, trained into a role subservient to man, pursuing man's object. They've been encouraged to be vicious in man's name, and they're quite frightening dogs. "You can't trust an Alsatian," my mother always used to say.

But the Alsatian that Alison sees has shed all that. It has reverted to its primeval self.

BRANS: Its learned role has been stripped off with its skin. —You know, that's unsettling. I would have thought I could read an *English* novel with no cultural gaps, no difficulty in understanding. But because I didn't know about Alsatians in police work, I missed your point.

DRABBLE: Oh, but I wouldn't have thought of my point consciously unless you had raised the question. I think one of the reasons it's an Alsatian that pisses on Kate's skirt is that the Alsatian is a frightening dog. If it had been a little fluffy dog, the incident would have been funny rather than actually rather awful.

BRANS: And you see I thought it was funny, and I couldn't quite understand why Kate was so shaken.

DRABBLE: But of course that's because they are frightening dogs. They've sniffed out that there's something wrong with you, and they're going to get you.

BRANS: It can smell Kate's depression or low spirits.

DRABBLE: Right.

BRANS: What about the innumerable references to "gold" and "golden" in your books, even in two of your titles— *Jerusalem the Golden* and *The Realms of Gold*? Can you, without too much limiting the meaning, say something about what that symbol means to you? Were you thinking at all of "the golden mean," of "the middle ground," to quote another of your titles—the reconciliation between extremes?

DRABBLE: I'd like to point out, though, that "the middle ground"—which I didn't know when I originally chose the title, but learned shortly afterward—is a nautical term referring to a dangerous, submerged reef on which ships founder. But I didn't intend that, certainly. On the other hand, I think I am quite interested in "the golden mean," the idea of balance and harmony.

BRANS: Gold is desirable, but it's also threatening, like the woman Chloe whom Ted is attracted to on the plane. She has a gold pencil, gold bracelets, and she's tawny, "lion-colored," predatory.

DRABBLE: Yes, she has a different kind of riches.

BRANS: But she's dangerous. I was pleased with Ted for not pursuing her.

DRABBLE: Yes, he'd had enough of that kind of wealth, hadn't he?

BRANS: You see the golden mean, the balance in the party at the end of *The Middle Ground,* which also made me think of the dinner party in *To the Lighthouse.* Mrs. Ramsay even has the same indifference toward what she will wear that Kate has. Her children decorate her like a Christmas tree, and she really doesn't care.

DRABBLE: Yes, the important thing for both women is that people should be together and should enjoy the occasion. And both of them have drawn together such disparate people. Yes, I like that very much.

BRANS: How do you decide in your books what kinds of wisdom you give to a female character, and what kinds you give to a male character? For example, Anthony Keating at the end of *The Ice Age* is clearly moving away from people and toward God. He doesn't make that sort of Meister Eckhart leap to the place where only God can comfort, but he's obviously contemplating it.

But Alison, his female counterpart, is earthbound by her love for her child. Are you pointing to some essential difference between men and women?

DRABBLE: That was a rather curious book in that I decided to write it largely through the male persona. In order to do that, I had to make Alison slightly unsympathetic to myself. I don't mean that I don't sympathize with her. I mean that I had to make her a different kind of person from my other female protagonists in order not to be tempted to write too much through her. Because I do feel very tempted: it's easier for me to write through the female point of view.

So when I was constructing that book I rather deliberately made Alison a very different sort of person, markedly different from Anthony, in order to force myself to think largely through Anthony's thoughts. For the first half of the book I was rather conscious of that, whether he was thinking like a man or not. Then I began to forget about it, which I think meant that I just got to know him and to know what he was thinking about the world he lived in. I had to work quite hard on exploring the technicality of the financial world in which he lived.

BRANS: Very complicated, wasn't it?

DRABBLE: Yes, I did a lot of research, and very interesting it was, too. But I had to do that in order to think as he thought, whereas I could easily do Alison, because I knew without looking what kind of world she lived in, what kind of problems she had.

BRANS: She's almost exactly the opposite of you, though, of what you said about yourself earlier. You say you always say yes, and Alison is a woman who has consistently said no. So that although one sympathizes with her—I was tremendously sympathetic to her—she's nevertheless not a woman you'd want to be like.

DRABBLE: No, she's more an illustration of what one wouldn't want to be like. Though I can see exactly why she is like that and how it has happened to her life.

BRANS: Do you think she regarded sacrifice as a great virtue?

DRABBLE: I think she did. It's horrible, but I think just in terms of the culture in which we live, women who do have ill children feel guilty and take it upon themselves and try a sort of sacrificial expiation.

BRANS: Being selfless, not thinking of oneself, is considered a desirable quality for women.

DRABBLE: Yes indeed, that is the ideal—not to take on the most challenging thing, not to push oneself but to be seen to have the other virtues. And that is very inhibiting and depressing. I suppose I cheat somewhat by giving Alison some very good reasons to be the way she is, objectively good reasons to be sacrificial.

BRANS: But of course she makes the choice between her two children. Alison keeps our sympathy even in rejecting Jane, her older daughter, because Jane is a brat, but you show Jane's brattiness to be symptomatic. When Alison sacrifices herself to Molly—

DRABBLE: She's also sacrificing Jane. Yes.

BRANS: And that's wrong! She shouldn't do that! —I really feel as if I know this woman. And in fact I feel that way about all of your women, more than any other women in contemporary fiction. Kate is me, I am Kate. What she goes through, I mean.

DRABBLE: You know her experiences very well.

BRANS: Yes. Does it make you uncomfortable at all to know that women do see themselves in your heroines and look to your books for an understanding of themselves?

DRABBLE: No, not at all. I'm delighted. I think women should feel that. Sometimes there are moments when I am writing, sometimes over an incredibly trivial incident, that I know a lot of women are going to know exactly what I mean. Sometimes its very triviality becomes a kind of passport into other people's consciousnesses, just some very silly thing—for instance, the difficulty of folding fitted sheets into proper squares.

BRANS: Or the chopping of vegetables. I remember what an impression it made on me when, oh, who was it?—

DRABBLE: Yes, it was Frances Wingate in *The Realms of Gold,* who's quite a good cook and who doesn't mind chopping vegetables. And that's something women, you see, would understand. There was one of the Michael Caine films, a mid-sixties film, on television the other night. And a man said to me when we were talking about this film, "That was the first film made in which a *man* was shown chopping vegetables." Cooking became fashionable for men in a certain social bracket 'round about then. But then he said, "But you could see it wasn't really Michael Caine, because he wasn't in the frame with the hands that were chopping."

A very interesting observation for a man to make in 1986, to show that he'd noticed and noted that particular incident. Come to think of it, the man who made that observation (I don't know him very well) is reputed to be a very good cook and a vegetarian, so he would obviously have picked this out with some interest and identified with it as a woman might. It was obviously something in his own realm of experience.

BRANS: Does that mean, do you suppose, that we're moving toward unisex or some such thing?

DRABBLE: That was his point. It would be nice to think so. I do hope that we are. Because I don't like the sort of divisiveness and antagonism which the women's movement occasionally brings forth and the statement that all men are part of the oppressive—

BRANS: That no man can chop vegetables?

DRABBLE: Exactly. And what one wants is for everybody to be able to be both things actually.

BRANS: At the conclusion of *The Waterfall,* Jane Gray says, "One can't have art without morality." Do you agree with her? Is art an essentially moral function?

DRABBLE: Yes, I think so. As I remember, it's a slightly ironic comment. It's nothing to do with poetic justice, is it? All I was meaning is that every artistic decision in writing a book actually involves a judgment of life as well as of art. That art is intimately connected with morality. Art isn't just something that exists separate from life but is very intimately connected with our judgments of life. To me, living art is an art that's informed by life, by which I don't mean moral in the Victorian sense of preaching the virtues of church and state and family, but simply deeply concerned with choices that are not purely aesthetic. I don't see the purely aesthetic as being divorced from our moral or human being. It's part of it.

BRANS: I was thinking of the controversy that rages between the aesthetes on the one hand and the moralists on the other.

DRABBLE: Yes, and it continues to rage. My husband tends to use the word "aesthetic" instead of "moral" rather provocatively, because he thinks we use the word "moral" far too much when we don't really mean moral. I really do stick to the view that, as almost all life is political, so almost all life is moral. Every choice is in some way a moral choice, and art, living art, is a reflection of this constant process of questioning, assessing, choosing. It's not a construct made on the side.

BRANS: It's not a game.

DRABBLE: *It is not a game.* That I most entirely do believe. And when I hear people talk about "fictive games" and "metafiction" and "the play" of this or that writer—well, I actually don't think it is a game. I think it's far more serious.

BRANS: The most serious thing, for me.

DRABBLE: It is! Well, exactly. And somehow the word "aesthetic" tends to be used in a diminishing way.

BRANS: *The Needle's Eye* ends with a glorious final image, of the stone lion on the shore, which you describe as "a beast of the people. Mass-produced . . . , but it had weathered into identity. And this, she hoped, for every human soul." I wondered if you think that is what going through experiences does for us, this weathering into identity. And is this then an achievement of grace? Because the lion doesn't do it to himself, does he?

DRABBLE: No, the weather does it. Or it's a cooperative action.

BRANS: And that word "mass-produced," but it's "weathered into identity"—it seems to me there's something very profound there.

DRABBLE: Yes, I thought so! That remains to me a symbol of a lot of what I mean. We're told we live in a collectivist age, where we think of people not as identities but as numbers or statistics or mass movements or migrations.

That is true. We are numbers, and we are mass-produced as people.

But to me the miracle of human existence is that we are millions on the planet, increasing millions, and can be seen statistically—and yet every single one of us is unique and grows differently from the others and we all have identities. We have to remember that, that every human soul is a human soul. That's the extraordinary quality in the ordinary. The thing about the mass production is that one doesn't have to be a very expensive, rare, valuable, aesthetic object, one doesn't have to be a million-dollar painting or a lion carved at Thebes or a bit of the Elgin Marbles. One can just be an ordinary, machine-made lion, and yet that very thing absorbs impressions.

And there's a political significance too, or for me there is. We tend to deprive of identity people who are in categories that we don't ourselves belong to. "Oh, they're Asians" or "Oh, they're engineers" or "Oh, they're computer freaks." Yet all these people are actually individuals; there's an extraordinary identity within each apparently dull person.

There are some people who are obviously extraordinary. Virginia Woolf, for example. She was extraordinarily gifted, extraordinarily neurotic and extraordinarily unhappy, extraordinarily distinguished, extraordinarily beautiful, and she came from an extraordinary heritage. There are other people with none of those qualities but who are nevertheless extraordinary.

BRANS: The Arnold Bennetts?

DRABBLE: It takes more insight to see that they are each extraordinary. I'll tell you one thing more about the Alexander Palace, which is where *The Needle's Eye* ends. I'm sure you've never been there because no one ever has. It's a huge palace in North London which was built, I think, at the end of the nineteenth century as a sort of early radio station and it was meant to be a cheap version of the Crystal Palace. It was for the working class more than for the suburbs, for roller skating and dog shows, cheap pleasures. It's burned down several times, and been through many vicissitudes.

I'm very touched that my youngest son, who is now a landscape gardener, is building the most beautiful garden for the people up at the Ally Pally, as we call it. It's somehow very satisfactory to me that he's so thrilled about this commission that they've got, and he's very proud of it. Of course he was only a baby when I wrote the book, a little lad. So it's rather nice that this symbol of the Ally Pally has attracted him in another generation.

It's still very much a sort of democratic fun spot. He's building this garden, and he's very pleased. He's always had this thing that he didn't want to join the middle classes or go to university; he wanted to be the working man. And he comes home every night covered in cement and mud, looking quite wonderful, and he's been off to the Ally Pally, among the beasts of the people. I love that.

photo by Nancy Crampton

ABOUT THE AUTHOR

BORN in Mississippi, Jo Brans was educated there and at the University of Texas at Austin. From 1970 to 1986 she was a member of the Department of English at Southern Methodist University in Dallas.

Brans, who lives now in New York City, has won numerous grants and awards for her work, including the John H. McGinnis Award for Nonfiction. She is the author of *Mother, I Have Something to Tell You,* published in 1987, and is currently at work on a new book on the subject of positive change.

INDEX

Abduction from the Seraglio (Mozart), 100
abortion, 129, 131, 223
Acastos: Two Platonic Dialogues (Murdoch), 173
An Accidental Man (Murdoch), 178, 186
Adler, Alfred, 7
The Adventures of Augie March (Bellow), 3, 25
The Adventures of Huckleberry Finn (Twain), 163
Aeneid (Virgil), 39
"After the Party" (Thomas), 110–112
agrarian society, collapse of, 158–161
Akhmatova, Anna, 105, 106, 109–110, 114, 116
Alexander Palace, 240–241
Alsatians (dogs), 232–233
Amateurs (Barthelme), 80
American Academy of Arts and Letters, 35, 150
Amnesty International, 144
"anathematization of the world," 93–95

Andreas-Salomé, Lou, 107
anger, in humor, 94
Anna Karenina (Tolstoy), 119, 179, 180
anti-Semitism, 114
Aquinas, Thomas, 14
Ararat (Thomas), 105–106
architecture, modernist, 81–82
"Aria" (Barthelme), 98
Aristotle, 210
Armstrong, Kate (Drabble's character), 218, 220–222, 223, 224, 227–228, 229, 232, 233, 234, 236
Arnold Bennett (Drabble), 217, 219, 230, 231
Arrowby, Charles (Murdoch's character), 175, 187–188
artist, mind of, 212–213
Ashbery, John. Work: *Three Poems*, 98
As I Lay Dying (Faulkner), 68, 83, 107
Atlantic magazine, 22, 34
Atwood, Margaret, xviii, xix, xxi–xxii, 125–147; on abortion, 129, 131; on affirmative view of life, 141–142; biographical sketch,

125–128; definition of feminism by, 128–131, 145; diversity of works, 138; and metamorphosis theme, 139–141; on open-ended symbolism, 138; political views of, 142–146; on portraying characters of the opposite sex, 135–136; on pregnancy, 129–131; on prescience of writer, 126; on receptivity of readers, 133–135; on relationships between men and women, 131–132; on unrealistic expectations about men and women, 136–137; on writer's responsibility to readers, 146–147; on writing and nationality, 132–133, 134; writing process of, 138–139. Works: *Bodily Harm,* 125, 126, 135, 141–142, 143; *The Edible Woman,* 125, 126, 138; "Giving Birth," 129–130, 131; *The Handmaid's Tale,* 125, 126–127; *Lady Oracle,* 125, 138; *Life Before Man,* 125, 129, 130, 135, 136–138; "Power Politics," 131; *Second Words,* 126; *Surfacing,* 125, 127, 129, 142, 143; *Survival: A Thematic Guide to Canadian Literature,* 125–126; "There Is Only One of Everything," 131–132

Austen, Jane, 144

Baltram, Edward (Murdoch's character), 174

Barthelme, Donald, xvii, xviii, xix, xxi, 77–101; on "anathematization of the world," 93–95; biographical sketch, 79–81; on collage principle, 79; on connection between teaching and writing, 98–100; definition of realism, 95; on deterioration of language, 86; on expression of emotion, 96–97; on Hemingway, 90–91; on influence of father, 81–84; on interpretation of writer's intent, 100–101; on men's notions about women, 84–85; on morality in fiction, 91–92; on narrative tension, 90; on prospects for human life, 95–96; on social change, 87–88; structural innovations of, 77, 79, 80–81, 88–89, 97–98; on work of other writers, 92. Works: *Amateurs,* 80; "Aria," 98; "Brain Damage," 80; *City Life,* 80; *Come Back, Dr. Caligari,* 80; *The Dead Father,* 80–81, 82–84, 93, 97; *Forty Stories,* 80; *Ghosts* (projected), 80, 86; *Great Days,* 80, 94, 95; *Guilty Pleasures,* 80; "How I Write My Songs," 98; "Nothing," 99; *Overnight to Many Distant Cities,* 80; *Paradise,* 80; *Sadness,* 80; "The Shower of Gold," 99; *Sixty Stories,* 80, 97; *Snow White,* 80, 84–86, 87, 93; *Unspeakable Practices, Unnatural Acts,* 80, 207

Barthelme, Frederick (Rick), 77, 82

Barthelme, Pete, 82

Bateson, Gregory, 94

Bayley, John, 173

Beattie, Ann, 77

Beaux Arts architectural tradition, 81

Bell, Vanessa, 219

Bellow, Saul, xiii, xiv–xv, xvi, xvii, xix, xxi, xxii–xxiii, 1–31, 40, 45, 55, 200, 203, 224–225, 227; acquaintance with Cheever, 46–47; on Berryman's demise, 25–26; biographical sketch, 1–4; on connection with readers, 5–7, 14–17; and female characters, 27–30; on linearity of criticism,

24; on love of family, 21–22; on modern world's denial of the soul, 7–9; on mystification of literature, 12–14; on teaching of literature, 9–12; on writer's games, 19–20. Works: *The Adventures of Augie March,* 3, 25; *Dangling Man,* 3, 5, 27, 47; *The Dean's December,* 3–4; *Henderson the Rain King,* xiv, 3; *Herzog,* xiv, 3, 16–18, 28, 30–31; *Humboldt's Gift,* 3, 7, 18–22, 27, 28–29; "Leaving the Yellow House," 28; *Mr. Sammler's Planet,* 3, 22–24, 27; *More Die of Heartbreak,* 4; *Seize the Day,* 3; *The Victim,* 3

Bennett, Arnold, 219, 230, 231, 240

Berryman, John, xxii–xxiii, 18, 19, 25–26, 94. Work: "Homage to Mistress Bradstreet," 110

Bible, the, 139, 153

Birthstone (Thomas), 103, 105, 112, 116

The Black Prince (Murdoch), 175

blacks: in chain gangs, 161–162; as characters, 64–65; dehumanization of, 163

Bloom, Harold, 171, 174

Bloomsbury group, 220, 230, 231–232

Bodily Harm (Atwood), 125, 126, 135, 141–142, 143

The Book and the Brotherhood (Murdoch), 171

Booker McConnell Prize, xvi

Book of Ecclesiastes, 11

Borges, Jorge Luis, 77

Bourke-White, Margaret. Work: *You Have Seen Their Faces,* 151

"Brain Damage" (Barthelme), 80

The Bride of the Innisfallen (Welty), 58

The Brigadier and the Golf Widow (Cheever), 35

Brown, Tallis (Murdoch's character), 191

Bruno's Dream (Murdoch), 175, 190–191

Buddhism, 184

Bulgaria, 156–157

Bullet Park (Cheever), 35–36, 39

Bundren, Addie (Faulkner's character), 107

Bundren, Anse (Faulkner's character), 107

Burde, Hilary (Murdoch's character), 175

Burke, Kenneth, 165, 166

Byatt, A. S., 217, 218

Byron, George Gordon, Lord, 139

Caine, Michael, 237

Caldwell, Erskine, xvii, xix, xxi, 149–170; biographical sketch, 149–152; on censorship, 152–153; on collapse of agrarian society, 158–161; on creation of characters, 167–169; on cruelty, 161–163; on cultural environment of readers, 156–157; on descriptive technique, 155–156; on the enlargement of personal horizons, 165–166; family background as impetus to writing career, 153–154; on independence of writers, 169; on journalism and fiction, 154–155; on morality in fiction, 169–170; on regional writing, 157; on religion in rural Georgia, 164–167. Works: *Call It Experience,* 151–152; *God's Little Acre,* 149, 166–167, 168; *Journeyman,* 149, 165; *Tobacco Road,* 149, 155–156, 163; *Tragic Ground,* 149; *Trouble in July,* 149; *You Have*

Seen Their Faces, 151

Caliban (Shakespeare's character), 8

Call It Experience (Caldwell), 151–152

Campbell, Joseph, 81, 89–90. Works: *The Hero with a Thousand Faces,* 89; *The Masks of God,* 90

Canada, national literature of, 132–133

Canadian Civil Liberties Union, 144

Canadian Governor General's Award, xvi

Cantabile, Rinaldo (Bellow's character), 26–27

capital punishment, 117–118

Carroll, Lewis, 77

Carver, Raymond, 77

Cash (Welty's and Faulkner's characters), 68

Cassandra, 114

Catcher in the Rye (Salinger), xv

Cato (Murdoch's character), 189

Caulfield, Holden (Salinger's character), xv

Celtic imagination, 108–109

censorship, 152–153

Central Intelligence Agency (CIA), 142, 143

chain gangs, 161–162

chance, as governing principle of life, 173–174, 175, 176

characters: creation of, 62–64, 167–169; of opposite sex from author, 27–30, 135–136, 235; power over readers, 202–204; revelation through dialogue, 61–62

Charleston farmhouse, 219

Cheever, Fred, 49–51

Cheever, John, xv, xvii, xix, xxii, xxiii, 33–55, 88; acquaintance with Bellow, 46–47; biographical sketch, 33–36; choice of vocation, 51–52; and Christianity, 40–41; on force of memory, 39–40; on loneliness, 54–55; on morality in fiction, 44–45, 200, 201; novel vs. short story, 48–49; on reading his own work, 47–48; relationship with brother, 49–51; residence in New York City, 52–54; on self-destruction, 55; on sexual explicitness, 42–44; on storytelling, 40; on writer's contribution to literature, 45–46. Works: *The Brigadier and the Golf Widow,* 35; *Bullet Park,* 35–36, 39; "The Death of Justina," 48; *The Enormous Radio,* 35; *Falconer,* 36, 42–44, 49, 51; "The Geometry of Love," 47; *The Housebreakers of Shady Hill,* 35; *Oh What a Paradise It Seems,* 36; *Some People, Places, and Things That Will Not Appear in My Next Novel,* 35; *The Stories of John Cheever,* 35; "The Swimmer," 48–49; *The Wapshot Chronicle,* 33, 35, 48; *The Wapshot Scandal,* 35; *The Way Some People Live,* 34; *The World of Apples,* 35

Chekhov, Anton, 34, 68

children: imperfect, 223–224; parents' control of, 229; relationship with parents, 121–122

China, 156

Chloe (Drabble's character), 234

choices: entrapment by, 223–224; making, 220–224; moral, 238–239

Christianity, 11, 12, 40–41; and metamorphosis, 140; in rural Georgia, 164–167; and virtue, 183, 184

Citrine, Charlie (Bellow's character), 3, 19–22, 24, 27, 28, 29

Citrine, Julius (Bellow's character), 22

City Life (Barthelme), 80

Civil War, matriarchal legacy of, 71–72

clairvoyance, 5–6, 15

Clark, Eleanor, 46

Cohen, Morris R., 7

collage, as principle of narrative structure, 77, 79

The Collected Stories (Welty), 58

Collier's, 34

Come Back, Dr. Caligari (Barthelme), 80

comedy, in tragedy, 69–70

Committee on Social Thought, 2

Compson, Caddy (Faulkner's character), 69

Compson, Quentin MacLachan (Faulkner's character), 69

Conrad, Joseph, 9

cotton picking, 158

The Coup (Updike), 92

Covici, Joan, 4

Covici, Pascal, 4

Cowley, Malcolm, xiii, xx, 45. Work: *The Portable Faulkner* (ed.), 68

Crader, Benn (Bellow's character), 4

Crane, Hart, 55

creative process, xix–xx

criticism: as intellectual faddism, 12; and interpretation of writer's intent, 100–101; linearity of, 24; New, xiv, 101, 195

Cronkite, Walter, 157

cruelty, 161–163

Crystal (Murdoch's character), 186

culture: commodification of, 12; conditioning of reader's perceptions by, 156–157; elite, 13–14; homogenization of, 157–158

Cummings, E. E., 52, 53

A Curtain of Green (Welty), 58

Dalloway, Clarissa (Woolf's character), 217

Danby (Murdoch's character), 190–191

Dangling Man (Bellow), 3, 5, 27, 47

"Dave Garroway Show," 38

The Dead Father (Barthelme), 80–81, 82–84, 93, 97

The Dean's December (Bellow), 3–4

"The Death of Justina" (Cheever), 48

Delphic oracle, 114

Delta Wedding (Welty), 59, 71

description, technique of, 155–156

dialogue: experimentation with, 97; revelation of characters through, 61–62

Diana (goddess), 41

Dickens, Charles, 215

Dickinson, Emily, 110, 232

Diderot, Denis. Work: *Rameau's Nephew*, 27

Didion, Joan, 34

dinosaurs, 138

Dr. Zhivago (Pasternak), 119

dogs: sinister, 232–233; virtue of, 178

Donatello. Work: Madonna and Child, 106

Dorina (Murdoch's character), 186

doubles, 3–4

Drabble, Judge John Frederick, 217

Drabble, Margaret, xviii, xix, xxi, 215–241; on Alsatian dogs, 232–233; on Bennett, 230, 231; biographical sketch, 215, 217–219; on convergent sex roles, 237–238; diversity of works, 219–220; on endings, 225; on everyday life, 230–231; on first-person vs. third-person narrative, 225–227; on generosity, 231–232; on the "golden mean," 233–234; on individual identity in mass culture, 239–241; on learning love, 227; on making choices, 220–224; on morality in fiction, 238–239; on permanence of friendship, 227–230; portrayal of male characters, 235; on sacrificial love, 236; on triumph of character, 231; on women and children, 223–224; women's identification with heroines of, 236–237; on Woolf, 230, 231. Works: *Arnold Bennett*, 217, 219, 230, 231; *The Garrick Year*, 217; *The Ice Age*, 218, 224, 232–233, 234–236; *Jerusalem the Golden*, 218, 222–223, 233; *The Middle Ground*, 218, 220–222, 223, 224, 227–229, 232, 233, 234; *The Millstone*, 217, 224; *The Needle's Eye*, 218, 239–241; *The New Oxford Companion to English Literature*, 218–219; *The Radiant Way*, 218, 223; *The Realms of Gold*, 218, 228, 233, 237; *A Summer Bird-Cage*, 217; *The Waterfall*, 218, 238

Drabble, Marie, 217, 229, 233
dreams, 189

Earle, Edna (Welty's character), 59
Eckhart, Miss (Welty's character), 70–71, 72
Edel, Leon, xiv, xx
The Edible Woman (Atwood), 125, 126, 138
Effingham (Murdoch's character), 187, 188–189
Elena (Thomas's character), 105, 122–123
Eliot, T. S., 13
elitism, 13–14

Elizabeth (Atwood's character), 137
The Enormous Radio (Cheever), 35
Erdman, Lisa (Thomas's character), 104, 105, 112–115, 119, 122
erotic love, 106, 110–114, 116–119, 120, 174–175, 211–212, 227, 230
Evans, Walker, 54
Evelyn (Drabble's character), 229, 232
existentialism, 173, 180
experience, non-autobiographical representation of, 62–63
The Eye of the Story (Welty), 58

fact, vs. value, 180–181
Fairchild, George (Welty's character), 59
Fairchild, Robbie (Welty's character), 59
Falconer (Cheever), 36, 42–44, 49, 51
family: love of, 21–22; tension within, 58–60, 72–75
A Farewell to Arms (Hemingway), 91
Farragut, Ezekiel (Cheever's character), 36, 49, 51
Faulkner, William, xiii, xix, xx, 47–48, 64, 68–70, 132, 134. Works: *As I Lay Dying*, 68, 83, 107; *The Portable Faulkner* (Cowley, ed.), 68; *The Sound and the Fury*, 69
feminine principle, 107–110
feminism: expectations about men, 137; and freedom of choice, 129–131; ideological, 128–129, 145; as outcome of writer's observations, 128
fiction: comparison with philosophical systems, 207–209; connection with politics, 207; descriptive technique in, 155–156;

distinction from nonfiction, 193; and journalism, 154–155; as metaphorical construction, 195–196; transformation of readers by, 201–204. *See also* novel; short story

Fiction and the Figures of Life (Gass), 93, 197, 201

filth, and virtue, 191

Finnegans Wake (Joyce), 13

The Fire and the Sun: Why Plato Banished the Artists (Murdoch), 173

The First Winter of My Married Life (Gass), 196

Flaubert, Gustave, 3

Flavin, Dabney Fairchild (Welty's character), 59

Flavin, Troy (Welty's character), 59

Fleisher, Von Humboldt (Bellow's character), 3, 18–19, 26

Fletcher, Virginia, 152

The Flute-Player (Thomas), 103, 105, 110, 112, 116, 122–123

formalism, vs. morality, 198–201, 238–239

Forty Stories (Barthelme), 80

fratricide, 49, 51

freedom: and clarity of perception, 173, 174; maximization of, 210; in relationships, 228

Freud, Sigmund, xx, 7, 40, 104, 114, 115, 117, 181, 187

Freudian psychology, and sibling relationships, 50

friendships, permanence of, 227–230

Frost, Robert, 114, 116

Frye, Northrop, 125, 139

Furber, Reverend Jethro (Gass's character), 196, 211, 212

Futurists, 89

Gainsborough, Thomas, 177

Gardner, John, 77, 209; friendship with Gass, 199–200. Work: *On Moral Fiction*, xxi, 44–45, 91–92, 199–201

The Garrick Year (Drabble), 217

Garroway, Dave, 38

Gass, William, xviii, xix, xxi, xxiii, 193–214; on artist's mind, 212–213; biographical sketch, 193, 195–197; comparison of philosophical and literary systems, 207–209; defining "the good," 209–210; on fiction as metaphorical construction, 195–196; friendship with Gardner, 199–200; on literary politics, 207; on morality in fiction, 91–92, 198–201; on purified imagination, 213–214; on rewriting of *Omensetter's Luck*, 206–207; on sexual metaphors, 211–212; structural innovations of, 193, 204; on theft of *Omensetter's Luck* manuscript, 204–206; on transformation of reader by fiction, 201–204. Works: *Fiction and the Figures of Life*, 93, 197, 201; *The First Winter of My Married Life*, 196; *Habitations of the Word*, 197; *In the Heart of the Heart of the Country*, 196; "The Next Time," 213–214; *Omensetter's Luck*, xxiii, 91, 196, 197, 198, 204–207, 211, 212; *On Being Blue: A Philosophical Inquiry*, 197, 213; "The Order of Insects," 212–213; "The Pederson Kid," 196; "A Philosophical Investigation of Metaphor," 195; *The Tunnel*, 202–203, 204, 207, 210; *Willie Masters' Lonesome Wife*, 197, 204; *The World within the Word*, 197

"The Geometry of Love" (Cheever), 47

Georgia: chain gangs and mule

teams in, 161–163; Christian fundamentalism in, 164–167; collapse of agrarian society in, 158–161; racism in, 163
Ghosts (McBain), 86
Ghosts (projected novel of Barthelme), 80, 86
Gibson, Graeme, 126
Ginsberg, Allen, 19
"Giving Birth" (Atwood), 129–130, 131
God's Little Acre (Caldwell), 149, 166–167, 168
The Golden Apples (Welty), 58, 70–71, 72, 75
"golden mean," 233–234
The Good Apprentice (Murdoch), 171, 174
Goodman, Benny, 35
"grass captain," 108–109
Gray, Jane (Drabble's character), 238
Great Days (Barthelme), 80, 94, 95
Greek mythology, 41, 139
Grimm's Fairy Tales, 139, 140
Guggenheim Fellowship, xvi, 2, 197
guilt: family, 136–137; racial, 64
Guilty Pleasures (Barthelme), 80

Habitations of the Word (Gass), 197
The Handmaid's Tale (Atwood), 125, 126–127
Hannah (Murdoch's character), 186–187
happiness, and virtue, 190–191
Hardy, Thomas, 225
Hartley (Murdoch's character), 187–188
Hattie (Bellow's character), 28
Hawthorne, Hazel, 53
head culture, canon of, 7–8
Hemingway, Ernest, 3, 77, 90–91. Works: A Farewell to Arms, 91;

The Sun Also Rises, 90–91
Hempel, Amy, 77
Henderson the Rain King (Bellow), xiv, 3
Henry and Cato (Murdoch), 189
The Hero with a Thousand Faces (Campbell), 89
Herzog (Bellow), xiv, 3, 16–18, 28, 30–31
Herzog, Moses (Bellow's character), 3, 17–18, 28, 30–31
Hilda (Murdoch's character), 188
Hinduism, 184
Hitler, Adolf, 118
Hogo (Barthelme's character), 84–85, 87
Holroyd, Michael, 217, 219, 238–239
"Homage to Mistress Bradstreet" (Berryman), 110
Homer, 14, 39
"The Honeymoon Voyage" (Thomas), 121
hotel, symbolism of, 113–114
The Housebreakers of Shady Hill (Cheever), 35
"The House of Dreams" (Thomas), 120
Howells Medal for Fiction, xvi, 35
"How I Write My Songs" (Barthelme), 98
Hugo (Drabble's character), 227–228, 229
Humboldt's Gift (Bellow), 3, 7, 18–22, 27, 28–29
humor: anger in, 94; and terror, 116; in tragedy, 69–70
Huysmans, Joris Karl, 44

Ibsen, Henrik, 86
The Ice Age (Drabble), 218, 224, 232–233, 234–236
identity, individual, and mass pro-

duction, 239–241
imagination: Celtic, 108–109; purified, 213–214
incest, 69
India, 140
intent, writer's, interpretation of, 66–68, 100–101
In the Heart of the Heart of the Country (Gass), 196

Jackson, Phoenix (Welty's character), 64, 65–66
James Tait Black Award, xvi
Janet (Drabble's character), 228
Japan, 156
jealousy, sexual, 230
Jeeter (Caldwell's character), 150
Jerusalem the Golden (Drabble), 218, 222–223, 233
Jo (Thomas's character), 105
Jorge (Gass's character), 196
journalism, and fiction, 154–155
"The Journey" (Thomas), 121
Journeyman (Caldwell), 149, 165
journeys, 109, 119–120, 121
Joyce, James, 13, 14, 116. Work: *Finnegans Wake*, 13
Juliet (Shakespeare's character), 117
Jung, Carl, 40, 90

Kafka, Franz, 77, 83
Kant, Immanuel, 209, 210
Keating, Anthony (Drabble's character), 234, 235
Keats, John, 110, 111. Work: "La Belle Dame sans Merci," 111
Kilian, Karl, 83
King, Julius (Murdoch's character), 191
Kirstein, Lincoln, 53–54
Kürten, Peter, 116–119

"La Belle Dame sans Merci"

(Keats), 111
"The Lady of Fetishes" (Thomas), 107
Lady Oracle (Atwood), 125, 138
language: displacement of objects by, 211, 212; modern deterioration of, 86; as trap, 175
Lardner, Ring, 77
Lasha (Atwood's character), 130, 137, 138
Lawrence, D. H., xxii, 109
learning, and virtue, 185, 186
"Leaving the Yellow House" (Bellow), 28
Le Corbusier, 82
Leda and the Swan (statuette), 106
Lessing, Doris, 218
Letter to Queen Victoria (Wilson), 98
Levertov, Denise, 51 52
Life Before Man (Atwood), 125, 129, 130, 135, 136–138
Lisa (Murdoch's character), 190–191
Literary Festival (Southern Methodist University), xiv, xv
"Livvie" (Welty), 66, 68, 71, 101
Lockhart, Jamie (Welty's character), 58
loneliness, 54–55
Losing Battles (Welty), 59, 61–62, 69, 70–71, 72–75
love: as entrapment, 186–188; equality in, 131–132; erotic, 106, 110–114, 116–119, 120, 174–175, 211–212, 227, 230; of family, 21–22; fraternal, 49–51; and happiness, 190–191; of imperfect children, 224, 236; learning of, 227; parental, 121–122, 227; of persons one never meets, 110; realism in, 188; and religious conversion, 40–41; selfless, 174, 183–184, 236; wounded, 18

Lynch-Gibbon, Martin (Murdoch's character), 175

McBain, Ed. Work: *Ghosts,* 86
McKelva, Becky (Welty's character), 59, 60
McKelva, Fay (Welty's character), 59–60
McKelva, Judge (Welty's character), 59–60
McKelva, Laurel (Welty's character), 59–60
MacLain, Eugene (Welty's character), 75
Maddocks, Melvin, 79, 127–128
Madeleine (Bellow's character), 18, 28
Madonna and Child (Donatello), 106
Mandelstam, Osip Yemilyevich, 122
Mann, Thomas, 13
Mark (Murdoch's character), 174
Marx, Karl, 7
Marxism, 184
The Masks of God (Campbell), 90
mass media: and deterioration of language, 86; homogenization of culture by, 157
mass production, and individual identity, 239–241
Masters, Babs (Gass's character), 197
matriarchy, of postbellum Mississippi Delta, 71–72
Matthews, Charles, 132
meaning, failure of, 79
meditation, 183
Melville, Herman. Work: *Moby Dick,* 11, 133–134
memory, as force, 39–40
men: as characters of female writers, 135, 235; and convergent sex roles, 237–238; and erotic love,

110, 111, 112, 116–119, 174–175; fetishization of women by, 107; intrinsic differences from women, 135–136; relationships with women, 84–85, 131–132, 186–188, 227–228, 229–230; unrealistic expectations about, 136–137
metafiction, 196, 239
metamorphosis, 139–141
metaphors: as building blocks of fiction, 195–196; sexual, 211–212
The Middle Ground (Drabble), 218, 220–222, 223, 224, 227–229, 232, 233, 234
Mies van der Rohe, Ludwig, 82
Miles (Murdoch's character), 175
The Millstone (Drabble), 217, 224
mines, symbolism of, 108–109
Mingo (Murdoch's character), 178
"Mr. Bennett and Mrs. Brown" (Woolf), 231
Mr. Sammler's Planet (Bellow), 3, 22–24, 27
Moby Dick (Melville), 11, 133–134
monologues, 97–98
Montaigne, Michel de, xxi
morality, connection with reality, 180–181
morality of art, xx–xxii; as affirmation of life, 44–45; distinction from didacticism, 91–92; effect of fiction on readers, 201–204; vs. formalism, 198–201, 238–239; as proscriptive concept, 45; and purified imagination, 213–214; transitory nature of, 169–170; unavoidability of, 179–180
Moral Majority, 127
More Die of Heartbreak (Bellow), 4
Mortimer, Miss Julia (Welty's character), 59, 70–71, 72, 73, 74, 75
Mozart, Wolfgang Amadeus.

Work: *Abduction from the Seraglio,* 100
mule teams, abuse of, 162–163
murder, and eroticism, 116–119
Murdoch, Iris, xviii, xix, xxi,
xxiii, 171–192, 200, 209, 232;
American vs. British reactions
to, 178–179; biographical sketch,
171, 173–176; on corruptions of
moral philosophy, 180–181; and
erotic love, 174–175; on happiness, 190–191; on morality in
fiction, 179–180; and philosophy of chance, 173–174, 175–
176; on relationships between
men and women, 186–188; on
virtue, 173–174, 178, 181–186,
189–191; on visions, 188–190.
Works: *Acastos: Two Platonic
Dialogues,* 173; *An Accidental
Man,* 178, 186; *The Black Prince,*
175; *The Book and the Brotherhood,* 171; *Bruno's Dream,* 175,
190–191; *The Fire and the Sun:
Why Plato Banished the Artists,*
173; *The Good Apprentice,* 171,
174; *Henry and Cato,* 189; *The
Nice and the Good,* 174, 188; *The
Philosopher's Pupil,* 178; *The Sacred and Profane Love Machine,*
178; *Sartre, Romantic Rationalist,*
173; *The Sea, The Sea,* 175,
187–188; *A Severed Head,* 175;
The Sovereignty of Good, 173,
180; *Under the Net,* 175–176,
178; *The Unicorn,* 186–187,
188–189; *A Word Child,* 175, 186
Murray, Alison (Drabble's character), 224, 233, 235–236
Murray, Jane (Drabble's character),
236
Muse figures/poetry, 106–107,
108, 120, 122–123
My Son, My Son (author unspec-

ified), 120
mystification of literature, 12–14
myth, literary inversion of, 80–81

Napoleon, 193
narrative: collage principle in, 77,
79; first-person vs. third-person,
225–227; tension in, 90
Nate (Atwood's character), 136–
137
National Book Award, xvi, 1, 3,
35, 38
National Book Critics Circle
award, 197
National Medal for Literature, 58
Nazi exterminations, 104, 117
Nazism: and eroticism, 116–119;
and sexual repression, 112–113
The Needle's Eye (Drabble), 218,
239–241
"net, the," 175–176
New Criticism, xiv, 101, 195
*The New Oxford Companion to En-
glish Literature* (Drabble), 218–
219
New Republic, 34
New Yorker, 34, 42, 44, 49, 79
New York Post, 158
New York Times, 215
The Nice and the Good (Murdoch),
174, 188
Nietzsche, Friedrich Wilhelm.
Work: *Thus Spake Zarathustra,*
195
Nobel Prize for Literature, xvi,
1–2, 46, 55
"Nothing" (Barthelme), 99
novel: compared with classical
literature, 2; inherence of metamorphosis to, 140–141; vs.
short story, 48–49; writing endings, 225
nuclear arms freeze, 146

O. Henry Award, 58
O'Brien, Edna, 218
Oh What a Paradise It Seems
   (Cheever), 36
Ollerenshaw, David (Drabble's
   character), 228
Omensetter (Gass's character), 196,
   205, 212
Omensetter's Luck (Gass), xxiii, 91,
   196, 197, 198, 204–207, 211, 212
*On Being Blue: A Philosophical In-
   quiry* (Gass), 197, 213
*One Time, One Place: Mississippi in
   the Depression* (Welty), 57–58, 61
One Writer's Beginnings (Welty), 57
On Moral Fiction (Gardner), xxi,
   44–45, 91–92, 199–201
The Optimist's Daughter (Welty),
   59–60, 62–63
"The Order of Insects" (Gass),
   212–213
Ortega y Gasset, José, 14
Overnight to Many Distant Cities
   (Barthelme), 80
Oxford philosophy, 180

Paley, Grace, 92
Paradise (Barthelme), 80
Pasternak, Boris. Work: *Dr. Zhi-
   vago*, 119
Peacock, Bonnie Dee (Welty's
   character), 59
Pearson, Bradley (Murdoch's char-
   acter), 175
"The Pederson Kid" (Gass), 196
PEN International, 125
Perelman, S. J., 91
Perkins, Maxwell, 151–152
Philippa (Drabble's character),
   222–223
The Philosopher's Pupil (Murdoch),
   178
"A Philosophical Investigation of
   Metaphor" (Gass), 195
philosophy: of chance, 173–174,

175–176; comparison with literary structure, 207–209; corruption of, 180–181, 209; definition
   of "the good," 209–210
Plath, Sylvia, 110, 213
Plato, xx, 209
Platonism, 173
plot, and independence of characters, 168–169
Pocket Books, 104, 119
politics: connection with fiction,
   207; and labeling, 144–145; and
   power relations, 143–144
Pollock, Jackson, 55
Ponder, Uncle Daniel (Welty's
   character), 59
The Ponder Heart (Welty), 59
The Portable Faulkner (Cowley,
   ed.), 68
Porter, Katherine Anne, 58, 68,
   205
poverty, and collapse of agrarian
   society, 158–161
power, and social relations, 143–
   144
"Power Politics" (Atwood), 131
pregnancy, 129–131
Presidential Medal of Freedom, 58
Pritchett, V. S., 93
Prospero (Shakespeare's character),
   8
Proust, Marcel, 18
psychoanalysis, denial of the soul
   by, 7, 8
Pulitzer Prize, xvi, 1, 59
Pushkin, Aleksandr, 105

Rabbit Is Rich (Updike), 92, 93
Rabbit Redux (Updike), 93
race relations, 64–65
racism, 163
The Radiant Way (Drabble), 218,
   223
Rainey, Virgie (Welty's character),
   72, 75

Rameau's Nephew (Diderot), 27

Ramona (Bellow's character), 30

Ramsay, Mrs. (Woolf's character), 234

Ransom, John Crowe, 195, 196

Rather, Dan, 157

readers: cultural environment of, 156–157; and first-person narrative, 226–227; independence of writer from, 169; receptivity of, 133–135; sophistication of, 13–14; transformation of, by fiction, 201–204; writer's connection with, 5–7, 14–17; writer's responsibility to, 146–147

realism, 95; in love, 188; and morality, 180–181

The Realms of Gold (Drabble), 218, 228, 233, 237

"Recipe for a Canadian Novel" (author unspecified), 132

The Red and the Black (Stendhal), 10, 20

regional literature, 132, 133, 134, 157

religion: formalization of dream symbols in, 189; in rural Georgia, 164–167; and virtue, 183–185

Renal, Madame de (Stendhal's character), 20

Renata (Bellow's character), 28–29

Renfro, Gloria (Welty's character), 59, 69, 72–73, 74

Renfro, Granny (Welty's character), 59, 73

Renfro, Jack (Welty's character), 59, 72–74

repression, sexual, 112–113

Rich, Adrienne. Work: "Trying to Talk to a Man," 136

roaches, artist's response to, 212–213

The Robber Bridegroom (Welty), 58

Romeo (Shakespeare's character), 117

Rosamund (Drabble's character), 224

Rousseau, Jean Jacques, 4, 9

Russell, Bertrand, 7

Russia. *See* Soviet Union

Sabatini, Rafael, 91

The Sacred and Profane Love Machine (Murdoch), 178

Sadness (Barthelme), 80

Salinger, J. D. Work: *Catcher in the Rye,* xv

Sammler, Artur (Bellow's character), 3, 4, 6, 23–24

Sartre, Jean-Paul, 173

Sartre, Romantic Rationalist (Murdoch), 173

School of American Ballet, 54

Schopenhauer, Arthur, 28, 30

Schwartz, Delmore, 18

The Sea, The Sea (Murdoch), 175, 187–188

Second Words (Atwood), 126

Seize the Day (Bellow), 3

Selected Poems (Thomas), 105

self-destruction, 25–26, 50–51, 55

self-realization, 210

A Severed Head (Murdoch), 175

sexual explicitness, 42–44. *See also* erotic love

Shakespeare, William, 108

Shelley, Percy Bysshe, 139

short story: narrative tension in, 90; vs. novel, 48–49; structural innovations in, 77, 79, 88–89, 97–98, 193

"The Shower of Gold" (Barthelme), 99

Sing Sing prison, 42–43

Sixty Stories (Barthelme), 80, 97

Snow White (Barthelme), 80, 84–86, 87, 93

Snow White (Barthelme's character), 80, 85

social change, writer's effect on,
    87–88
Solomon, King, 11
Some People, Places, and Things
    That Will Not Appear in My Next
    Novel (Cheever), 35
sophistication: of readers, 13–14;
    and virtue, 181–182
Sorel, Julien (Stendhal's character),
    20
soul, the: denial of, by modern
    world, 7–9; and individual iden-
    tity, 239, 240
The Sound and the Fury (Faulkner),
    69
"Southern Ontario Gothic" writ-
    ing, 132
Southwest Review, xv
The Sovereignty of Good (Mur-
    doch), 173, 180
Soviet Union, 150, 156; totalitari-
    anism in, 114–116
Sphinx (Thomas), 105–106
Stalin, Joseph, 105
Stein, Gertrude, 77, 83, 98, 195
Stendhal, 13. Work: The Red and
    the Black, 10, 20
The Stories of John Cheever, 35
Story magazine, 34
storytelling, 40. See also short
    story
subconscious, the, 39–40
success, of writer, 20
suffering, contrasted with self-
    destruction, 55
suicide, Berryman's, xxii–xxiii, 26
A Summer Bird-Cage (Drabble), 217
Summit (Thomas), 106
The Sun Also Rises (Hemingway),
    90–91
Surfacing (Atwood), 125, 127, 129,
    142, 143
Survival: A Thematic Guide to Cana-
    dian Literature (Atwood), 125–
    126
Swallow (Thomas), 105–106

Swift, Clive, 217
"The Swimmer" (Cheever), 48–49
symbol(s): in dreams, 189; hotel as,
    113–114; interpretation of, 67–
    68, 101; mines as, 108–109;
    open-ended, 138; women as, 107

teacher, writer as, 15–16
teaching of literature: as commu-
    nity for literary culture, 9–11;
    connection with writing, 98–
    100; exploration of systems in,
    208; and intellectual faddism,
    11–12; and interpretation of
    writer's intent, 67–68, 100–101
Ted (Drabble's character), 229, 234
telephone, and deterioration of lan-
    guage, 86
television: and deterioration of lan-
    guage, 86; homogenization of
    culture by, 157
"There Is Only One of Every-
    thing" (Atwood), 131–132
Thomas, D. M., xvii–xviii, xix,
    xxii, 103–123; biographical
    sketch, 103–106; on Celtic
    imagination, 108–109; distaste
    for celebrity, 104; on erotic love,
    106, 110–114, 116–119, 120;
    and feminine principle, 107–110;
    on his mother, 121; on journeys,
    109, 119–120, 121; on Kürten
    the mass-murderer, 116–119; on
    love of persons one never meets,
    110; and Muse figures, 106–107,
    108, 120, 122–123; on parents
    and children, 121–122; on pros-
    pects for human life, 122; on
    symbolism of hotel, 113–114;
    on totalitarianism, 114–116.
    Works: "After the Party," 110–
    112; Ararat, 105–106; Birthstone,
    103, 105, 112, 116; The Flute-
    Player, 103, 105, 110, 112, 116,
    122–123; "The Honeymoon
    Voyage," 121; "The House of

Dreams," 120; "The Journey," 121; "The Lady of Fetishes," 107; *Selected Poems,* 105; *Sphinx,* 105–106; *Summit,* 106; *Swallow,* 105–106; *The White Hotel,* xix, 103–104, 105, 106, 112–119

Thomas, Harold, 109

Thompson, Will (Caldwell's character), 167, 168

Three Mile Island nuclear accident, 96

Three Poems (Ashbery), 98

Thus Spake Zarathustra (Nietzsche), 195

Tobacco Road (Caldwell), 149, 155–156, 163

Tolstoy, Leo, 8, 9, 87, 181, 201. Work: *Anna Karenina,* 119, 179, 180

Tom Swift (author unspecified), 39

The Torrents of Spring (Turgenev), 116

totalitarianism, 114–116

To the Lighthouse (Woolf), 217, 234

tragedy, presence of humor in, 69–70

Tragic Ground (Caldwell), 149

Trouble in July (Caldwell), 149

"Trying to Talk to a Man" (Rich), 136

The Tunnel (Gass), 202–203, 204, 207, 210

Turgenev, Ivan Sergeyevich. Work: *The Torrents of Spring,* 116

Twain, Mark. Work: *The Adventures of Huckleberry Finn,* 163

Ty Ty (Caldwell's character), 150, 166–167

unconscious, the, 8

Under the Net (Murdoch), 175–176, 178

The Unicorn (Murdoch), 186–187, 188–189

United Way, 210

"unselving," 174, 175

Unspeakable Practices, Unnatural Acts (Barthelme), 80, 207

Updike, John. Works: *The Coup,* 92; *Rabbit Is Rich,* 92, 93; *Rabbit Redux,* 93

value, vs. fact, 180–181

Vassiliou, Rose (Drabble's character), 218

Vendler, Helen, 127

Vico, Giambattista, 14

The Victim (Bellow), 3

Virgil. Work: *Aeneid,* 39

virtue: and clarity of perception, 173–174, 181–182; of dogs, 178; and filth, 191; and happiness, 190–191; and learning, 185, 186; as philosophical ideal, 209–210; religious, 183–185; and sophistication, 181–182; and visions, 189–190; and work, 182–183, 185, 190

visions, 188–190

Vonghel, Demmie (Bellow's character), 28, 29

Wapshot, Leander (Cheever's character), 33, 35

The Wapshot Chronicle (Cheever), 33, 35, 48

The Wapshot Scandal (Cheever), 35

Warren, Robert Penn, 38, 46

The Waterfall (Drabble), 218, 238

The Way Some People Live (Cheever), 34

Welty, Eudora, xv, xvii, xix, xxii, 57–76; biographical sketch, 57–60; on characters' realization of larger world, 72, 75–76; on creation of characters, 62–64; on family struggles, 58–60, 72–75; on Faulkner, 64, 68–70; on fictional treatment of race, 64–66; on narrative tension, 90; on postbellum Delta matriarchy, 71–72; on presence of humor in tragedy, 69–70; on purpose of writing, 61–62; on work as photographer, 61; on writer's intent, 66–68, 101. Works: *The Bride of the Innisfallen*, 58; *The Collected Stories*, 58; *A Curtain of Green*, 58; *Delta Wedding*, 59, 71; *The Eye of the Story*, 58; *The Golden Apples*, 58, 70–71, 72, 75; "Livvie," 66, 68, 71, 101; *Losing Battles*, 59, 61–62, 69, 70–71, 72–75; *One Time, One Place: Mississippi in the Depression*, 57–58, 61; *One Writer's Beginnings*, 57; *The Optimist's Daughter*, 59–60, 62–63; *The Ponder Heart*, 59; *The Robber Bridegroom*, 58; *The Wide Net*, 58; "A Worn Path," 64, 65–66

Werner, Hazel, 53

Werner, Morey, 53

West, Nathanael, 205

The White Hotel (Thomas), xix, 103–104, 105, 106, 112–119

Whitman, Walt, 6

The Wide Net (Welty), 58

Willie Masters' Lonesome Wife (Gass), 197, 204

Wills, Chill, 100

Wilson, Angus, 218

Wilson, Robert. Work: *Letter to Queen Victoria*, 98

Wingate, Frances (Drabble's character), 218, 228, 237

Winternitz, Mary, 34

Wittgenstein, Ludwig, 173, 195

women: as characters of male writers, 27–30, 135; and children, 223–224; domination of postbellum Delta society by, 71–72; and erotic love, 110–113, 114, 118–119, 120, 174–175; indecision of, 220–222; intrinsic differences from men, 135–136; as

Muse figures, 106–107, 108, 120, 122–123; relationships with men, 84–85, 131–132, 186–188, 227–228, 229–230; relationships with other women, 228, 229; sacrificial love by, 236; self-recognition in fictional heroines, 236–237; unrealistic expectations about, 137, 186, 187. *See also* feminism

Woolf, Virginia, 230, 232, 240. Works: "Mr. Bennett and Mrs. Brown," 231; *To the Lighthouse*, 217, 234

A Word Child (Murdoch), 175, 186

work, and virtue, 182–183, 185, 190

The World of Apples (Cheever), 35

The World within the Word (Gass), 197

"A Worn Path" (Welty), 64, 65–66

writer(s): connection with readers, 5–7, 14–17, 133–135; as contributor to stream of literature, 45–46; effect on social change, 87–88; as entertainer, 115; games of, 19–20, 210–211, 239; independence of, 169; intent of, 66–68, 100–101; and nationality, 132–133, 134, 156–157; portraying characters of the opposite sex, 27–30, 135–136, 235; prescience of, 126; responsibility to readers, 146–147; as teacher, 15–16

Yale Review, 150

Yeats, W. B., 115, 116, 117

Yevtushenko, Yevgeni, 105

You Have Seen Their Faces (Caldwell and Bourke-White), 151

Zed (Murdoch's character), 178

Zola, Emile, 225

Typesetting by G&S, *Austin*
Printing and binding by Braun–Brumfield, *Ann Arbor*
Design and production by Whitehead & Whitehead, *Austin*